PERRY M. SMITH

A HERO AMONG HEROES

JIMMIE DYESS
AND THE
4TH MARINE DIVISION

A Hero Among Heroes

Published by the
Marine Corps Association
Box 1775
Quantico, VA 22134

October, 1998

ISBN 0-940328-23-2

TABLE OF CONTENTS

PROLOGUE

He was a man of the deep South yet he was proudly and unambiguously American. Open faced and open hearted, he gave those around him a sense of comfort and well being. Whenever he was involved in any activity, others wanted to join in. If he was "doing it", whatever "it" was, "it" must be something worthwhile or fun or uplifting or adventurous. People, even those who had known him for a short time, just knew that if they were with him they would be safe and well taken care of. Even as a young man he exuded that sense of quiet competence and confidence which spoke volumes about his maturity and sense of purpose.

The red hair was very much a part of his persona. It was more auburn than red; it was not curly but had a natural wave. The hair was so rich and so full and he stood so tall and so straight that he could be spotted at a great distance—long before the others in his entourage would be recognized. People would see him and move naturally towards him. They clearly enjoyed his company and he, theirs.

He had fine individual skills, especially as a world class marksman, yet he was fundamentally a team person and a team player. He loved sports and played them with great energy. Not a great athlete by any means, he thrived in sports through sheer determination, the willingness to work very hard in practice, an ability to ignore pain and a total commitment to his team. He had a keen sense for what was right and what was wrong and hence saw things as black or white. People knew where he stood on issues—he left no doubt. He was, in a real sense, larger than life. He lived his life to the fullest and, like young Theodore Roosevelt or Winston Churchill, was a man of action who was impossible to ignore.

His love for things military dated back to when he was eight years old. A great mass of soldiers had assembled in the Augusta area for training as they got ready for combat in World War I. His family would invite young soldiers from the nearby camp to come by for Sunday dinner and he would listen intently as they described

1

their training and their commitment to saving democracy by joining the allies and defeating the Germans. From age fourteen, until he was killed twenty one-years later, he wore a military uniform—first at his military high school, then as a member of the cadet corps at Clemson College, next as an Army reservist, then as a Marine Corps reservist and finally on active duty with the United States Marines. He wore each uniform with pride, for it represented to him service above self, discipline, honor, tradition and esprit de corps.

There are very few who have the inborn ability to motivate and inspire people to do their very best to achieve a worthy goal, despite the obstacles, dangers, pain or exhaustion. Some would call it innate leadership; others might label it charisma, charm, personality or magnetism. Whatever it was, he had it in spades. He was clearly a leader by the time he walked into Richmond Academy in Augusta at age fourteen—many felt that his leadership skills were well developed at even an earlier age. He perfected these skills through the years so that when he led eight hundred men into combat, he was the epitome of a combat leader.

His name was Jimmie Dyess. His homes were Augusta, Georgia, Clemson College and the United States Marine Corps. This is his story.

INTRODUCTION

Writing biography is an inherently incomplete task, since no one can fully grasp the actions, motivations, influences and circumstances of another person's life. It is particularly difficult to capture the mind and motivations of a bona fide hero whose pattern of behavior is marked by extraordinary altruism and self-sacrifice. After more than ten years of research and writing, these realities have become very clear to me. Writing biography is very different from other non-fiction—and a much, much more difficult task.

Despite the difficulties and pitfalls, I persevered because this is a story which cries out to be told. The main setting for the Jimmie Dyess story is World War II and the events that led up to the first, and hopefully the last, truly global war. As far as grasping the full context of this war, I am quite fortunate. Although I never had the privilege of knowing Lieutenant Colonel Aquilla James Dyess, United States Marine Corps Reserve, the World War II period has been a very important part of my life.

I have dealt with World War II on three separate and distinct occasions in my life. My first experience, in December 1941, was quite a dramatic one. I was living with my family in Honolulu, Hawaii. My father was then an Army officer—a major, on active duty, in the Coast Artillery Corps. In the summer of 1940, after he had completed the Army Command and General Staff College at Fort Leavenworth, Kansas, he had been assigned to Hawaii. From June 1940 until December 1941, the whole Smith family had enjoyed an idyllic eighteen months in the beautiful, quiet and under-populated Hawaiian Islands. There were then just three hotels on Waikiki Beach; only about once a month was there a surge of tourists. This would occur when a cruise ship would sail, with great fanfare and excitement, into Pearl Harbor.

Suddenly and dramatically, on an early morning in December, my world changed. I was half way through the second grade and nine days short of my 7th birthday. Every Sunday morning my older sister, George Anne, who was eight years old, and I were

3

picked up from our home in Honolulu and taken by Army truck to Sunday school at a nearby military post. Sitting on benches in the rear of the large truck, we looked out the back as other "Army brats" climbed aboard along the way. In those days before air conditioning, people in Hawaii went to work (and to church on Sunday) quite early. My sister and I were in transit from about 7:30 to 8:00 AM each Sunday. Just before we reached the post on December 7, 1941, the Japanese commenced their attack on Pearl Harbor, Hickam Field and a number of other vital military targets.

An Army captain who met us at the main gate made a foolish decision. Rather than herding all of the children into a basement until the attack was over, the captain ordered the driver to turn around and to take us home immediately. It was a wild ride that morning as the truck careened along the same roads we had just traveled so serenely and innocently. Since my sister and I had been among the first to be picked up, we were among the last to be delivered back to our home. Fortunately, no Japanese fighter pilot elected to roll in to strafe that truck full of small children, so we all made it safely back to our homes.

After being evacuated to the mainland in February, 1942, my family moved around a great deal throughout the remainder of World War II. In the late spring of 1942, I was asked to give a short talk about my experiences on the morning of the 7th of December. Hence, I gave my first public speech at age seven to my second grade class in St. Cloud, Minnesota. In a way, I was already somewhat of a mini-celebrity, since I had not only been in Hawaii when the attack took place, but had also witnessed a part of it up close and first hand. From 1942 through 1945, I gave similar speeches to cub scout dens, Sunday School classes and elementary school classes in Zanesville, Ohio; Wilmington, North Carolina; and Richmond, Virginia, as my mother, grandmother, sister and I followed my father from assignment to assignment during the remainder of the war. My memories of those early days of World War II remain quite vivid, perhaps because I told my story so many times to so many audiences.

My second encounter with World War II took place in the mid 1960s. As a military scholar pursuing a Ph.D. at Columbia University, I spent a year researching and writing a book about military planning during that war. Much of my research was accomplished in Washington, D.C., and at Maxwell Air Force Base, Alabama, as well as conducting interviews throughout the country. Going through the dusty War Department files (from 1941 to 1945) got me deeply interested in the events of World War II.

My third encounter with World War II was a very long one, extending from 1986 to 1998. I returned intellectually once again to the period of the early 1940s to research and to write this biography. For twelve years I studied the life and death of Lieutenant Colonel Dyess—the man who was Jimmie to most of his family and friends and "Big Red" or "Red Dyess" to his fellow Marines. I decided to write the biography of Jimmie Dyess, the father-in-law I never met, after four events took place.

In 1986, at the invitation of the U. S. Army, my wife, Connor, and I flew seven thousand miles from Washington, D. C. to the island of Roi Namur in the Marshall Islands. Connor had been asked to help dedicate Roi Namur as a national historic landmark and to honor the Marines who had participated in the 1944 battle for these islands. Her father had fought there, had been killed in the final assault on the last Japanese pillbox and had earned a Medal of Honor on that tiny spot of land in the middle of the Pacific ocean.

Through waist-high jungle, Connor and I walked the battlefield of Roi Namur from Green Beach, where Dyess and his battalion had landed, to the place on the far side of the island where he was killed. The battlefield, which happily has never been ransacked by tourists, has been kept in wonderful order by a retired Marine who works on the island. Although we gained an excellent understanding of the battle for Roi Namur, we still didn't fully understand the role that Jimmie Dyess had played in that battle. The citation for his award of the Medal of Honor was very general and the specifics of his heroism in combat remained a mystery to us more than forty years after he was killed.

For conspicuous Gallantry and intrepidity at the risk of his life above and beyond the call of duty as Commanding Officer of the First Battalion, Twenty-fourth Marines, Reinforced, Fourth Marine Division, in action against enemy Japanese weapons, Lieutenant Colonel Dyess launched a powerful final attack on the second day of the assault, unhesitatingly posting himself between the opposing lines to point out objectives and avenues of approach and personally leading the advancing troops. Alert, and determined to quicken the pace of the offensive against increased enemy fire, he was constantly at the head of advance units, inspiring his men to push forward until the Japanese had been driven back to a small center of resistance and victory assured. While standing on the parapet of an anti-tank trench directing a group of infantry in a flanking attack against the last enemy position, Lieutenant Colonel Dyess was killed by a burst of enemy machine-gun fire. His daring and forceful leadership and his valiant fighting spirit in the face of terrific opposition were in keeping with the highest traditions of the United States Naval Service. He gallantly gave his life for his country.[1]

The October, 1986 dedication of the Roi Namur battlefield was described in a number of publications, including the newsletter of The 4th Marine Division Association, World War II. The fact that Connor Dyess Smith, the only child of one of the four Marines who had earned the Medal of Honor during that battle, had participated in the dedication ceremonies was highlighted in all of the articles.

This led to a magic day in February, 1988 when Connor received a letter from Frank Pokrop of Milwaukee, Wisconsin. Pokrop had served with Lieutenant Colonel Dyess both at Camp Pendleton in California and in the Marshall Islands. That letter changed our lives. This is what Pokrop wrote.

Dear Mrs. Smith:

The last newsletter of the 4th Marine Division Association WWII carried the story of the dedication of the RoiNamur battlefield, and your part in that ceremony. Although I was not in your father's battalion he has been very close to me for a number of reasons. I thought you might like to know.

As a 17 year old Marine I was assigned to Camp Pendleton to prepare for the formation of the new 4th Marine Division. We were told to make ready for our first major inspection and thus worked for hours to clean and shine everything. Early Saturday morning we were called to attention and this large, very military looking Colonel, approached the doorway to the Company room. He stopped at the entrance, put on a pair of white gloves, and reached up above the framework of the door running his fingers over that framework. He then looked at the gloves to see if there was any dirt on them. Seeing none he proceeded into the room to do the same to walls, bunks, bedsprings, and anything else in the room. That was my introduction to Colonel Dyess. Not being in his battalion I saw very little of him, except at a distance, during the remainder of our training in California.

Enclosed is a copy of the map we were given prior to the assault upon Namur. Without going into great detail, about halfway through the island I was ordered to take a patrol and scout ahead. The 6 of us reached the x points shown on the map. Unbeknown to us the rest of the troops were ordered to reform and hold at "Sycamore Blvd.". We had walked through the Japanese lines and were faced by the ocean at our front, a number of heavy machine guns on our left, and Japanese behind us and on our right. One man had been killed and four others wounded as we were exposed to close fire from three sides.

With no protection and heavy fire coming at us from a few feet away and dusk approaching we were certain to be killed. All of a sudden Colonel Dyess broke through on the right, braving the very heavy fire, and got all of us out of there. We were placed in the huge hole left by the enormous blockhouse explosion while Colonel Dyess fought off the continued Japanese fire.

The next morning Colonel Dyess was killed while leading his men up the parapet that held the enemy machine gun nests. As you may see, Colonel Dyess has never been out of my thoughts for these 43 years and he will always be there until I die. In the terminology of those days "he had guts."

In 1985, after the "Return to Iwo" I had finally received permission to visit Namur. I spent 5 hours, all alone, just walking through the areas I had walked through, or run, during the battle. I did not need a map as it was as though it was yesterday. I spent 2 hours in the few yards circled on the map just thinking about the men and the time. It was a deeply moving experience interspersed with prayers for those that did not survive.

Semper Fidelis

Thanks to Frank Pokrop, Connor and I now understood, in much more detail, her father's heroism during the battle for Roi Namur. In May, 1988, Connor, our daughter Serena, and I met Frank and his wife Maxine in Kohler, Wisconsin. Frank provided some additional information about the Fourth Marine Division as well as his personal reminiscences of Dyess. During our conversations, I mentioned to the Pokrops that Dyess had also won the Carnegie Award for heroism and explained the circumstances of his selfless heroism as a young man. As Connor, Serena and I discussed Dyess's courage in peace and war with the Pokrops, Frank made the point that it was a shame that the full story of Dyess's heroism had never been told or written down. Frank declared how wonderful it would be if someone would write a book about Dyess so that he could become a role model for young people, especially young Marines. Pokrop's suggestion stuck in my consciousness.

In the summer of 1989, The 4th Marine Division Association, World War II, held its annual convention in Las Vegas and Connor was an honored guest. At this convention, the Georgia chapter was to be named the Aquilla J. Dyess Chapter. Connor had been asked to receive the charter for the chapter on behalf of all the World War II veterans of the Fourth Marine Division living in Georgia. The warmth with which the thousands in attendance at the conference welcomed Dyess's daughter touched her heart and mine. Many of these veterans of World War II had vivid memories of Red Dyess, but the great majority had never met his daughter. Very few had had the opportunity to thank anyone in the Dyess family for his leadership or his heroism. They did so that day with a warm, standing ovation that continued on for many minutes. There were very few dry eyes in the audience that morning as they remembered a very special leader.

Those in attendance at this convention knew that Lieutenant Colonel Dyess had won the Medal of Honor but they did not know, until it was announced at the final banquet, that he had also won the Carnegie Medal. Once again, the applause was strong, sincere and sustained. With their applause, they saluted a man whom so many had known at Camp Pendleton, on the ship from San Diego to the Marshall Islands or in combat. They honored him for who he was, what he did, and what he symbolized.

The fourth event that played a role in my decision to write this book occurred six months after Connor and I had moved from Virginia to Augusta, Georgia in 1990. In the fall of 1990, after we became settled in our new home, I contacted both the Medal of Honor Society and the Carnegie Hero Fund Commission. I wanted to find out how many individuals had won both the Medal of Honor and the Carnegie Medal. Over the telephone, I asked the executive director of the Carnegie Hero Fund Commission many questions about the Carnegie Medal. He was very gracious, answered all my questions and agreed to send me background material on the award. It was at the end of this long telephone conversation when I asked the key question: "How many individuals have earned both

9

the Carnegie Medal and the Medal of Honor?" He quickly replied, "No one." He then explained that it is not possible for anyone to win both awards since military people are not eligible for the Carnegie Medal.

As politely as I could, I suggested that he might be incorrect. I suggested that someone might earn the Carnegie award as a young person, later enter the military, and then earn the Medal of Honor. As I recall his response, it was, "I never thought about that." When I explained that I had, in my home in Augusta, a Carnegie Medal that had been awarded to Aquilla James Dyess in 1929 and a Medal of Honor awarded to the same Aquilla James Dyess in 1944, he seemed quite surprised.

Next, I telephoned the executive director of the Medal of Honor Society. He was very helpful. However, he was not familiar with the Carnegie Medal and had no idea about who else, besides Dyess, might have earned both awards. I was in a real quandary since it was clear that I could get little help from the experts on either the Carnegie Medal or the Medal of Honor on how many others, besides A. J. Dyess, might have earned both awards. I soon came to the realization that I had only one choice. I must examine the complete list of winners of each award and see who were on both lists. Although this seemed like a very straightforward, albeit time consuming, approach, this search turned out to be a rather complex undertaking.

At my desk, I lined up both lists alphabetically—side by side. I started, slowly and carefully, going down the two lists—from Helmer Aakvik to William Zydiak on the Carnegie list; from Michael Aheam to Raymond Zussman on the Medal of Honor list. This comparison of names took me three full days. I came up with about twenty-five names (first, middle and last) which were exactly the same name on both lists. My immediate reaction was that there was nothing unique about someone earning both awards. But after careful examination of a few of these names and when these awards had been earned, I had a blazing flash of the obvious. Just because the name was the exactly the same on both lists, it didn't mean it was the same person. For instance, I found individuals who earned the Medal of Honor in the Civil War in the early 1860s whose names reappeared as earning a Carnegie Medal in the 1940s, 50s or 60s. Clearly, even though the name was exactly the same, it could not be the same person. I then gave each of these twenty-five names my very close attention. By carefully comparing birth date, place of birth and date of each award, it was rather easy to find the disconnects. I would cross a name off my list whenever it was crystal clear that it could not have been the same person who earned both awards. Slowly but surely the names which were on both lists and could possibly have been the same person became fewer and fewer.

By this process of elimination, I narrowed the number of possible double award winners down to two: Aquilla James Dyess and George Bradley. George Bradley had won the Medal of Honor in the battle of Vera Cruz in 1914. Also, George Bradley had won the Carnegie Medal in the early 1920s. At first, it appeared that George Bradley, born in 1881, had earned both awards. After doing further research, however, I discovered that there were two George Bradleys with the same year of birth as well as similar backgrounds and heroic accomplishments. Although they were both born in 1881, their births were on different dates and at different locations. At last, it was crystal clear—there was only one! Only one person in history had earned both awards. At that private yet very emotional moment, a decision was made. Frank Pokrop was correct; this unique story must be told. With tears welling up in my eyes, I told Connor that I had made a firm decision: a biography of her father had to be written and I would begin the research immediately.

It was then November, 1990 and soon I was hard at work researching the life of Jimmie Dyess. Little did I know at this time that, within two months, the Persian Gulf War would intervene suddenly in my life. When, in early January, 1991, Gail Evans, the vice president for booking at CNN, asked me to be a full-time CNN military analyst for the duration of the Gulf War, I did not anticipate that my decision to join CNN would so dramatically change my life. My television commentary during the six-week Persian

Gulf War, the book that I wrote on my CNN experiences and the many speaking and teaching opportunities which followed fully occupied my time for the next three years. Only in 1994 was I able to recommit myself to the serious research which this biography demanded.

When I first decided to write this book, I did so for the entire Dyess family, and principally for two very special people: Dyess's widow, Mrs. C. G. Goodrich (widowed in February, 1944, Connor Cleckley Dyess married Colonel Charles Grant Goodrich of the U. S. Army Air Corps in 1946) and his daughter, Connor, my wife for more than 35 years. I also wanted to write it for Dyess's sister, Sarah Dyess Ewing. But this biography has become much more than a gift to the family. Doing the research on this remarkable man has become an uplifting experience for me and for so many others who have assisted me. The more we read, the more we have said to ourselves, "What a man he must have been." Hence, this biography is, first and foremost, for Lieutenant Colonel A. J. Dyess, United States Marine Corps Reserve.

However, this book is more than a biography of an American hero, it is also the story of the men whom he led in combat. In the early 1940s this group of young men chose to serve their nation and the cause of freedom in the United States Marine Corps. They served in the 4th Marine Division as it fought its way across the Pacific in 1944 and 1945. To understand the Jimmie Dyess story, it is necessary to understand the men whom he led, trained, served with, and died for. Hence, this is more than the story of a hero and extraordinary leader; this is the story of a group of exceptional men.

Each year, for more than fifty years, the men of the 4th Marine Division of World War II have come together to celebrate their brotherhood and accomplishments and to thank their nation for the opportunity to serve in a time of great need. These men, who gave so much as young men, are patriots in the finest sense. It is to them, to their families and to their memory that I dedicate this book.

CHAPTER 1:

THE EARLY YEARS: 1909-1927

The Jimmie Dyess story begins in Augusta, Georgia, in 1909 and ends in the Marshall Islands in the Pacific in 1944. Who was this man and what events in his early life shaped him to be the kind of person who was so willing to risk his life to save others? The answer to these questions are to be found in his familial, religious, cultural, community and economic environment and in certain key events in his early life.

Aquilla James Dyess was born in Augusta, Georgia, on January 11, 1909. He was the third of four Dyess children. His father, Maurice Dyess, was the founder and president of the Augusta Lumber Company, a small but well established firm which specialized in high quality millwork for architects and builders throughout the Southeast. Mr. Dyess was a reserved and rather austere man. He had few hobbies, worked six days a week and when asked about golf, he loved to say, "The Augusta Lumber Company is my golf." Mr. Dyess was a devout Presbyterian and a long-time Rotarian, having served as president of the Augusta Rotary Club in the early 1920s.

The Dyess family has a very rich history in America. The first of the Dyesses emigrated from Wales to Virginia in 1635 and by the early 1640s other Dyesses had also sailed to the colony of Virginia. The primary motivation was to escape the very high tax rates in Wales at the time and, just as importantly, to seek a new life in the untamed world that was America. Most of the original Dyess emigrants were farmers and many of these early immigrants thrived in their new homeland. By the 1660s, various Dyesses were buying parcels of land as large as 1200 and 1350 acres in various counties of Virginia. The spelling of Dyess varied quite appreciably in 17th century America. There seemed to be a family relationship among those with the following names: Dyos, Dyes, Dyess, Dyas, Dyass, and Dias. In the 18th century, however, the Dyess spelling seems to have dominated the family tree and does so until today.[2]

By the middle of the 18th century, a segment of the Dyess family had moved South—to the colony of South Carolina. Jimmie Dyess's great-great-grandfather, Thomas Dyess, was the fourth of six brothers from Barnwell County, South Carolina. Three of Thomas's older brothers fought in the Revolutionary War but Thomas, who was born in 1768, was too young to have fought in that war.

Jimmie's great-grandfather, William Dyess was born in Wilkinson County, Georgia, in 1802, and his grandfather, Aquiler James Dyess, was born in 1848 in Macon County, Georgia. The name Aquiler appears often in the Dyess family tree in the 18th and 19th century. Why it was changed from Aquiler to Aquilla when Jimmie was born in 1909 is not known. What is clear is that the portion of the family tree which is directly traced back from Jimmie to his great-great-grandfather is directly linked to the soil, to the rural south and to the states of Georgia and South Carolina.

Many of the men of the Dyess family fought on the side of the South in the Civil War. The most poignant story of the Dyesses in combat is of the five Dyess brothers who fought together at the battle of the Wilderness in 1864. During an attack by Union soldiers, one of the brothers, Ely, was killed. The four other brothers were denied permission from their commander to recover Ely's body. The commander feared that the risks were too high in the face of a continuing strong Union advance. The memory of having to retreat from the battlefield and of leaving Ely behind was a heavy one on all of these brothers for the rest of their lives. Like so many who were killed in that long and tragic war, Ely was never found or properly buried.[3]

Jimmie Dyess's mother was Sallie Weatherly Dyess. She came from Hazelhurst, a small farming town in South Georgia. Like the Dyess family, the Weatherlys had roots in the deep South and also like the Dyesses these roots were in both rural Georgia and rural South Carolina. She was the mother of the four Dyess children who were born from 1904 until 1915. Louise was the oldest child; Guyton was the oldest boy; then came Jimmie and, six years after Jimmie's birth, Sarah, the youngest, was born. They were all born at a time when America was thriving economically, large families were common and taxes were low. Hard work and self-discipline were highly valued among the middle class all across America.

Aquilla James Dyess was a healthy, happy, robust, energetic boy with a great shock of unruly dark red hair. As a very young man he decided that he hated the name Aquilla and wanted to be known simply as Jimmie. Although he picked up many nicknames along the way including "Pinky," "Red" and "Big Red," he clearly preferred Jimmie. When he completed a personal letter, he signed it, "Jimmie." His mother and sisters called him James, but they were clearly the exception.[4]

The Dyess family were faithful Christians; as dedicated Presbyterians they lived by a strict code of personal behavior and family discipline. Church membership, attendance and support were a significant part of their lives. Although they lived in the small village of North Augusta, South Carolina, which was situated on the east bank of the Savannah River, they attended the First Presbyterian Church across the river in downtown Augusta.

This church had a long history of service to the Augusta community. Throughout the 19th century it had been led by a number of distinguished pastors, including a man of indomitable character and theological distinction, Joseph Ruggles Wilson. Wilson was pastor of the First Presbyterian Church of Augusta for twelve years during, and immediately after, the American Civil War. He had a powerful influence on many Augustans, including, most profoundly, his own son, Thomas Woodrow Wilson. After a distinguished academic career, Woodrow Wilson would become, in 1913, the 28th President of the United States. Woodrow Wilson spent his formative years in Augusta and at the First Presbyterian

Church. In fact, during his 67 years, he lived longer in the Wilson home on 7th Street in Augusta, Georgia, than at any other location, including the White House.

The Presbyterian values and lifestyle to which the young Woodrow Wilson was exposed in the middle part of the 19th century had changed very little in the fifty years from the time Wilson left Augusta and Jimmie Dyess was born. Hard work, Sunday church attendance, support for the community, patriotism and abstinence from alcoholic beverages were deeply held commitments of Augusta Presbyterians. In the Dyess household, consumption of alcohol was strictly forbidden. During Jimmie's youth, there were never any alcoholic beverages allowed in the Dyess home nor was there any drinking by any of the Dyess family at any location.

At about the time of Dyess's birth, the city fathers of Augusta began an aggressive "ballyhoo" to advertise the Garden City of Augusta as a great place to live and visit. They took this initiative for a number of reasons. Manufacturing and cotton farming were both in decline, population was stagnant (at about 40,000), and the Medical College of Georgia, which was located in an out-of-date facility, was in danger of being moved from Augusta to Atlanta. Augusta thus began to aggressively advertise for aviation schools, National Guard encampments, Army camps, and, most of all, tourists from up North. Augusta leaders came up with all kinds of innovative ways to attract both tourists, who would "winter" in Augusta from January through April, and permanent residents.[5]

A big breakthrough came in 1911, two years after Dyess was born, when Wilbur Wright, the world famous inventor and aviation pioneer, accepted an invitation from the Augusta city fathers to open a winter aviation school. Flying in open cockpits in the winter time was a frigid undertaking in the hometown of the Wright brothers, Dayton, Ohio. Wilbur, one of the great visionaries of all time, understood that if aviation were to thrive it needed to be expanded into the South where, because the flying weather was both better and warmer, it could become a year-round proposition.

In this prewar period, other famous people were invited to Augusta, and many came. Ethel Barrymore, the actress; Booker T. Washington, the educator; Eugene Debs, the famous Socialist, all came for performances or speeches. In these boom times, wealthy Americans were becoming fascinated with celebrities. They flocked to the same spots that these celebrities frequented.[6]

In 1911, the governor of New Jersey, Woodrow Wilson, took a vacation in Augusta. Already being talked about as a potential presidential candidate, Wilson, the renown scholar and gifted orator, visited his boyhood home and church. He also went to watch the acting debut of the famous Georgian athlete, Ty Cobb. At the time, Cobb was the most talented baseball player in a game which had become, during the first decade of the 20th century, the rage of the American sports scene. Cobb also was the most famous baseball player in the world (Babe Ruth would come along a few years later). In this period immediately prior to World War I, President William Howard Taft visited Augusta three times, in 1909 and 1911 when he was the president, and again in 1914 after Woodrow Wilson had defeated both Taft and Theodore Roosevelt in the great three-way presidential race of 1912.

When Dyess was seven, on March 22, 1916, a fire broke out in downtown Augusta. In the high winds the fire quickly spread and all of downtown was soon in flames. Thirty-two blocks and some 746 buildings were destroyed, including historic St. Paul's Episcopal Church and many of the finest homes in Augusta. Although the building which housed Augusta's daily newspaper, The Augusta Chronicle, had been gutted by fire, the staff was able to get out a two page edition the next morning. The editorial reflects well the community spirit of Augusta in the days of Jimmie's youth.

If we know Augustans, and we think we do, Augusta will awake today to a new energy and determination: to rebuild what the flames have destroyed, and to build better than before.

For be it known, Augusta has faced disasters before...

Augusta knows something of adversities and how to overcome them.

The lesson she had learned is that reverses test the mettle of cities as they do of men; that obstacles spur us to greater effort and determination and that the surest and quickest way to overcome a loss is to begin at once to repair it.

So let's all join in bright and early this morning; wash the smoke off our faces, shake the cinders off our clothes—wade right in to show what old Augusta really can do when she tries.[7]

That is exactly what happened and young Jimmie watched as the citizens of Augusta, with little outside assistance, rebuilt the city. The fire was a devastating blow for Augusta but, like so many tragedies, it had a positive aspect. Soon after the great fire, a construction boom began and many new homes were built. The housing boom took place not only in the downtown area but also on "The Hill" in the Summerville area. Now that many well-to-do people owned automobiles, it had become quite practical to live four or five miles west of downtown, on the lovely wooded hill which overlooked the town. "The Hill" had many advantages. It was less vulnerable to flood and fire, it was slightly cooler in the summer, and the building lots were larger and less expensive. Although the Dyess family was not part of this initial surge to "The Hill", they eventually (in 1929) moved their home to 2556 Walton Way in Summerville.

When Jimmie celebrated his eighth birthday in January, 1917, war clouds were on the horizon. Popular opinion about the World War I was split in Augusta, where there was much anti-British sentiment. Those of German descent looked for and found support from the many in Augusta who had Irish blood. The "Easter Rising" in Ireland in 1916 had been followed by the brutal British suppression of the Irish independence movement. This bloody suppression had enraged most Irish-Americans and had reinforced their strongly anti-British feelings. Hence, these Irish-Americans joined the German-Americans in opposition to America's joining in a war in support of Britain. But January, 1917, was the month that the German government made a major strategic mistake. Germany publicly announced that it would extend its submarine campaign to include all ships, neutral as well as belligerent. This meant that American ships were in grave danger. On February 3, a German submarine sunk the American liner Housatonic off the coast of Sicily.[8] This sinking caused public opinion in Augusta and throughout America to shift swiftly and dramatically against Germany. On April 2, 1917, a town meeting was held and the citizens of Augusta adopted a resolution which stated that declaration of war was the only course for America.[9]

Hence, there was strong local support when President Woodrow Wilson, on that same day, asked the Congress to declare war on Germany. This decision to enter World War I with a huge commitment of troops affected the entire nation. There was an immediate need to expand dramatically the small American military establishment and to train soldiers for the combat they would face on the western front in France. The Augusta leaders, who had proven themselves so skilled in attracting business, commerce and tourism to Augusta, moved quickly and put in a bid to the War Department for an Army camp. Approval from Washington followed soon thereafter and a surge of soldiers into Augusta commenced.[10]

By autumn of 1917, 36,000 soldiers, mostly from Pennsylvania, had arrived, nearly doubling the population of the metropolitan area of Augusta. Eight-year-old Jimmie Dyess saw soldiers everywhere. They would spark an interest in military matters which would stay with him for the rest of his life. With the arrival of these soldiers came a surge in patriotism throughout the Augusta area. These young men were not Damn Yankees; they were patriotic Americans doing their duty and were warmly welcomed by the community. America was unified in a common cause and a common mission—to save Western democracy and to win "the war to end all wars."

In the next year and a half, America played a major role in defeating Germany. On November 11, 1918, all of America celebrated the end of the Great War. Nine year old Jimmie felt this outpouring of patriotic jubilation which permeated the Augusta area. Our soldiers were coming home, a new decade was coming and Americans and Augustans alike were confident that the good times would roll.

Since the 1920s were the most formative years in Dyess's life, it is important to examine the context of America and Augusta at this exciting, uplifting time. By 1920, America had passed the 100 million mark in population (the census of that year showed 105 million), making it more populous than France, Germany, Great Britain, Italy or Japan. The United States' economy had become the largest of any nation in the world. Since 1900, life expectancy in America had increased from 49 to 54 years and by 1920 the illiteracy rate had dropped to 6%.[11] The vast majority of Americans were Caucasians (89 per cent) and the biggest minority group were Negroes (as African-Americans were called in the 1920s) with about 10 per cent of the population. Georgia had a population of 2.2 million people (Florida, by contrast, had only 900,000). Augusta, Georgia's second oldest and third largest city (only Atlanta and Savannah had more people), had 52,000. The ratio between whites (60 per cent) and Negroes (40 per cent) in Augusta had remained fairly steady for many decades. The white and Negro neighborhoods were closely interspersed and the Negroes who worked in the homes and gardens of the whites normally walked to and from work.

By far the most significant event of Jimmie's pre-college years occurred in 1919. He was then ten; his older brother, Guyton, was fourteen; Louise was sixteen and little Sarah was four. That summer, a major family tragedy occurred that impacted Jimmie's life in a particularly traumatic way. After this event, the Dyess family would never be the same. Guyton was on a Boy Scout camping trip in the third week in July when he became quite ill. He was brought home for care, but his condition deteriorated quickly. He had contracted typhoid fever and the doctors could do nothing to save him.

Within a few days he was dead. These were the days before peni-
cillin and other "miracle" drugs so it was not uncommon for people to die quite quickly and unexpectedly from disease or infection.
Guyton had been the pride and joy of both his parents and his death
had a shattering impact on everyone in the family.

Shortly after his death, Jimmie's father, in a moment of great
grief, told him, "the wrong boy died." From that moment on, there
are indications that Jimmie, for the rest of his life, was driven to
prove himself to his parents. The family went through an extended
period of mourning and it is clear that Guyton's parents never fully
recovered from the loss of their most favored son.[12]

The years of Dyess's youth marked the era of greatest segregation in the South, even more so than in the period immediately after
the Civil War. However, it was not just racial segregation. It was a
multifaceted segregation based on race, social class and sex. A
Supreme Court decision of 1896 (Plessy vs. Ferguson) had made
racial segregation the law of the land. By the time Dyess was born,
rest rooms, drinking fountains, buses and streetcars had became
segregated (whites filled buses from front to back and blacks from
back to front). The only public high school for blacks, Ware High
School, had been closed in 1897. Those black children who might
be inclined to go on to high school had no publicly-funded institution to attend. Some bright young black children would attend
small and informal "private" high schools. These schools, which
received no public funds, provided classes held in the homes of
black women who had some education beyond grammar school.
The most prominent of such schools in Augusta was Lucy Laney's
Haines Institute.

There was also a small private college for blacks, Paine College,
which offered both high school and college level courses. Some of
the brighter and more ambitious black children from Augusta
would enter Paine College without a formal high school education.
However, Paine College received most of its students from other
Southern cities which still provided some public high school education for black children. Although Paine College managed to sur-

vive in these difficult times, it did not become a full-fledged college for higher education until after World War II. In sum, only a few black students got an academic education beyond grammar school. But the black children were not alone; poor white children also faced many barriers. Public funds for education were largely reserved for white students of the middle and upper classes.

Segregation among whites in Augusta was based on social class. The white workers in the cotton mills tended to live in Harrisburg, a poor section of town which was immediately adjacent to the cotton mills. Harrisburg had elementary schools, but no high school. Hence, children of the mill workers rarely continued their schooling beyond the eighth grade. At age fourteen, most of these children began full-time work. Many of the adults of Harrisburg were from families of recent European immigrants who had moved to America starting in the 1880s. They were largely Irish or Scottish of Anglo-Saxon stock. Most worked at low wages in the mills and factories of Augusta, being paid once a week— often in silver dollars. Eight dollars a week was a common wage in the mills. The majority of these mill and factory workers, as well as the white families from small farms in the area, were political supporters of southern populism.

The populist movement, which had grown very strong in the period from 1890 to 1910, was a grass roots effort by small farmers and poorly paid factory workers to oppose the "fat cat" monopolists who were exploiting them. William Jennings Bryan from Nebraska was the great American populist leader whose spellbinding oratory electrified the American political landscape. After his "cross of gold" speech at the democratic national convention of 1896, the ideas of the "Great Commoner" spread like wildfire throughout rural and small town America. Bryan was the candidate of the Democratic Party for the American Presidency in 1896, 1900 and 1908. However, the Republican party, which had captured the support of the rich and, more importantly, most of the fast-growing middle class was dominant in these boom times. Bryan, whose appeal was to the small farmer and industrial and mill workers, was soundly defeated in all three of these presidential elections. Bryan and his enthusiastic supporters did make progress in Washington. Some of his programs included a shorter work week and the control of some of the excesses of the monopolists, such as child labor and extremely hazardous working conditions.

Within the populist movement there was a branch that had a dark side, one which espoused white supremacy and was largely responsible for the disenfranchisement of the black voter in the South. This movement was very strong politically when Dyess was growing up in the Central Savannah River Area. The closing of Ware High School was a direct result of the strong political clout of Augusta populists.

The Augusta Jewish community was small, but it was included in the city's mainstream of white, upper middle class families. Often excelling in academics, Jewish children attended both of the two public high schools for whites, The Academy of Richmond County and Tubman High School. After going off for higher education, many returned to Augusta to became respected business leaders, attorneys or medical doctors.

In those days, the sexes were segregated during the high school years. After attending elementary school together, boys and girls were separated during the "dangerous" teenage years when they were becoming sexually attracted to one another. White boys and girls attended separate high schools (Richmond Academy for boys and Tubman for girls) and only when they went on to The Junior College of Augusta (which opened in 1925), did men and women again attend classes together.

After the sharp, but short, recession in 1920-21, there was strong, sustained economic growth throughout the country for the next eight years. In the early 1920s, middle class Americans in the South tended to have large families with three or more children. They owned one automobile (usually a Ford which they bought for about seven hundred dollars). They lived in large, two story, homes with four or five bedrooms, indoor plumbing and a telephone, and sent their children to public schools. In the early 1920s, there were no Augusta suburbs to speak of, paved roads were rare and only recently had middle and upper class Augustans switched from horse-drawn buggies to automobiles. The vast majority of Augustans of all social classes moved from place to place by street-car, on bicycles or on foot.

In 1923, fourteen-year-old Jimmie Dyess, along with the other male freshmen, put on a military uniform and entered the Academy of Richmond County for the four-year curriculum. An all male military school since its founding in the 18th century, Richmond Academy was a public school for white young men of the middle and upper classes. That year also marked the grand opening of Augusta's new Bon Air Hotel. Located on the Hill, it was very large and quite elegant. It attracted the rich, the famous and those who liked to be around the elegant and the glamorous. Tourist traffic surged to its highest level in history. In April, President and Mrs. Harding visited Augusta and stayed at the Bon Air. The President played golf at the Augusta Country Club while the baseball fan in the family, Mrs. Harding, attended spring training games among major league teams. Augusta was becoming quite a resort city as wealthy Yankees came South during the cold winter months for lawn tennis, horseback riding, golf, badminton and other outdoor sports. The height of the tourist season was from January to April when the weather was mild with high temperatures in the 60s during the day—perfect weather for most sports. Most stayed not for a week or two but for three or four months.

In those halcyon days of the 1920s, when Yankees dreamed of a warm spot to spend the winter months, they did not normally think of Florida, Arizona or the Caribbean Islands. The great attraction which Florida would provide for tourists of later generations had not yet materialized. Florida was a bit too far to travel by train and the devastating Miami hurricane in September, 1925, turned American speculators away from Florida and back towards the Garden City of Augusta, the neighboring resort city of Aiken, South Carolina and other southern resort areas such as Ashville, North Carolina.[13]

The year 1924 was a particularly eventful one for Augustans with many memorable events taking place. Not to be outdone by a character who called himself the "human spider" and who had climbed Augusta's Lamar Building in previous years, another daredevil, the "Great Zarelli", walked a high wire across Broad Street at noon each day for a week in late January, 1924. Appreciative citizens tossed pennies and an occasional nickel into a hat that was passed through the crowd. The world's greatest tennis player, Bill Tilden, won the South Atlantic Tennis Tournament at the Augusta Country Club's new courts and a young golf sensation from Atlanta, Bobby Jones, played a round of golf in Augusta for the first time. Also in 1924, Anna Pavlova, perhaps the greatest ballerina of all time, danced at the Imperial theater at the height of Augusta's winter tourist season.[14]

All of these exciting events occurred during Dyess's teenage years, and he witnessed many of them. Although the Dyess family lived across the Savannah River in North Augusta, South Carolina, all of their work, school, church and social activities took place in Augusta proper. It was an easy and inexpensive trolley ride from home to school, church and the other centers of activity in Augusta. Dyess developed a great interest in sports and in anything having to do with the military including marching, marksmanship, aviation and hiking. With the major exception of the death of Guyton, life for the Dyess family was very good in the 1920s.

The local citizens of Augusta were benefiting from the new hotels being built, the land speculation and the tourist trade. A 1925 bond issue to build new roads to accommodate the growth in hotels and tourists passed by a vote of 5633 to 178, the closest approach to unanimity ever reached in the history of Augusta. There also was an ambiance which attracted many. Yale professor William Lyons Phelps explained Augusta's appeal quite well. "It has the finest winter climate, the people are hospitable and charming; the hotels are all that the most fastidious person could desire. Furthermore, for some reason, jazzy, noisy, pretentious, flashy people do not come hither; I dare say Augusta is too quiet for them. The hotels are filled with interesting men and women and those who think that good conversation is a lost art should enter our hotel some morning and stop, look and listen."[15]

Augusta was conveniently located on a major rail line coming down from the north. Although the first New York to Florida commercial airplane stopped in Augusta in December, 1925, reliable airline service from the northern states to Florida would wait until after the Great Depression of the 1930s. America and Augusta were on a roll in the rollicking years of the 1920s. The United States had bailed out the democratic states of France and England in the Great War. America had not had a major economic crisis since 1895. The United States not only had the world's largest national economy but its economy and population were growing faster than any of the other industrial nations. Also, the vast majority of Americans felt safe behind the great oceans that had protected them so well from external military attack for more than a century. Warren Harding of Ohio had campaigned in 1920 on a slogan of return to normalcy. After being elected to replace Woodrow Wilson, Harding followed a conservative course which included a return to isolationism that had been America's strategic policy for most of its one hundred and forty year history. To the great majority of Augustans it was prudent, patriotic and comfortable being an isolationist. Harding died a few months after his 1923 vacation in Augusta but his successor, President Calvin Coolidge, continued the conservative and isolationist course that had been established by his predecessor.

For the Dyesses these good, optimistic times were to be enjoyed not with the raucous frivolity of the flappers and the illegal speakeasies but with church, picnics, sports, family outings and honest, uplifting hard work. If anyone had suggested to the members of the Dyess family in the mid-1920s that lurking just over the horizon was a huge world-wide economic depression that would be followed immediately by the most devastating war in the history of mankind, they would have quickly rejected this prediction.

In this environment Jimmie seemed to be attracted to well-organized, purposeful activities. He loved and thrived in the Boy Scout movement which was very robust in Augusta in the 1920s. He was a member of Troop Four, sponsored by the First Baptist Church. Troop Four was the largest of the Augusta Boy Scout troops, probably because the Baptists outnumbered all the other religious denominations. In fact, the First Baptist Church was the largest of all the churches in the entire region. Since the Dyesses were Presbyterians, it is not clear why Jimmie chose Troop Four, but perhaps it was because many of his friends were Baptists. They may have encouraged him to join their troop rather than the one associated with the First Presbyterian Church.

In 1925, Dyess was one of five Boy Scouts (along with Bill Weltch, Russell Blanchard, Bill Wall and Parks Hende) who were selected to represent Augusta on a trip to Washington, D. C. to attend the International Boy Scout Jamboree. These boys were not only lucky to have been selected to go, but most fortunate in their means of transportation. Bill Wall's father held an important job on the Georgia and Florida Railroad. Mr. and Mrs. Wall, the five Boy Scouts, and a cook all traveled together to Washington in a private railroad car. During the entire jamboree, they all lived on this rather luxurious car, which was placed at a siding near the magnificent Union Station in Washington. During some leisure time, the five young Augustans, resplendent in their Boy Scout uniforms, went for a walk through a park near the White House. Mrs. Calvin Coolidge, the First Lady, was walking her dog. She saw the scouts and greeted them in a very friendly manner as they passed by, giving the boys quite a tale to tell when they returned to Augusta. They not only had visited the nation's capital, but had been greeted personally by the President's wife.[16]

During his early teenage years, Dyess was a quiet-spoken and modest boy, but he also held some very firm opinions and, at times, demonstrated that he had quite a temper. One issue that really angered him was the desire by the adult who was the Boy Scout leader of Troop Four to have the young Scouts sing together at public gatherings. Dyess had very strong feelings about the Boy Scouts and which activities were part of the mission and which ones were not. Dyess felt that singing performances for the public were completely inappropriate for Boy Scouts. So strong was his view that he not only argued with the adult scout leader whenever he scheduled a performance but, on a couple of occasions, threatened to leave the event if the Scouts were forced to sing. Despite these differences with his leader, Dyess stayed active in the Boy Scout movement, worked hard to earn merit badges, and eventually earned the rank of Eagle Scout.

When Dyess reached the age of sixteen, he joined with Mr. Reggie Dales of Augusta to form a Sea Scout Troop from among the senior scouts in the area. When the United States Navy gave the troop a boat, a number of the Augusta Sea Scouts, including Jimmie, went to the coast of South Carolina to fetch it. It was a twenty-foot life boat that was in terrible condition. For a week the scouts lived in Georgetown and practiced their nautical skills on this derelict. When it was time to leave, Jimmie approached the elderly man who manned the boat and did other chores around the dock. By now a self-confident teenager, the young man extended his hand, stating his thanks for the services rendered by this old man. The worker was so touched by the sincere appreciation of young Dyess that tears filled his eyes. There would be many others who, in the years ahead, would be touched by the thoughtfulness of this tall, strapping redhead.

Dyess spent all four of his high school years (from 1923 to 1927) at the Academy of Richmond County. This venerable school was the oldest incorporated institution in Georgia, having been established on July 31, 1783. In the 1920s, young white men in Augusta had only two choices when the time came to attend high school. One was a small Catholic school in downtown Augusta, the other, the public military school, commonly called Richmond Academy. When Jimmie was a high school sophomore, a small junior college was created. It occupied a few rooms of the Richmond Academy building. From that point forward, the school yearbook, the Rainbow, covered both the high school and the junior college. Although Dyess never attended the junior college, the young lady he would marry studied there for a year. This junior college moved to the old Augusta arsenal in the Summerville area and in 1958 became Augusta College. In 1996, Augusta College became Augusta State University.

Although Dyess played a great deal of football for the Richmond Academy team, his greatest successes came not in sports but in military drill. There was military competition in numerous areas of cadet life. Especially important was the competition in close order drill, where the cadet units could highlight their marching ability. Dyess won more prizes for his drill leadership than any other cadet in his class. In 1927, the year of his graduation, there were 654 boys in the four-year high school. Sixty graduated in 1927, including "Pinky" Dyess, now a tall, handsome football player who was also an officer (a second lieutenant) in the cadet corps. His biographical sketch in the 1927 yearbook was brief:

"Pinky won his letter on the football team this year and played some real football to get it. He is also a lieutenant and is one of the most popular boys in the class."[17]

This rather bland summary might be compared with the more graphic descriptions of a couple of his classmates, including Harry E. Dawson, who appears just above Dyess in the yearbook.

"Sleepy has dozed in and out of the school for four years. It is a mystery how he gets any of his lessons for it appears that he is always thinking of something a million miles away from where he is. However, he is still with us so he must have some special system of apprehending, which is unknown to us."

Also, there was Eugene A. Woodward, who already knew what profession he would pursue while still in high school.

"An aspiring young dentist came to us not so many years ago and has been 'pulling' along ever since. 'Gene' expects to enter Cleveland Dental College at its next term of school. We all hope his profession will be painless, and that he builds up a prosperous business."

The class prophecy covered all sixty boys in the graduation class. It was predicted that two boys would become admirals, and that others would become coal miners, dance or golf instructors, or automobile racers. It was forecast that "Pinkie" Dyess and two of his classmates, "Ginnie" Flint and Parks Hende would head to Hollywood to replace the current romantic leading men of the silent screen, Richard Dax, Ronald Colman and John Gilbert.

The last few paragraphs of the 1927 Class Day Oration by Gus Speth, Jr. captured wonderfully well the altruism, spirituality and boundless optimism of these young men of Richmond Academy in Augusta of the 1920s.

It has been said that life is a grim battle and this world a great battlefield. Yes, it is true, this world is a great battlefield and today its battles are being constantly fought between the forces of good and the forces of evil. Never before has justice been so attacked and threatened by injustice, honesty by dishonesty, love by hatred, temperance by intemperance, fidelity by infidelity and mercy by cruelty. These great forces are always at warfare—some trying to uphold great principles of truth and integrity others to tear down and destroy. With this great thought, it behooves each of us to take a look into the future on which rests our destiny. What is the first thing we should have in mind? I cannot better answer this question than in the words of Daniel Webster, who, when asked what the greatest thought of his mind was, promptly replied. "My responsibility to my God." This ought to be the basis and inspiration of the great career we go out to seek. Another thought we should constantly keep in mind is an answer to a question asked the richest man in our country. He was asked what his greatest desire and ambition was. His reply, "To serve my fellow man." These are the fundamental avenues of service that lead to ultimate success and happiness. As some one has said, what we do for ourselves is temporal and dies with us, but what we do for others is eternal and lives for ever. We who have been blessed with a college [Speth was in the Junior College] education, must be of service to the untutored by extending a helping hand, for unless we lift them up they will pull us down, and with us the entire fabric of our civilization.

The sacred voice of inspiration has told us that there is a time for everything; time to work, time to play, and time to pray. These are the elements of humane character, with which God has endowed each of us. But, fellow classmates, it is reserved for each of us to be the great alchemist as we work out the proper formulas for each of our lives. How we compound these elements in our lives will measure the degree of our progress and our success. We become the architects of our own fortunes, the masters of our own destinies. Then let us cherish these thoughts and give them meaning in our lives. Great men live for today and perhaps the day after today, but their great deeds for others live on through the centuries.

Friends, as we stand on the height of cultural development, the education that this school has given us, let us put ourselves in the place of the young man Abraham, to whom God committed the great task of founding a nation. God led him into the world and said: "Lift up now thine eyes, and look from the place where thou art northward, and southward, and eastward, and westward: For all the land which thou seest, to thee will I give it . . ." We, fellow classmates, are like this young man, the world is ours to take, but we must possess the courage to do or die, faith in God, in our fellow men, and in ourselves. Let us lift up our eyes and behold the limitless riches of the future.

Fellow classmates, with sublime faith and hope and courage we turn now to face the challenge of the greatest century in all the history of the world. These physical bodies of ours shall know alike the inexorable degree of nature. But may this unconquerable spirit of youth sustain us triumphant to the end. Far down the years may the heroic figure of gray Ulysses inspire us to purpose yet to sail beyond the light of all the Western stars until we die.[18]

This period in the history of the Academy of Richmond County was a rich one. There were many cadets of the classes of 1926 and 1927 who would go on to considerable success in sports and in life. Ed Mulherin, who chose the same college as Dyess, soon became the star quarterback for the Clemson varsity football team. Tyrus Cobb, Jr., the son of the great baseball player, was also a fine athlete; his great love was tennis. Young Ty had a gentle nature and, unlike his volatile father, made friends easily. After graduation from college, Cobb became a doctor and quietly practiced medicine in the small town of Dublin, Georgia for many years. Henry Pund became an All-American center on the Georgia Tech football team and later became a vice president of Bethlehem Steel. Richard Sheridan, one of Richmond Academy's most gifted athletes, met a tragic death when he broke his neck playing football for the United States Military Academy. He was the first athlete to be memorialized at West Point. Russell Blanchard, Dyess's close friend in the Boy Scouts, would become a very successful banker, and serve for many years as president of the Georgia Railroad Bank. Two of Dyess's friends at Richmond Academy had very successful careers in the military. Ed Montgomery graduated from the Naval Academy, becoming a Marine Corps officer and an aviator. He flew in combat during the battle for Okinawa, served on active duty for thirty years and retired as a brigadier general. Macpherson Williams had a long and distinguished career in the U. S. Navy and was promoted to rear admiral before he retired.[19]

There are many stories about Dyess from his days at Richmond Academy. When Jimmie first arrived, he was, like all of his classmates, outfitted with a uniform and sent out to the parade field to learn close order drill. Unfortunately, he had such a large head that no hat could be found that would fit him. Seventy years later, a number of people still remembered watching the new freshman class marching on the drill field with one tall lad with no cap. Dyess's rich abundance of flaming red hair made him stand out even more in the formation.

Later in his high school years when he had grown quite large (six foot one and 180 pounds), Dyess was helping out the track team which was competing against Lincolnton High School. The man who served as Richmond Academy track coach was Professor G. C. Cordle, a well respected history instructor. He was a man of small size but of big heart and great enthusiasm. The Lincolnton coach, a large and rather pompous man, told Cordle, "Coach, if we beat you today, I will take you and roll you down the infield." As the track meet continued Richmond Academy fell farther and farther behind. Coach Cordle went over to Dyess and said, "Come with me." Cordle then walked up to the Lincolnton coach and said, "I want to introduce you to my personal bodyguard." Richmond Academy lost the track meet but coach Cordle was never touched. For many years after Dyess was killed, Coach Cordle told that story with pride and affection. This is just one of many times when Jimmie Dyess would come to the assistance of someone in need.

As the rambunctious years of the 1920s raced by, the Augusta economy, social life and sporting activity thrived. In 1927, the year Dyess graduated from Richmond Academy, the New York Giant baseball team was invited to hold its spring training in Augusta. The Giants accepted, so Augusta had not only a fine baseball team to draw tourists but also the most famous manager of the era, John J. McGraw. Also in 1927, Augusta's most famous citizen, Ty Cobb batted .357 in what was to be his "final" season. Cobb changed his mind and played again in 1928. During his last year in baseball, Ty Cobb became the first American baseball player to become a millionaire—one step ahead of Babe Ruth.[20]

During his high school years, Dyess spent much of his spare time at his father's firm, the Augusta Lumber Company. In the 1920s, the company was especially successful and was considered the best firm in the entire region for the production of high quality millwork, windows and doors. Since there was an ongoing building boom in the Augusta area, this fine millwork was in great demand by the builders of homes, hotels, guest houses and country clubs.

When Dyess left home in 1927 for college, he decided to pursue studies in architecture. It was a natural choice for someone who had grown up watching his father's firm serve the needs of the architects and builders in the area. Dyess expected that when he would return to Augusta in four years there would be excellent job opportunities, either at the Augusta Lumber Company or within the robust construction business in the Central Savannah River Area. Little did he know what traumatic events and dramatic changes would take place in the world, in America and in Augusta during the next four years.

CHAPTER 2:

CLEMSON 1927-1931

The summer of 1927 brought the next big challenge in Dyess's life, for he was off to Clemson College, or as it was then called, Clemson Agricultural College of South Carolina. Dyess chose Clemson for a number of reasons, but two were fundamental. First of all, he wanted to play college football. Clemson was not at the top in the football rankings and did not attract the very best of the high school athletes. But Dyess felt the Clemson football program was ideal for him. He thought that he would have a better chance of making the team at Clemson than at one of the bigger football powers. Also the Clemson coach had a fine reputation of building a good program with the athletes he had. The second strong attraction that Clemson had for Dyess was that it was then a military school. From its founding in 1889, Clemson had been a military institution where every student wore a uniform all of the time on campus. Dyess had so enjoyed the military regimen of the Academy of Richmond County that he looked forward to the order, discipline and camaraderie that had defined Clemson College since its founding.

During the decade before Dyess arrived, there had been a great deal of turbulence at Clemson. On a number of occasions, the cadets held major protests against food that was "unfit for human consumption," the harsh discipline of military life, and the scarcity of weekend passes for the cadets. In October, 1924, the most serious of a series of student walkouts took place. This incident led to the dismissal or suspension of two hundred and fifty students including R. F. "Butch" Holahan, the president of the senior class and a football star. Holahan was suspended for consuming alcoholic beverages, then considered a serious offense indeed, not only because prohibition was the law of the land, but also because it was a serious violation of the rules of Clemson College. When an institution of just over a thousand students loses two hundred and fifty, the impact, to say the least, is traumatic.[21]

But the cadets were blessed by the arrival in 1925 of a new president, "the Plowboy Scholar," Enoch Walter Sikes. By the time Dyess arrived in the summer of 1927, Sikes had solved many of the problems that had so enraged the Clemson cadets. In addition, most of the suspended students had been allowed to return and were back on campus. The food in the mess hall was vastly improved and a more liberal policy on weekend passes and visiting privileges had been established. Dr. Sikes would provide enlightened and compassionate leadership at Clemson from 1925 to 1940. Most of these years were difficult ones for Sikes and the college, for when the Great Depression hit, funding support was hard to obtain for the students, the faculty and the college.[22]

The Clemson campus of the present day gives little evidence of how small and rural the area was in the 1920s. The town of Clemson then numbered only a few hundred people, most of whom were either faculty or administrative people at the college or their family members. There was one gas station, one drug store and one general store. Most of the roads were unpaved. Located 100 miles due north of Augusta in the extreme northwest corner of South Carolina, Clemson was a three hour automobile trip for Jimmie when he enrolled in September, 1927.

By the time Dyess arrived at Clemson, the college had expanded modestly to a student body of about twelve hundred cadets and a faculty and staff of about one hundred. President Sikes knew every faculty member and every cadet by name. As he walked the campus in his slow and rambling style, he would take the time to stop and visit with cadets, faculty and staff. Long before the management guru of the 1980s and 1990s, Tom Peters, invented the term "Management by Walking Around", Sikes was practicing it every day on the campus of Clemson. President Sikes was a wonderful role model for the cadets of Clemson College. Jimmie Dyess, who was so interested in leadership, observed Sikes at close hand, particularly during the last two years when the financial situation grew increasingly grim for the school and for so many of the students. Sikes, who seemed to thrive in difficult times, worked hard to keep the program on track and to help the cadets find sources for financial aid so they could stay at Clemson and complete their education.

Life on campus then consisted mainly of studies, military drill, parades and sports. There was the close comradeship among the students that often exists at small colleges in remote locations. Since this was the period when the temperance movement was at its height and prohibition was in full swing, intoxicated behavior was largely absent from the Clemson scene. Moonshine was available, of course, and there was plenty of it being produced in the illegal stills in the nearby hills of South Carolina, Georgia and North Carolina, but on campus, alcohol was rarely found. An exception would sometimes occur on weekend nights, when a few of the more daring cadets would, surreptitiously, share a flask of corn liquor.

The greatest shortage on campus, however, was not alcohol but girls (in those days, no one used the term "woman" to describe an unmarried female in her late teens or early twenties). Of course, none of the cadets were female, and there were very few "town girls" whom the cadets might ask out for a date. The closest places where large numbers of girls could be found were the South Carolina towns of Anderson and Greenville. So when weekends arrived and cadets got permission to leave the campus, they would hitchhike to one of these towns in hopes of finding female companionship. They would almost always travel in their uniforms, for there was a better chance that someone would give them a ride. Throughout the region, Clemson cadets were widely respected for their good manners and self-discipline. They would bring with them a change of clothes and would normally spend most of the weekend out of uniform. When it was time to return to campus, they would change back into their Clemson uniforms, stick out their thumbs and catch a ride back. Although the cadets loved these weekends away from the barracks, life off campus was really pretty tame. The parties, dances and dinners in Anderson and Greenville were not only closely chaperoned but also quite sober affairs.

For those who did not get weekend passes, Saturday night dances on campus were the highlight of many weekends. Invitations would go out far and wide and the girls would be driven to and from the dances. By the late 1920s, the automobile had become the most common form of transportation to get visitors to Clemson. Most cars arriving for the dance carried a number of girls; the driver would normally be the mother of one of them who would serve as both driver and chaperon. At the end of the dance on Saturday evening, she would drive the girls back home.

Football was a hugely important part of Dyess's life his first three years at Clemson. He was a starting end on the freshman football team and, like most of his teammates, played on both offense and defense. What he lacked in skill, speed and size he made up with great competitiveness. He suffered many injuries—to his hip, his shoulder and his knee—but he was always willing to ignore the pain and eager to get back into the game. In late September, 1927, Jimmie hurt his hip practicing against the Clemson varsity team and missed at least one game as a result. However, the 1927 season was a grand one for Dyess and his fellow freshman football players. The team was undefeated and would provide many of the stars of the Clemson varsity team in the next three years.

As the autumn of 1928 approached, Dyess had great hopes of being a member of that varsity football team as an upperclassman. These hopes were realized and he made the team both his sophomore and junior years. As a sophomore, he was moved from end to tackle. This was the year that Dyess played on the same offensive and defensive line with the great O. K. Pressley, the unanimous choice as All-Southern Conference center in 1928, Pressley's senior year. Like Dyess, Pressley would later join the Marine Corps. Retiring as a brigadier general, Pressley would, later in life, be named to the College Football Hall of Fame.

Pressley's recollections of college football in the late 1920s are quite vivid. "Protective devices were optional and only consisted of thin shoulder pads, a helmet, built like a skull cap, with no knee pads or face masks. I can remember when many college players did not wear a helmet during a game." Players would often hit each other with their fists and, on occasion, kick opponents in the face when they were down. It was a common practice for players to work on the injury of an opponent in an attempt to knock him out of the game. In a game with South Carolina, O.K. recalled that every player on the first team, except one, was carried off the field in a stretcher. The eleventh player walked off the field voluntarily and gave it over completely to the second team.[23] Hence, because of injuries to players on the starting team throughout the football season, Dyess got plenty of playing time even though he was not a regular member of the starting team.

By the time his junior football season rolled around, his coach had shifted Dyess again, this time from tackle to center. An article in the school newspaper, The Tiger (November 6, 1929), captures the respect with which Dyess was held. Clemson had just played the powerhouse team of the University of Kentucky. Please note the colorful style that the student sports writer used to describe Dyess's exploits both on and off the field.

> *Dyess relieved Metz Gresham in the first half and immediately made himself noticeable. He hurt his shoulder on the first play, but refused to have time taken out.*
>
> *Shortly afterwards a sickening tackle was made by the red-head of a big Kentucky back as he hit the line of scrimmage. Dyess, seeing but one way to stop the Colonel, flung the injured shoulder into the runner and both went down as if they were shot. It spelled the finish for Dyess as he was hurt too badly to continue.*
>
> *He showed up better than any lineman the Tigers had in the entire game.*
>
> *Keep it up Jimmy boy—we open with congratulations to the scrappiest, pluckiest little red-head we know.*

Although Dyess was by now about six feet one inch tall and weighed about 190 pounds, he was labeled "little". This may be because he was now playing in the center of the line where the biggest players operated. The shoulder injury did not end his football career but 1929 was to be his last as a college football player. Dyess wanted to play as a senior, but a serious knee injury, which he sustained towards the end of his junior year, ended his football career. The damaged knee would bother him, off and on, for the rest of his life.

With his college football career at an end, Dyess's interest in sports now shifted from football to the rifle team. Rifle was a minor sport at Clemson and was sponsored by the Reserve Officers Training Corps. Dyess had been a member of the rifle team ever since he was a freshman, but by the late fall of his junior year he was devoting increasing attention to his skills as a marksman. During his senior year, Dyess served as captain of the team and led the Clemson College rifle team of 1930-31 to an especially noteworthy record. It was the second best among college rifle teams in the South. Dyess was one of two Clemson cadets selected for the regional ROTC team (the Fourth Corps Area ROTC team). This team was made up of the best marksmen in a twenty-five college area throughout the South.

In 1930 as a college senior, he competed in the National Team Matches at Camp Perry, Ohio, as a member of this regional ROTC team. These marksmanship championships featured over one hundred teams from all over the country. Most of these teams were made up of mature adults who had been shooting competitively for many years. Even though the ROTC team was composed of young and inexperienced marksmen, it earned 14th place. In the long history of these national open rifle championships, this was the highest ranking ever scored by any ROTC team.

Upon returning to Clemson after the rifle championships in 1930, Cadet Major A. J. Dyess and his teammate, Cadet First Lieutenant F. H. Crymes, were presented special awards before the assembled Corps of Cadets at a retreat ceremony on the 26th of September. This was a fine beginning for Dyess's senior year. At age twenty-one, Jimmie was not just a fine college marksman but had established himself as one of the best marksmen in the nation.

Therefore, it is not surprising that, six years after graduation from Clemson, Dyess would become one of the Marine Corps' top marksmen and would lead the Marine Corps Reserve Rifle Team to an even higher team standing in these same national championships.

Although he did not play football his senior year, Dyess was otherwise very busy. As a cadet major and commander of the first battalion, he was one of the five highest-ranking officers in the cadet corps (there was one colonel, one lieutenant colonel and three

Cadet Major Jimmie Dyess at Clemson College. Jimmie played varsity football, was a nationally acclaimed college marksman and served as a cadet major in the Clemson Cadet Corps. At the time, Clemson was an all male college with an enrollment of about 1200 cadets. Jimmie graduated from Clemson in 1931.

majors). In addition to his military duties and being rifle team captain, he was the president of both the Inter-Fraternity Council and the Minaret Club (students studying architecture), and vice president of the Georgia Club (for those undergraduates whose home towns were in Georgia) and the Kappa Phi Fraternity.

Even without football, there continued to be many opportunities to play sports both at Clemson and when he was home during the summer months. Although Dyess, like his father, considered golf a "sissy game," he loved tennis, badminton and horseback riding. In fact, horseback riding would have a direct role in drawing his attention to aviation. Dyess was not a great equestrian by any measure, but he, like all of the Dyesses, enjoyed riding. The new family home on Walton Way had a barn in the rear of the house. There were two horses stabled there (Apple and Canterbury) and when Dyess was home from Clemson he would often saddle up and head out into rural Georgia, or on occasion, into rural South Carolina. His home was near the outskirts of town so he would find plenty of open country soon after leaving the barn.

One summer, while Dyess was still a cadet at Clemson, his home was visited by a young Augusta high school student named Campbell Vaiden, who rode by on his horse. Campbell was not there to meet Jimmie but to visit his younger sister, the lovely Sarah Dyess. To Vaiden's considerable disappointment, Sarah was not home that day but Jimmie was. Noticing how downcast Vaiden was, Dyess suggested that they take a ride together. Campbell readily agreed and off they rode toward Daniel Field with its sod runways and bi-wing airplanes.

The airport manager of the time, Frank Hulse, noticed them as they rode up. Hulse, who later became the president of Southern Airways, was in his early twenties at the time. On a lark, Hulse suggested that the two young men might enjoy a short airplane ride. Neither Vaiden nor Dyess had ever flown in an airplane, but both young men quickly agreed. Hulse strapped them in, side-by-side, into the front cockpit. It was a tight squeeze, but both young men had a seat belt. Hulse climbed into the rear cockpit, fastened his seat belt and taxiied out to the grass runway. This open cockpit bi-wing airplane was a wonderful acrobatic craft and Hulse intended to demonstrate its full range of capabilities to the two young men.

The airplane ride was a wild one, while the impressions of the two aviation neophytes were in stark contrast. The high school student, Campbell Vaiden, and the college undergraduate, Jimmie Dyess, both enjoyed the early part of the ride. Then, as the pilot approached the Savannah River, he abruptly turned the aircraft upside down. From that moment on, the reactions of the two passengers were very different. As soon as the acrobatics began, Dyess fell in love with airplanes and aviation. As loops, rolls, Immelmans and Cuban eights continued, Vaiden was terrified while Dyess cried out for more. The final maneuver was a dive at the ground followed by a sharp pullout and a straight ahead landing. When they touched down, Vaiden vowed never to fly again. He kept that vow for many years. In fact, it was more than twenty years before he took another trip in an airplane. [24] By contrast, Dyess was so taken with flying that he tried, on a number of occasions, to become a military aviator, only to be turned down because of imperfect eyes.

Before completing the story of Dyess's college years, it is important to examine more carefully the event that he so rarely talked about—that day at the beach in the summer of 1928.

CHAPTER 3:

EARNING THE CARNEGIE MEDAL: 1928

It was during the summer between his freshman and sophomore years that Dyess was to demonstrate vividly a part of his character that was to mark the rest of his life. When people were in trouble, Dyess had a compelling desire to help out, irrespective of what dangers he faced. Let me tell the story of Dyess's earning the Carnegie Medal by using the words and recollections of those who witnessed Dyess's actions when he first demonstrated great courage.

The date was July 13th, 1928. The place was the beach on the Atlantic Ocean at Sullivan's Island on the coast of South Carolina, just a few miles north of Charleston. A nineteen year old young man with striking auburn hair was walking along the beach. Jimmie Dyess had just completed his freshman year at Clemson and was enjoying a vacation of sun and surf with his family. A violent summer storm had blown up unexpectedly; it produced high winds and huge waves. What happened next is best related in the newspaper story that appeared a few days later in the Augusta newspaper. Please take note of the wonderfully descriptive words and phrases used by the reporter.

MRS. ROSCOE HOLLEY SAVED FROM DROWNING AT SULLIVAN'S ISLAND

Detailed information has reached Augusta relative to the near drowning of Mrs. Roscoe Holley of this city which occurred at Sullivan's Island last Friday afternoon. Mrs. Holley was in the surf which was exceedingly rough. The tide began to ebb and she was being rapidly taken out to sea. Several attempts at rescue were made and given up because the parties attempting were not

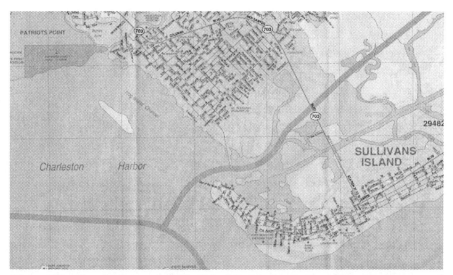

Map of Patriots Point and Sullivan's Island, South Carolina. Dyess earned the Carnegie Medal when he saved two women off the coast of Sullivan's Island in the summer of 1928. On the retired aircraft carrier Yorktown at Patriots Point is the home of The Medal of Honor Society.

expert swimmers and realized the hopelessness of their efforts. There were no surf boats available, no life guards on the spot at the time. Finally when all hope of rescue seemed gone, a young Charleston lady, Miss Barbara Muller, with courage and bravery unsurpassed, started out in a last ditch attempt to save the drowning girl. At this point 'Jimmy' Dyess an Augusta boy who had been bathing further down the beach came upon and realizing the situation went immediately to the rescue without pause to consider the danger involved in such an attempt in such a heavy sea. Both he and Miss Muller reached Mrs. Holley after she had been carried, perhaps, two hundred yards out. While both the rescuers were expert swimmers, it looked for what seemed to be an interminable time to the observers who stood in breathless suspense on the beach, that the trio was doomed to certain destruction. Finally it could be seen as they appeared from time to time at the crest of the huge waves, that they were gaining slowly and after about thirty minutes, they reached the beach and safety, where Jimmy's training in the Boy Scouts was of further service in aiding the resuscitation. When seen by a Chronicle reporter, 'Jimmy' said, 'Huh, that's nothing: what else could a man do? If there is any credit it is due Miss Muller, the bravest girl I ever saw. It looked for a time that we were all gone for a long stay but luck was with us.' On lookers give high praise to Miss Muller for a display of bravery and self sacrifice seldom equalled and never surpassed and add that but for the strength and cool headedness of Jimmy Dyess both girls would undoubtedly have been lost.[25]

For the valor he had displayed, Jimmie Dyess was nominated for the Carnegie Medal, a medal that has been awarded since 1904 to heroes who risk their lives in peacetime to save others. He received

Both sides of the Carnegie Medal. The Carnegie Medal is awarded to heroic Americans and Canadians who, at risk to their own lives, save or attempt to save the life of another. It is America's highest award for heroism by civilians. Dyess was presented the Carnegie Medal in 1929.

the award the next year—1929. The circumstances of Dyess's heroism that summer day at the beach are well documented. What is remarkable about the event is that he saved from drowning not one but two people. Also, he rescued them, not one at a time, but both at the same time. With no life guards along the wide beach at

Sullivan's Island, the sea became a very dangerous place whenever a storm appeared. Then, as now, when a storm began to build up, prudent swimmers would quickly leave the ocean and return to the safety of the beach. Mrs. Roscoe Holley made the mistake of staying in the surf too long and of being caught by the storm. Barbara Muller, who dived into the surf to assist, was able to swim out to Mrs. Holley. However, she did not have the strength to accomplish the rescue. For the rest of his life, Dyess, when asked about his heroism, would always give credit to Barbara Muller. She also earned the Carnegie Medal that day, but if it had not been for Jimmie Dyess, she might have won it posthumously.

There are other aspects of Jimmie Dyess's heroism that July day which need to be emphasized. It was not just his strength and swimming ability that saved the lives of two women. His cool-headedness also played a major role. Mrs. Holley had swallowed a lot of water and was very weak from fighting the waves and undertow. Jimmie Dyess's ability to analyze the situation, his strength and swimming skills and his will to prevail all played important roles. However, what was absolutely crucial was his ability to calm the women, especially the desperate Mrs. Holley, to gain their trust and to get them both to hang on to him as he slowly swam back to shore.

When they finally reached shore, a small group of onlookers picked up Mrs. Holley and moved her far enough onshore to get her away from the waves. However, they laid her out with her head higher than her body. Dyess, despite his exhaustion from swimming the two women to safety, ran up to Mrs. Holley, picked her up and placed her so that her head was lower than her body. He realized that she needed to get rid of the sea water that she had swallowed. Jimmie started giving her artificial respiration. Mrs. Holley coughed up a great deal of water and soon revived.[26]

Although his heroism was highlighted in the Augusta Chronicle immediately after the rescue, few people in Augusta or at Clemson understood the significance of the award. Apparently, he rarely discussed it with his friends. He was a real hero, yet he never publicly acknowledged his heroism on that extraordinary day when he dove, without hesitation, into the surf to save the lives of two strangers. Already, by age 19, Dyess had displayed two of the three most important qualities of a great leader: courage and compassion. Over the next few years, he would develop the third quality, competence.

To fully understand the implications of his actions on Sullivan's Island in 1928 and why they led to his being nominated for and earning the Carnegie Medal, it is useful to understand what the Carnegie Medal is, who created it, why it was established, who is eligible (and not eligible) to receive it and how difficult it is to earn.

Who was Andrew Carnegie and why did he establish the Carnegie Hero Fund Commission to honor outstanding acts of self-

Andrew Carnegie was one of America's most successful industrialists. He also was one of America's premier philanthropists. He gave away more than 95% of his wealth. Of the many organizations he started, the one he was most proud of was the Carnegie Hero Fund Commission which he founded in 1904. This commission honors civilian heroes.

less heroism? The saga of Andrew Carnegie, who established so many foundations, institutions and organizations to pursue worthy causes and assist people, is a very American story in the rags-to-riches, Horatio Alger, tradition. Although Carnegie started his professional life with very modest means, he soon became extremely wealthy, very powerful and world famous. In today's terms, Carnegie would be described as an aggressive entrepreneur. He set the mold that Bill Gates would follow more than a century later. Carnegie worked very hard and took many risks on his way to fame and fortune. He took full advantage of the business opportunities that America presented to aggressive, innovative, visionary men immediately prior to, during, and after the American Civil War. Although not the first of the American philanthropists, Carnegie would, in his long life, give away more money than any private citizen in history. He was a truly remarkable American. His story is well worth telling.

Born in Scotland 1835, Andrew Carnegie spent his first thirteen years in the village of Dunfermline, which was just to the north of the city of Edinburgh. By the 1830s, Dunfermline had become a one industry town. His father, William Carnegie, as well as most of the men, women and children of the village, was engaged in the linen weaving business. William Carnegie operated a hand loom and at the time of Andrew's birth was a successful small business man with four looms in his home and three employees. William Carnegie was Andrew's hero and the boy spent many hours each day sitting by his dad's side as he worked long hours at the loom each day. Initially, it was an idyllic life for small Andrew, who was a boy with unusual energy, curiosity and a zest of life. He was described, even at any early age, as an optimist and a dreamer.

However, life for the Carnegie family was destined to become very rough and very traumatic. By the time Andrew was twelve, the industrial revolution in Britain was in full swing. The big industrial looms began to produce cloth very cheaply. In the summer of 1847, a large steam-powered weaving factory began operation on Pitmuir Street in Dunfermline. Although 400 men found work in this noisy and dirty factory, dozens of local handweavers, who could not compete with the low prices of the factory, were put out of work.

That same summer, William Carnegie came to the stark realization that there were no longer any buyers for his hand woven linen. In the harsh winter of 1847-48, Will tried desperately to find work among the many manufacturers in the region, but to no avail. When his son would greet him at the door at the end of a long and discouraging day, William would say, "Andra, I can get nae mair work." With no income from Will, Andrew's mother, Margaret, tried to take up the slack by sewing shoes by hand and working in a tiny retail shop. The income that she produced could not adequately feed and clothe the large Carnegie family.

The year 1848 would set a record in emigration by the British to America. In all, 188,233 British citizens would leave for America. Among this group were the impoverished Carnegie family, reluctant to leave their beloved Scotland, but desperate to find employment in the promised land of America. Driven out of Scotland by poverty, they sustained themselves on their arduous journey with the hope of a brighter future.[27] In the Carnegie family there was one who saw this trip to America as a great adventure. Young Andrew loved the great squared-rigged sails of the crowded ship and while many were desperately seasick on this fifty day voyage, he loved the adventure and suffered no seasickness at all. Upon arriving at New York Harbor, the Carnegies took the cheapest possible route to Pittsburgh—by boat via the Hudson River and the Erie Canal. Margaret's two sisters lived in Allegheny, a suburb of bustling, dirty and crowded Pittsburgh.[28]

By this time all the family savings were depleted and work needed to be found quickly. Mr. Blackstock, a respectable Scotsman, offered both Will and his thirteen year old son, Andrew, jobs in one of his cotton textile mills. Andrew's first job was as a "bobbin boy", earning the meager pay of $1.20 a week—less than five cents per hour. Andrew hated his job. The hours were very long and work was boring. But he took great satisfaction in making an economic contribution to his family. Because he was such a happy and energetic boy, he was soon offered $2.00 a week in a factory that man-ufactured bobbins. This increase in Andrew's income was enough to allow his father to return to his beloved hand loom to make rough table cloths which he would then try to sell door to door.

Because Andrew was such an industrious teenager and had such great enthusiasm and charm, he was able to move up the job ladder rather quickly. His big break came when, at age fourteen, he inter-viewed for and received a job as a messenger boy in a telegraph office. The pay was $2.50 a week.[29] Young Andrew would lie awake at night memorizing the names, faces and addresses of hun-dreds of people who were to be his regular customers. Often, with an urgent message in hand, he would find the man on the street and deliver the telegram with a friendly greeting on the spot. This prompt, personal service usually resulted in a small tip for Andrew.

Soon, Andrew became the unofficial organizer of all the mes-senger boys in the telegraph office and he established rules which improved the efficiency of the whole operation. His boss, realizing how much Andrew contributed, would quietly give Andrew a bonus each month (usually $2.50). Andrew would dutifully bring all his pay home to his mother. Before he was fifteen, Andrew was pro-viding the main financial support for the Carnegie family. As a result of his continuing success as a breadwinner, the Carnegie fam-ily was able to borrow some money to buy a nicer home. Within three years after arriving penniless in America the Carnegie family was thriving. There was one very sad exception, Andrew's father. Will, who became more and more depressed with his inability to sell the cloth from his land loom, never adjusted to life in America.

Young Andrew was so hard working, creative and utterly charm-ing that his talents were recognized by many businessmen in the Pittsburgh area. At age eighteen, he accepted a job offer from the Pennsylvania Railroad Company and moved rapidly up the man-agement ranks in that dynamic young corporation. Now his vision-ary talents began to pay off. He realized that, as the company expanded and train trips became longer, people might appreciate sleeping accommodations. Carnegie borrowed some money and invested in a small sleeping car company. Then, he encouraged the executives of the Pennsylvania Railroad to introduce sleeping accommodations on some of the longer routes. Sleeping car service was an instantaneous success for the Pennsylvania Railroad, the sleeping car company and the Carnegie family. For the rest of his life, one of Andrew's favorite quotes was, "Blessed is the man who invented sleep."[30]

The executives of the Pennsylvania Railroad soon realized that the young Carnegie had great potential as a future executive. In 1859, at age 24, Carnegie was given a major promotion. He was named head of the Western Division of the Pennsylvania Railroad. He jumped into this job with a hands-on attitude. In those early days of railroads, engines often broke down. Also, it was quite normal for whole trains to derail. Carnegie would, on many occasions, work throughout the night with the repair teams making sure problems were solved quickly and the trains got through.

When the Civil War broke out, President Lincoln recruited Carnegie to help provide logistics and communication support to the Union Army. Carnegie witnessed the first battle of the Civil War at Bull Run and had the opportunity to see up close the bloodshed, death and devastation of war. For the rest of his long life he worked to find ways to prevent war. In his words, "War must become as obsolete as cannibalism."

After the war, Carnegie aggressively pursued new technologies and new investment opportunities. He became convinced that wooden railroad bridges were becoming obsolete and that bridges made out of steel would be stronger, safer and would last much longer. He invested in a small company, the Keystone Bridge Company, which made steel bridges. This was his first step into the new business of steel. It proved to be a timely and brilliant step, for it was in the steel business that Carnegie would make his greatest fortune. In 1865, he resigned from the Pennsylvania Railroad and never had to work full time again. In 1868, he moved to New York City and became, for a while, an investor and a capitalist.

By age 33, he was a very wealthy man, earning more than $50,000 per year (a quart of milk cost a nickel in those days, a newspaper—two cents). However, he soon became bored with investing and returned to the world of high level management. He developed a business strategy of vertical organization: owning everything in the manufacturing process from ore to final product. He was a perpetual optimist and "All is well since all grows better" was one of his favorite expressions. By middle age, Carnegie was making money in the infant oil business, iron and steel, bridges, railroads, the telegraph and steamships.

In 1889, Carnegie wrote and published an essay, "The Gospel of Wealth," portions of which were soon widely quoted throughout the world. Carnegie's thesis was that after a man became rich, he should distribute the surplus for the general welfare. This was a radical idea in the era of wealthy monopolists in America. Despite the heavy criticism of many of his rich friends and colleagues, Carnegie soon demonstrated that he was a man of his word. After he had made his case to the world, he vigorously followed his own advice and began to give away large sums of money to worthy causes. Despite his generosity he had, by the end of the 19th century, amassed a huge fortune. These were the days in America before income taxes; if people made vast amounts of money they could keep it all.[31]

In 1901, at age 66, Carnegie consolidated all his businesses into the United States Steel Corporation and sold it for $480 million to his close friend and neighbor, J. P. Morgan. In today's dollars, this would be a sale price of more than 12 billion dollars. When the day arrived to consummate the sale, Morgan came to Carnegie's house so they could both sign the simple paper that made the sale legal. Morgan said to him, "Congratulations, you are the richest person in the world."

Andrew Carnegie devoted the rest of his life (the next 18 years) to charitable endeavors.[32] Through the non-profit Carnegie Corporation of New York, he gave money to build 2811 public libraries, including 1946 in the United States, 660 in Great Britain, and 156 in Canada.[33] Prior to this time, there were private and society libraries but no free libraries for the general public. His commitment to the intellectual development of the common person had a profound impact on the American society and the growth of an educated middle class. Also, he founded the Carnegie Institute of Technology (now part of the Carnegie-Mellon University) in Pittsburgh, the Carnegie Endowment for International Peace in Washington, D.C. and the Carnegie Endowment for the Advancement of Teaching. In 1904, he established the Carnegie Hero Fund Commission in the United States and a similar commission in Great Britain in 1908.[34]

As an older man, Carnegie worked almost as hard giving away money to good causes as he did amassing his great fortune during his younger years. By the time he died in 1919, Carnegie had established himself as the world's most generous philanthropist. He also became a role model for other wealthy Americans like John D. Rockefeller, Andrew Mellon, Henry Ford and W. K. Kellogg, who, in turn, established foundations to help the handicapped, disadvantaged children, the elderly and other needy individuals and groups. These extraordinary philanthropists also established academic institutions, museums, libraries and other organizations that would serve the public at large. The people of the United States of America, which has the largest number of philanthropic organizations of any nation in the world, owe a considerable debt to the model established by Andrew Carnegie. Every American citizen who has ever received a grant from a private or public foundation should probably acknowledge the enlightened vision and generosity of Andrew Carnegie.

What inspired Carnegie to start the Carnegie Hero Fund Commission was his great interest in, and concern for, people who had risked their lives to save others. As he read about these heroic people in newspapers or heard about them from friends and colleagues, Carnegie was deeply touched by their unselfish acts of valor. Many of these courageous people, in their efforts to save a life, had injured themselves badly. Others had died during their heroic acts and left behind families which soon became destitute. America, at the turn of the 20th Century, had no safety net—no social security system or workman's compensation. In many cases, there was no way for injured heroes to pay for hospital expenses or to find work if they were permanently injured. Hence, the primary purpose of the Carnegie Hero Fund in the early years was to assist financially those who needed help after their acts of selfless courage.[35]

Of the more than 25 institutes, foundations, special funds and associations that Carnegie established during his nearly twenty years of full-time philanthropy, the Carnegie Hero Fund was his pride and joy. All of the others had been suggested to him. The Carnegie Hero Fund was his idea and his alone. He took great satisfaction in establishing, publicizing and participating in the implementation of this unique and enlightened program.

In 1904, Carnegie gave a grant of five million dollars for the specific purpose of helping these heroes and their families financially. This was a large sum of money in those days (it would be roughly comparable to 80 million dollars today). Remember that the average wage for a working person in 1904 was less than three dollars a day and less than seven hundred dollars a year. In the early years of the Carnegie Hero Fund, the top priority was providing financial aid to the heroes and their families. However, it also sought to provide public recognition for these heroic acts both by presenting to recipients a Carnegie Medal for their extraordinary valor and by publicizing their acts of courage.

Since 1904, the Commission has given away more than twenty million dollars to assist Carnegie Medal recipients or their families. In most years, the Commission has paid all of its expenses out of the income from the endowment and has not had to reduce the principle at all. In fact, the endowment has grown through the years. Through skillful investing and sound management, the endowment has increased from the original five million dollars to about twenty million dollars today.[36]

In more recent years, with the advent of social security and widespread insurance and pension support for most working Americans and their families, the need to assist financially the Carnegie heroes and their families has diminished quite significantly. However, financial support, when it is needed, remains an important part of the mission of the Carnegie Hero Fund Commission. In recent years approximately ninety people (Carnegie Medal recipients themselves or family members of Carnegie Medal recipients who lost their lives in acts of heroism) have been receiving monthly checks. Each year, the Commission reviews the financial needs of each individual receiving monetary compensation to insure the monthly stipend is still needed. If, for instance, when a child of a Carnegie Medal recipient, killed during an act of heroism, has finished his or her education and obtained a job, the financial support to that young adult is normally discontinued.[37]

It is very difficult to earn the Carnegie Medal; many hundreds of people are nominated every year from throughout Canada and the United States but fewer than 100 each year receive the award. Just saving a person's life does not qualify someone for the award. Only those who risk their lives voluntarily "to an extraordinary degree" qualify for consideration. The risk of life to save a family member does not make one eligible. In addition, certain categories of people are not normally eligible for the medal, including life guards, firemen, policemen and military personnel, no matter how heroic their efforts were to save the lives of others.

As stated on the 75th anniversary of the founding of the Carnegie Medal:

> *The Carnegie Medal is awarded to one who, at the risk of his own life, saves or attempts to save the life of a fellow man.*
>
> *There must be conclusive evidence that the person performing the act voluntarily risked his own life to an extraordinary degree in saving or attempting to save the life of*

> another person, or voluntarily sacrificed himself in an
> heroic manner for the benefit of others.
>
> The act of rescue must be one in which no direct fami-
> ly relationship or other full measure of responsibility
> exists between the rescuer and the rescued.
>
> The act must have been performed in the United States,
> Canada or the waters thereof and must be brought to the
> attention of the Commission within two years of the date
> of rescue.

The medal itself was carefully designed to display important, meaningful, symbology.

"Mr. Carnegie's embossed profile dominates the front of the medal. On the reverse side in low relief are shown the geographical outlines of the United States and Canada, the countries to which the Fund applies. In higher relief the seals of these countries are shown, with the United States below the inscription plate, and Canada and Newfoundland at the top left and right respectively.

"Relief work surrounding the inscription plate reveals a sprig of laurel underneath and sprigs of ivy, oak, and thistle at the top. Laurel typifies glory; ivy, friendship; oak, strength; and thistle, persistency. Encircling the relief work is a quotation from the New Testament (John XV, 13): *Greater love hath no man than this, that a man lay down his life for his friends.*"[38]

There is, of course, a paradox regarding this last point. In fact, the Carnegie Medal goes beyond this passage in St. John's Gospel about laying down a life for a friend. The Carnegie Medal is awarded for someone who is willing to lay down his life, not for a friend, colleague or family member, but for a complete stranger.

Reading the citations of Carnegie Medal winners can be an uplifting experience, for it makes one realize the extraordinarily selfless nature of certain people. Whether the event occurred in 1910, 1928, 1955 or 2001, the message is universal. To illustrate the kind of act that has qualified individuals for the award, let me cite two examples from 1979, the 75th year of the Carnegie Medal.

"Bronze Medal awarded to Gary Lane Parker, who rescued Gerry D Smith while he was in a runaway motorboat, Killeen, Texas, March 26, 1978. When his parents and younger brother were thrown out of an outboard motorboat and into deep water in a reservoir, Gerry, aged 19 months, was left alone in the runaway craft, which made erratic circles taking it ever nearer a rocky cliff. Parker, aged 25, automobile mechanic, entered a boat which was then piloted on the same circular course by an Army captain and from which vain efforts were made to snag the runaway with a rope. Parker then moved onto the bow of the captain's craft and when the two boats were parallel, leaped across the gap between them and grasped the railing of the runaway. Climbing into the runaway boat as it continued circling, Parker stopped the craft before any harm could come to Gerry."

" Bronze Medal awarded to Joanne Betts, who died after rescuing Patrice L Schmidman from an armed assailant, Omaha, Nebraska, June 23, 1978. In a public park Patrice, aged 9, was knocked down by a 15 year old boy, who then began stabbing her with a steel arrowhead. Joanne, aged 14, schoolgirl, jumped onto the boy's back and knocked him off Patrice, who then ran to get help. When others arrived, Joanne was found dead from stab wounds she had received. Patrice recovered from her wounds."[39]

CHAPTER 4:

THE DEPRESSION YEARS IN AUGUSTA: 1931-1940

Jimmie was in his junior year at Clemson when Augusta was hit by three major disasters. In October, 1929, heavy rains caused a monstrous flood. The levee failed along the Savannah River and a forty-six foot high wall of water smashed into the Fifth Street bridge that connected Augusta with North Augusta. Much of downtown Augusta was flooded and many businesses and homes were destroyed or badly damaged. In the same month, the stock market crashed and, soon thereafter, the normal tourist flow from the North diminished dramatically. The flood, the crash and the abrupt drop-off in the tourist trade combined to devastate Augusta economically. Since Dyess was busy with his studies, his cadet duties and his football practices and games, he probably didn't realize how seriously Augusta's fortunes had deteriorated until he came home for vacation in the summer of 1930. For the rest of his life, Augusta would never return to the buoyant, optimistic, uplifting atmosphere that had so shaped his life as a youth.[40]

Although the Augusta Lumber Company was clearly impacted by the Depression, it was able to keep most of its work force and make a small profit throughout the 1930s. Hence, the ongoing economic crisis had only a modest impact on the lifestyle of the Dyess family. Mr. Dyess was able to send Sarah off to a private women's college, Mary Baldwin, in 1932, with only a minor strain on the family finances.[41] But for the vast majority of citizens, Augusta in the 1930s was not a happy place for many reasons. There were thousands of Augustans out of work, not temporarily but permanently. For the very first time, Augustans came to the realization that they could not solve their problems themselves. Always in the past, whenever there had been a major fire, flood or economic depression, Augustans would get together, pool their time, talent

59

and resources, and begin the rebuilding process. The impact of the Great Depression was so severe on both Augusta and the outlying farming communities that the entire area required federal programs to help weather a period of economic deprivation that would last for more than a decade.

Desperate times also caused people to reach out for radical solutions, and the Cracker Party—with its strong emphasis on white supremacy—became the dominant force in Augusta politics. In fact, it was not until 1945 that the Cracker Party's control over local politics was broken. Prohibition, which had been in effect in Georgia since 1908, stayed on until 1938 even though the federal constitutional amendment was repealed in 1933. Yet there was much alcohol consumption in Augusta in the speakeasies along Broad Street (often referred to as "Whiskey Row") and from the bathtubs of many homes. This illegal behavior did not affect the Maurice Dyess family. In fact, although Jimmie would take an occasional drink after he graduated from Clemson, it was only after he was married in 1934 that having a cocktail become an occasional evening activity.[42]

If there were a worst time in American history to graduate from college and seek employment, it was the 1930s. When Jimmie Dyess and his classmates graduated from Clemson in 1931, unemployment throughout the nation had skyrocketed and would soon reach 25 percent. Although America had weathered a number of serious depressions in the 19th Century, the length and the scope of the depression of the 1930s exceeded anything in previous American history. All were touched by it, many were destroyed by it but Jimmie Dyess was strengthened by it. Of course, he was helped by the fact that his father gave him a job. His pay was very low at the Augusta Lumber Company, but at least he had steady employment.

From the time Dyess graduated from Clemson and returned to Augusta in the summer of 1931 to when he was called on active duty in the Marine Corps in November 1940, there were a number of significant events in his life. The most important of these were his decisions in 1931 to work for his father and to join the Army Reserves; his marriage to the former Connor Cleckley in early November 1934; the birth of their daughter, Connor Cleckley Dyess, in late August 1935; his determination, in 1936, to leave his job at the Augusta Lumber Company and to form a small construction company; his decision to leave the Army reserves and join the Marine Corps reserves, also in 1936; the failure of his small construction company in the "Roosevelt Depression" of 1937; and his return to the Augusta Lumber Company.

Accepting a job in 1931 as a timekeeper for the Augusta Lumber Company was an easy decision. There were just no other options. Companies large and small in Augusta were laying off workers or were going out of business. Joining the Army reserve unit in Augusta was also an easy decision for Dyess. He loved the military and he also enjoyed getting the small amount of extra income which duty with the Army Reserves would provide. The fact that he had been in a uniform since he was fourteen, that he was an excellent leader (both on the parade ground and in training maneuvers in the field), and that he was an expert marksman, made his transition into the Army Reserves a smooth one.

His transition into the Augusta Lumber Company was a breeze. Dyess had worked part time at his father's firm during his high school and college years and had earned a degree in architecture from Clemson. His rapport with both Augusta Lumber Company employees and with customers was based on his previous work experience and on the technical and intellectual competence he had gained at Clemson. His father felt that Jimmie should start at the bottom and that is exactly what he did. Earning less than a dollar an hour, Dyess had little choice but to live at home and to eat most of his meals with his family.

The handsome Dyess was admired by young ladies in Augusta and he had dates with many of them. However, soon he was spending most of his social time with Connor Cleckley, a lovely, vivacious and popular young woman, who was two years younger than Dyess. Connor had many interesting and unusual experiences in her youth and was more well traveled than the vast majority of her Augusta contemporaries. She had not only lived in England for almost two years but had traveled widely throughout Europe. Her father, until the family moved to England in 1924, was a well-respected dentist in Augusta.[43]

Connor's older brother, Hervey Cleckley, even as a young man, was recognized as an extraordinary individual. In time, he would become a world famous psychiatrist and best selling author. Hervey was eight years Connor's senior and by the time he reached high school, it was clear to many Augustans that he was a gifted young man. Quite a scholar in high school, he was best known for his athletic skills in football, track and field and boxing. After graduating from Richmond Academy in 1920, Hervey attended Princeton University, but was so homesick that he soon transferred to the University of Georgia. Although a modest and reserved man, he was a big man on campus who starred on the football and track teams and graduated very high in his class academically. In his senior year at the University, he was chosen for the most coveted of all post graduate scholarships. In competition with outstanding scholar athletes from all around America, Hervey was selected to be a Rhodes Scholar.

This selection led to a major family debate. Hervey was honored and pleased to have been chosen for this prestigious scholarship and wanted to attend graduate school at the most distinguished university in the world, Oxford University. However, he remembered his homesickness at Princeton just a few years earlier. Hervey announced to the family that he would turn down the Rhodes scholarship unless the entire family accompanied him to England. After a vigorous family discussion, Dr. Cleckley, who was in his sixties by this time, made a decision to give up his dental practice. In the summer of 1924, the whole Cleckley family packed up for England, where they fully expected to spend the next two years. [44]

Connor, who was thirteen when the family sailed for Europe, would not have a happy time in England. A shy and sensitive person, Connor went through a major cultural shock when she enrolled in a prestigious English girls' school. To state that she was not made welcome at the Headington School for Girls, Oxford, would be an understatement. During her first year at Headington, the British girls and the teachers treated her with disdain. Upper class English people in the 1920s tended to view Americans as culturally, socially and educationally deficient. Teenage English girls in the era of the British Imperium and of Pax Brittiania could be particularly cold towards all foreigners, especially those from the former colonies. Fortunately, the second year at Headington was somewhat better for Connor. In fact, she was elected "form leader" of the upper fourth form, the equivalent of president of her class. However, seventy years later Connor still shudders at the thought of those two miserable, cold years in England.[45]

Dr. Cleckley died suddenly during the latter part of Hervey's second year at Oxford. Connor and her mother returned to Augusta in the Spring of 1926. Connor was ecstatic to be back with her childhood friends again, where the houses and classrooms had central heating and where the climate was generally quite mild. She entered Augusta's Tubman High School and graduated in 1929. She then attended the Junior College at the Academy of Richmond County for a year and in the fall of 1930 was off to Sweet Briar College. Located in the beautiful rolling foothills of the Blue Ridge Mountains near Lynchburg, Virginia, Sweet Briar had been founded in 1901 and had been granting the A. B. degree since 1910. The mission of this woman's college remains the same a century after its founding. Its aim is to prepare women to be active, responsible members of a world community. Its curriculum is organized on the premise that a foundation in the liberal arts and sciences enhances the development of creative abilities and encourages the individual to continue to learn long after leaving Sweet Briar.[46]

Mrs. Cleckley made a decision when she drove up with Connor to enroll her at Sweet Briar College which turned out to be a major mistake. Rather than enrolling Connor as a freshman, Mrs. Cleckley insisted that she enter the sophomore class. Connor's roommates, who knew each other from their freshmen year together, considered her an outsider and were not kind to her. Although

63

she made four good friends (Mary and Helen Lawrence, Teresa Aikinson and Sarah Meador) Connor was severely homesick and decided to return to Augusta permanently after only one year at Sweetbrier. Just as Dyess was graduating from Clemson in the summer of 1931 and returning to Augusta, Connor was also return-ing home to stay.[47]

Connor still remembers the very first time she saw Jimmie soon after she returned from England. Dyess was still in high school and she saw him being driven by his father to Richmond Academy. Her immediate reaction was very strong and very positive. She thought Jimmie was the most handsome man she had ever seen and was immediately attracted to him. Jimmie also noticed Connor and, a couple of years later, he invited her to Clemson for a dance. Again, she was quite smitten by the handsome football player in his sharp cadet uniform who was so popular with his fellow cadets.

Fate clearly played a role in the summer of 1931 for not only had they returned to Augusta at the same time, but Connor and Jimmie were also to be neighbors for the first time. Dyess, who lived with his family on the hill in Summerville, was working six days a week and was doing weekend and summer drills with the Army Reserves. Connor was living on Monte Sano Avenue only a few blocks away from the Dyess home. Connor had many beaus, including Bill Thurman (younger brother of Senator Strom Thurman) and the tall, handsome and charming Dick Allen, who would later become mayor of Augusta.

Although Jimmie dated a number of young ladies after graduat-ing from college, he found himself wishing to spend more and more time with Connor. Slowly a romance was blossoming between the tall, strong redhead from Summerville and the lovely young lady who lived nearby. The romance between Jimmie Dyess and Connor Cleckley was in many ways an idyllic one, but it was not without its ups and downs. These were two strong-willed people who would, on occasion, have fiery arguments. One of the low moments of the romance occurred after a particularly intense dis-agreement. Jimmie had decided that the chemistry between the two was just not right and that his upcoming date with Connor would be his last. Connor's mother, realizing that these two young people were having quite a tiff, suggested to both of them that they "kiss and make up." That kiss turned the corner in their romance which soon blossomed again.[48]

Jimmie Dyess and Connor Cleckley in the summer of 1934 at about the time they became engaged to be married. Connor, who had lived and studied in England and traveled widely throughout Europe, was two years younger than Jimmie. When this picture was taken, Jimmie was 25 and Connor was 23.

The First Presbyterian Church of Augusta. The boyhood church of Woodrow Wilson; the Dyess family attended this church regularly. Jimmie and Connor married here on November 7, 1934.

By the autumn of 1933, the Connor Cleckley and Jimmie Dyess courtship had become quite serious. However, since Dyess had not asked Connor to marry him, it was socially quite important that she continue to have dates with other men. On the other hand, Connor felt that Jimmie should not date others because that would mean he would have to ask them. Both young people understood that under the unwritten rules of the 1930s it was not appropriate for Dyess to date other women since he was now so serious about his relationship with Connor. But it was important, since she was not engaged to be married, that, if Connor were asked by other men for dates,

Wedding Party. On Connor's right is Hervey Cleckley, her older brother. Cleckley, a Rhodes scholar and a psychiatrist, later became world-famous for his work with the sociopathic personality and with multiple personalities. His book, The Three Faces of Eve, *was a best seller and the film earned Joanne Woodward the 1957 Oscar for best actress.*

Wedding picture of Jimmie and Connor Dyess, November, 1934.

she accept these invitations. Since she was vivacious and pretty, Connor was asked out often. On many evenings, Dyess's only recourse was to date Connor after her escort for the evening dropped her off at home. Hence, there was a period of a few months, when many of the rendezvous between the two took place about midnight. Strange as it may seem today, this double standard where the woman dated many men and the man dated only one woman was well accepted throughout Augusta in the 1930s.[49]

It wasn't until the summer of 1934, three years after he had returned to Augusta, that Jimmie Dyess asked Connor Cleckley to marry him. Wedding arrangements were planned in the late summer and early fall. The wedding was held in the First Presbyterian Church in Augusta at noon on November 7, 1934. Although no invitations were sent out, the church was packed. The day was unusually cold for Augusta, and almost everyone in the church left their overcoats on throughout the ceremony. The strong-minded Connor decided that there would be no wedding reception. Soon after the wedding was concluded, the wedding party went back to Connor's home. The newlyweds had some pictures taken and then jumped in their new car and headed south. Dyess had been given the car by his father as a wedding present. It was the first automobile he had ever owned. Jimmie was twenty five, Connor, twenty three, when their life together began. The newlyweds honeymooned on the east coast of Florida, stopping at many spots on the drive to and from Miami. The honeymoon was short, for Maurice Dyess, always the tough taskmaster with his son, insisted that he return quickly to his job at the Augusta Lumber Company.[50]

After the marriage, Dyess and his bride lived in the home of Connor's widowed mother in order to save on expenses. A couple of months after the wedding, Connor learned that she was pregnant. For reasons that are hard to fathom today, it was considered rather inappropriate in those days for any young bride to become pregnant so quickly after the marriage. Most young marrieds in the 1930s were postponing their babies since the economic times were so dismal and no job was secure. Dyess was earning only $150 per month at the Augusta Lumber Company. This was barely enough to cover the expenses of a man and his wife. Thankfully, Connor received a small monthly check from her mother to help cover the additional expenses which the arrival of the new baby would entail.[51]

August 29, 1935, was a banner day for Jimmie and Connor Dyess, for it marked the arrival of a bouncing baby girl, Connor Cleckley Dyess. "Baby Connor" was a large baby, at eight pounds, and she was born with a full head of jet black hair. This hair soon fell out and was slowly replaced by the rich auburn hair of her father. Baby Connor was to be the only child of the marriage of Jimmie and Connor. The small family continued to live in the Cleckley home for an additional year. Only in 1936, two years after the marriage, was the young Dyess family able to afford to rent a small home of their own.

Also in 1936, the Marine Corps announced that a new reserve battalion was to be formed in Augusta. Dyess was greatly attracted to the Marine Corps and its grand traditions. In addition, Dyess learned that the Marine Reserves would do more training each year than the Army Reserves. This meant more pay for Marine Corps reservists than for Army personnel of a comparable rank. Also, the Marines had a richly deserved reputation as being among the very best marksmen in America. Army First Lieutenant Dyess applied for and was granted an interservice transfer. Hence, he became one of the first members of the new 19th Marine Reserve Battalion of Augusta.

With a wife and a new baby, it was time for Dyess to make another important decision. He chose to leave the Augusta Lumber Company and join with Brad Bennett (also an Augusta Lumber employee) to form a small construction company to build residential houses in the Augusta area. Dyess wanted to be free from that stern disciplinarian, his father, Maurice Dyess. He also hoped to make more money to support his family. Dyess was twenty-seven years old at the time, had been married for two years and had a year-old child. Dyess had known Brad Bennett since Jimmie had been in high school and began working part time at the Augusta

Lumber Company. Brad was six years older, had extensive work experience and was very strong on the sales and marketing side of the Augusta Lumber Company.

Starting a small construction business in the middle of the Depression was a considerable risk. The new partners built a number of small homes but the phone in the office didn't ring very often and, within a year, the business folded. Dyess had to go back to work for his father. The failure of the business may have been related to the so called "Roosevelt Depression" of 1937-38 when the American economy took another major nose dive. It would not be until 1941 that the build up for World War II finally pulled America out of its longest, deepest and most agonizing economic depression.

Soon after Dyess joined the 19th Marine Battalion, he took the initiative to join the Marine Corps Reserve marksmanship team. The skills he had developed at Clemson served him well and, within a few months, he was not only a full-fledged member of the team, but also one of its coaches. With this team, he competed in the annual National Rifle Association national championships which were held at Camp Perry in Ohio. In the 1920s and 1930s, these marksmanship championships were major events with nationwide publicity and many dignitaries in attendance. In the days before television, professional football Superbowls and NCAA final-four basketball championships, there were only five sports that received national attention (golf, baseball, tennis, horse racing, and marksmanship). The press gave lots of coverage to the baseball World Series, three great horse races (The Kentucky Derby, the Preakness and the Belmont), the U.S. Tennis Open at Forest Hills, New York and a few golf tournaments such as the PGA, the U. S. Open and the National Amateur. The Masters, first held in Augusta in 1934, was not a closely followed championship in the mid-1930s. It was not until 1937, when Gene Sarazen made a double eagle on the final round on the 15th hole to forge into the lead and win the championship that the "Augusta Invitational" became widely known as the Masters and began to rank at the same level as the United States Open and the PGA. The only other national sports championship that drew large numbers of reporters was a championship in which Jimmie Dyess competed in 1930 and again in 1937 and 1938.

The Marine Corps was especially well represented at the annual marksmanship championships in 1937. The Commandant of the Marine Corps (from 1936 to 1943), Major General Tom Holcomb, had, as a young officer prior to World War I, been a member of the Marine Corps marksmanship team. He attended the 1937 national championships with both nostalgia and great pride. That year, a team made history by winning the team championship for the fifth consecutive year. That team was the United States Marine Corps marksmanship team. But Holcomb's pride extended beyond the Marine Corps active duty team. There was another team representing the Marine Corps at these championships whose performance was also very impressive: the Marine Corps Reserve marksmanship team. When this team first competed at these national championships in 1935, it had the 50th best score (out of 113 teams). But in the next two years the skills of the team improved dramatically. In fact, the improvement was so rapid that some pundits accused the Marine Corps Reserve of actively recruiting the best civilian marksmen and signing them up as Marine Corps reservists just so they could compete for the Marine Corps Reserve Team. This accusation was false but there was an effort to carefully select the team from among those who were already Marine Reservists and who were outstanding marksmen as well. Also, the leaders of the Marine Corps Reserve made a strong commitment to give the team members a considerable amount of practice before the championships.

First Lieutenant Aquilla James Dyess, an outstanding college marksman in 1930, was selected as one of twelve members of the 1937 Marine Corps Reserve Team even though he had been a Marine for less than a year. The team membership was made up of both officers and enlisted men and all were reservists. Dyess won a number of marksmanship ribbons at the 1937 and 1938 national championships. As might be expected, he also earned the highest recognition for regular marksmanship qualification within the

Marine Corps, earning the top ranking (expert) in pistol, rifle, automatic rifle and bayonet. These marksmanship skills would serve him well after he was called to active duty, when he trained his Marines at Camp Pendleton and when he led them into combat.

In the four years from 1936, when the 19th Battalion was established in Augusta, to 1940, when the battalion was called to active duty, Dyess played many roles and had many successes. Although only a first lieutenant, he was assigned as a company commander of Company C of the 19th Battalion. Each summer the Augusta Marines would travel by railroad to Parris Island, South Carolina, for an intensive two weeks of training. There the training day would start at 5:15 each morning. Much of the time was taken up with marksmanship, and Lieutenant Dyess would instruct his young Marines in rifle, automatic rifle, pistol and bayonet. There was also close-order drill each day. Dyess, who had been drilling troops ever since his high school years, easily gained the respect of his fellow Marines as he enhanced the discipline of his company on the parade field.

While Dyess provided lots of enlightened leadership to his young Marines, he also made some mistakes. On one occasion, the men of the 19th Battalion were on the train from Augusta to summer camp when a fight broke out between two enlisted Marines. A third enlisted Marine jumped between the two in an attempt to break up the altercation. For his efforts he got hit hard in the face. He swung back to subdue the perpetrator just as Lieutenant Dyess appeared on the scene. Dyess was very angry that his Marines were so undisciplined that they were fighting among themselves. He made a snap decision, breaking from corporal to private the man who had attempted to end the fight. Although he was later challenged about his decision, a stubborn streak would not allow Lieutenant Dyess to acknowledge that he might have made a mistake.

Through his work with the Augusta Lumber Company and in his own short-lived construction company, and through his military responsibilities with both the Army Reserves and the Marine Corps

Reserves, Dyess cultivated a wide circle of friends and admirers. Many would look to him for advice and support during those years of the Great Depression. Dyess had the technical skills as well as the self-confidence, maturity and leadership ability that people found attractive. Also, he was always looking for ways to help others. Claud Caldwell, now in his 90s, remembers with great affection two things that Dyess did for him in those tough days of the Great Depression. In 1934, Caldwell was working at a very low salary as a purchasing agent for the city of Augusta. At his request, Dyess tried hard to get him a commission in the U. S. Army Quartermaster Corps. Dyess approached Captain Cook of the Army Reserves, encouraged Caldwell to take the "Series 10" examination and, in due time, Caldwell received his reserve commission. During the two years they were together in the Army Reserves, Dyess worked hard with Caldwell to make him a good marksman. Sixty years later Caldwell gives Dyess great credit for Claud's eventually earning all three legs on his pistol Expert's Badge. When Caldwell lost his job with the City of Augusta in 1935, Dyess escorted him to Washington to try to find work with the one of the many federal agencies that blossomed during Roosevelt's New Deal. This time, Dyess's efforts to help Caldwell did not succeed, but it was an example of Dyess doing his best to help a friend in need.[52]

As the storm clouds of war grew in Asia, Africa and Europe in the late 1930s, Americans began to examine critically their military establishment. What they saw was not impressive. Funds were so short during the Depression that the equipment and training of the military forces was terribly deficient. On the year that war broke out in Europe, 1939, the United States had the sixteenth largest military in the world—about the size of the military of Portugal or Bulgaria. America was a giant, but a sleeping giant. Even though much of the rest of the world was in flames and war was getting ever closer to our shores, the American political culture was caught up in an era of strong isolationism which refused to fund and support well-equipped and well-trained military forces. However, there was one area where the United States military services were doing an outstanding job. All four of the military services were developing the doctrines, the strategies and the tactics that would serve them well if America were to be drawn into combat. The Marine Corps was particularly creative in the interwar period between World War I and World War II. This creativity was to have a huge payoff when America finally entered the war.

CHAPTER 5:

THE MARINE CORPS PRIOR TO WORLD WAR II

Jimmie Dyess's relationship with the United States Marine Corps is bound up with both the history and the traditions of the Corps. Marines take great pride in the fact that the Corps was created before there was a Declaration of Independence, before there was a United States of America and, before there was a United States Navy. The birth date of the United States Marine Corps was November 10, 1775 and every year on that date, this birthday is celebrated with considerable fanfare all over the world. Since Marines serve in American embassies in more than 200 nations, this means that the Marine Corps birthday is the most widely celebrated birthday of any American organization or institution.

Of course, before there was an American Navy and Marine Corps there was, in Britain, the Royal Navy and the Royal Marines. In the eighteenth century, the Royal Navy needed to have Marines for a very basic reason—to maintain order aboard ship. Many British sailors were non-volunteers; in fact, most seamen in the 18th century had been recruited the hard way—they had been obtained, totally against their will, by the "press-gang" method and served sulkily at their unsought posts. The Royal Marines, an all volunteer force of officers and enlisted men, were posted on each warship with musket or pistol in hand to keep the "bluejackets" of the British Navy in line and to prevent mutiny.

In the fall of 1775, John Adams chaired a committee that would recommend the formation of a United States Navy. The thinking of John Adams and his committee was that if there was to be a Navy, first there must be a Marine Corps to insure order and discipline aboard ship. Originally, Marines were "...the police of a man-of-war, serving as the captain's orderlies, mounting guard at gangways and maintaining order among the crew." Since the United States Navy never used "press gang" methods to recruit sailors and since the American Navy was quite small throughout most of the 19th century, the United States Marine Corps was also very small—less than 5,000 officers and men.

In the years before World War I, the Marine Corps was such a small military service that most Americans could not differentiate between a Marine and a sailor. In the aftermath of the Spanish American War, there were no well-known Marine Corps heroes, such as the Navy's "Hero of Manila Bay," Admiral George Dewey, or the Army's "Rough Rider," Teddy Roosevelt. In fact, at the time of Jimmie Dyess's birth, in early 1909, there was a serious debate in America about the disestablishment of the Marine Corps. In the autumn of 1908, President Theodore Roosevelt, encouraged by some Marine Corps critics within the Navy, issued an executive order removing Marines from naval ships. Many knowledgeable observers at the time felt that this was a first step that would lead to the demise of the United States Marine Corps. Fortunately, the Corps had some powerful friends in high places in the Congress and in the Navy itself. Admiral Dewey himself wrote to the House of Representatives Naval Affairs Committee supporting the continuation of the Marine Corps.[53]

Some key leaders in both houses of the United States Congress, knowing that Roosevelt would soon step down from the Presidency, took steps to save the Marine Corps from extinction. This confrontation between the Congress and the White House served the Marine Corps well, for it led to a vigorous national debate on the value of a separate Marine Corps. In addition, the American press was very helpful in outlining the many contributions the Marines had made to the nation, both in war and peace. Happily, when Dyess was just two months old (March, 1909), the Marines were restored to duty on naval ships as a direct result of a strong initiative of the United States Congress and the blessing of the new President, William Howard Taft.[54] Hence, the Marine Corps was secure as a separate military service as the tensions between and among the great powers in Europe grew and as storm clouds of impending war appeared on the horizon. Tragically, war broke out in Europe in August, 1914, and the "Great War" commenced with a fury and a casualty rate on the battlefield that was beyond anything experienced in the history of warfare. The devastation caused by machine guns, artillery and the tanks combined with the nasty European weather to make life at the front miserable for all soldiers on both sides for four long years. Since the Americans did not join on the side of the allies until late in the war, the full force of American military power on the battlefield was not felt until the summer of 1918.

During the American involvement in World War I, the Marines endeared themselves in the hearts of all Americans with their heroism in combat on the Western Front. Growing rapidly from its prewar size of less than 6,000 officers and men, the Marines reached an unprecedented size of more than 70,000 by war's end. Approximately 30,000 Marines were shipped to France. They fought in eight battles and suffered more than 12,000 casualties. For the very first time in its 140 year history, the Marine Corps fought in large formations and was forced to deal with the complex problems which arise in major military engagements. Ironically, the Marine Corps' very success in World War I brought into question, once again, its continued independence. Since it had engaged in the kind of large scale warfare that was the heart and soul of the United States Army mission, many influential Americans in the immediate postwar period urged the union of these two military services. Hence, the 1920s was destined to become a time of extraordinary challenges for the Marine Corps. While Jimmie Dyess was growing into a strapping young man with great interest in the military, his destiny, the U. S. Marine Corps, was undergoing great institutional and doctrinal turbulence, uncertainty and change.

In the 1920s and early 1930s, there were five outstanding individuals (two Marine officers, a Congressman and two inventors) who played vital roles in the evolution of the Marine Corps from its precarious position at the end of World War I to its strong institutional and doctrinal position in the late 1930s. These five determined and visionary men made major contributions which helped to ensure that the Marine Corps would find a new and important mission — offensive amphibious operations. They also played a vital role in developing both the doctrine and the equipment that permitted it to be effective in the island invasions that would lie ahead. Three of these men also helped counteract the strong effort to disestablish the Marine Corps in the interwar period.

When the Great War came to a close in November, 1918, the Marine Corps was fortunate to have two visionary officers serving in key positions. Major General John Lejeune, who established the new Marine doctrine of amphibious warfare, and Major Earl "Pete" Ellis, who outlined an overall plan for retaking Pacific islands from the Japanese, played pivotal roles at a critical time. General Lejeune, the only U. S. Marine officer ever to have commanded an Army division (the Second Infantry Division on the Western Front during World War I), was probably the most forward-looking Commandant in the history of the Marine Corps. Since he served as Commandant for nine years (1920-1929), he had time to institutionalize and implement the vision which he and his most innovative staff officer, Major Ellis, created in the early 1920s.[55]

Immediately after the war, the troops of all the military services returned home and the nation began a period of radical demobilization. At the same time, the Royal Marines of the British Empire, upon which the U. S. Marines had been modeled in 1775, suffered serious budgetary cuts and, even more ominously, lost much of their supporting arms, including the highly competent and respected Royal Marine Artillery. Naturally, America's top Marine, General Lejeune, feared a similar fate for the U.S. Marine Corps or, even worse, the total disestablishment of the Corps.[56]

Lejeune decided to try to differentiate the Marine Corps from the Army and to restructure the Corps around a unique military capability. He chose amphibious warfare as the mission that would preserve the United States Marine Corps. However, tying the future of the Marine Corps to the mission of amphibious warfare was a risky approach since amphibious operations in World War I had gone very badly for the Allies. The most vivid example was the allied attack at Gallipoli. The Turks under the command of their charismatic military leader, General Kemal Attaturk, had pinned down on the beaches and badly mauled an amphibious assault force which consisted of mainly Australians and New Zealanders. Many military experts throughout the world had drawn the conclusion that amphibious attacks against beaches defended by modern, rapid-fire weapons made no military sense whatsoever.[57]

Even before World War I, military and naval experts had been raising serious questions about the utility of amphibious operations against defended territory. Captain Asa Walker of the U. S. Navy, in a 1900 article that appeared in the Naval Institute's *Proceedings* magazine, had written, "The landing of vast bodies of men and horses, with the artillery and stores, even under the most favorable circumstances and with the most perfect organization, presents great difficulties. If, then, we complicate these difficulties by subjecting the troops to the fire of a determined enemy, begun at long range and continued during the confusion attendant on disembarking, what but pre-eminent disaster can be the result?" In addition, a renown British military strategist, B. H. Liddell Hart, believed that amphibious assaults had "become impossible."[58]

But General Lejeune had the wisdom to understand that, with the proper doctrine, equipment, strategy and tactics, amphibious attack could play an important role in future warfare. He also sensed that the leaders of the U. S. Army had little interest in amphibious warfare and would be unlikely to compete with the Marine Corps for this mission, especially during this postwar period of budgetary austerity. Lejeune took the opportunity to redefine the Marine Corps and to establish a new paradigm that would legitimize, once again, a separate and independent United States Marine Corps. In the early 1920s, Lejeune and his staff of bright planners formulated an amphibious doctrine that would serve the United States as well as the Marine Corps well in the decades ahead.

Whereas General Lejeune was a nationally-known and well respected leader and visionary, Marine Major "Pete" Ellis was a shadowy figure. Ellis had a wide range of talents; he was a scholar, a war hero and a Japanese linguist. However, this brilliant thinker, writer and planner had a number of medical problems including a series of bouts with alcoholism. Ellis had carefully studied Japanese history and was very concerned that, in the aftermath of World War I, Japan would follow an aggressive policy of imperialistic expansion. In the period from 1919 to 1922, Ellis wrote extensively about Japanese military forces and doctrine and the potential threat that these forces posed to the United States. The more he studied the Japanese military establishment, the more he became interested in what the Japanese were doing in the islands of the Western and Central Pacific which they owned outright or were now governing under the mandate of the League of Nations.

In 1921, Ellis wrote and published a paper about future warfare in the Pacific that was both visionary and prescient. Even his estimates of the number of forces which would be needed to carry out a successful amphibious operation against an island of a specific size turned out, twenty years in the future, to be highly accurate. On July 23, 1921, General Lejeune gave his official blessing to Ellis's paper and it soon became the foundation of subsequent planning for amphibious operations in the Pacific in the 1940s.[59]

Ellis's plan and Lejeune's endorsement marked a major break from Marine Corps history. In the past, American Marines had been used primarily to maintain order on warships and to defend advanced bases. There was little Marine Corps tradition of offensive military operations. From 1921 onwards, the principal role of the Marine Corps would be to seize forward bases from an enemy. Ellis's intellectual breakthrough was not in identifying Japan as a potential enemy. Others had done that as early as 1907. Ellis's unique contribution was the development of the strategy, doctrine, tactics and techniques that would be involved in seizing an island base. No longer would Marines be a force solely for defensive operations.

Hence, starting in the early 1920s the Corps would focus most of its training and its resources on offensive action. This was a doctrinal shift of the first order and Pete Ellis became, like Alfred Thayer Mahan for the Navy and Billy Mitchell for the Army Air Corps, the intellectual father of the modern Marine Corps. In sum, Ellis defined, and Lejuene endorsed, the premier mission of the Corps: amphibious assault against heavily defended enemy islands. [60]

Since it was very difficult for Ellis to get accurate information on how the Japanese military was operating in their islands in the Central Pacific, he decided to take a systematic look for himself. It was to be a fateful voyage which would end abruptly in his death. In 1923, using false identity documents and taking full advantage of his ability to speak Japanese, Ellis boarded various Japanese ships and boats. He toured the Marshall and Caroline Islands, taking notes on commercial and military activities. Immediately after World War I, by a League of Nations mandate, the Japanese had been given custody of these two island groups, which had been German colonies prior to World War I. By the terms of this mandate, of Article 22 of the League of Nations Covenant, of the Five-Power Naval Treaty of 1922, the Japanese were forbidden from militarizing these small, but strategically important, islands. Japan was not allowed to establish military or naval bases, erect fortifications, give the natives military training or make any other military use of the islands.[61]

Ellis, extremely interested in whether the Japanese were, in fact, militarizing them, was a careful observer and note taker as he moved from island to island. Sadly his consumption of alcohol was prodigious during this trip. During periods when he was very drunk, he would tell his drinking buddies of the evening that he was on a secret spying mission. However, during his periods of sobriety he worked hard on his report. Unfortunately, the extensive report which he was compiling was never completed. Soon after he reached the island of Palau, in the Western end of the Carolines, he died. More than seventy years later, the exact circumstances of Ellis's death are still not known. However, a biography of Ellis, published in 1996, points to the fact that Ellis consumed two bottles of alcohol one evening and died that same night, May 12, 1923.[62] He was given these two bottles by Japanese military officials but there is no evidence they did so in hopes that the liquor would kill him. Of course, the Japanese military were aware of Ellis's speculation on a future war with the United States. Japan may not have wanted him to gain detailed geographical information to carry back to the United States. In any case, Ellis's notes were never found.

What is quite clear is that Ellis was on to something. The Japanese spent the twenty-one years, between the time they gained control over the Marshalls and the Carolines and the time they attacked Pearl Harbor, building airfields, ports and supply facilities on those islands. All of these facilities had a commercial value and there is no evidence that the Japanese were in specific violation of the terms League of Nations mandate or the Naval Treaty of 1922. However, there were many people, especially in Germany, Great Britain and America, who felt that one of the reasons for these many construction projects was to serve the Japanese military in the years ahead. The fact that the Japanese were so secretive about what they were doing on these islands and put such severe restrictions on foreign travel through them contributed to the myth of a large and ominous Japanese military buildup in the Central Pacific.

Despite the untimely death of its best and most prolific intellectual, the Marine Corps devoted a great deal of time and effort in the 1920s and early 1930s devising a doctrine for amphibious operations. However, the Marine Corps could not devote all of its assets to this new initiative. There were many preoccupations for the Marines throughout the fifteen years immediately following World War I. From 1918 to 1933, the Marines conducted numerous military operations in Central America and the Caribbean which can best be described as counter-guerrilla operations. Many of the Marine Corps officers, who would emerge as senior Marine commanders in the war against Japan, got combat experience in places such as Haiti and Nicaragua. Lewis "Chesty" Puller, who would have such a distinguished combat record in World War II, fought in more than a hundred small military actions in the 1920s and early 1930s and earned two Navy Crosses for heroism in combat. It was not until 1933, when Franklin Roosevelt became President and articulated and implemented his good neighbor policy towards Latin America that the Marine Corps ended this period of anti-guerrilla activity and returned to the United States. At last, the Marine Corps was able to devote its full attention to the development of the amphibious warfare mission.[63]

The third important personality in the story of the escape of the Marine Corps from institutional extinction was a small, dynamic, charismatic politician from New York City with the quaint nickname of "Little Flower." Many older Americans still remember Fiorello La Guardia very fondly. He is generally regarded as the most popular mayor (1933-1941) in the long and colorful history of New York City. One of the often cited stories about Mayor La Guardia was his reading on the radio, with great animation in his voice, the Sunday comic strips to the children of the city during a newspaper strike. Many adults would also listen in with great amusement. La Guardia later became well known for his outstanding work as the chief of the Office of Civil Defense during World War II and, later, as Director of the United Nations Relief and Rehabilitation Program which fed millions of displaced persons after World War II. What is not normally highlighted by historians is that La Guardia had a strong background and a high interest in the military.

Son of a United States Army bandmaster, La Guardia spent much of his youth at a military post in Arizona. After his father's discharge from the U. S. Army in 1898, the family moved to Italy and settled down in Trieste. While in Europe, young La Guardia joined the U.S. consular service and from 1904 to 1906 served as the acting American consular agent in the northeast corner of Italy at Fiume (now Rijeka in Croatia). Returning to America to continue his education, he served part time as an interpreter at Ellis Island, in New York Harbor, from 1907 to 1910. This was a time when there was a huge flow of immigrants to America. Most came from Europe and were processed through the important immigration center on Ellis Island.

Later, La Guardia chose a political career. As a New York Republican he was elected to the United States House of Representatives in 1916. When America entered World War I six months later, La Guardia took a series of unusual steps. He obtained a leave of absence from Congress, enlisted in the United States Army, learned to fly, and became a pilot in the U.S. Air Service, rising to the rank of major. He flew a number of combat missions out of the Italian theater of operations and made many public speeches to large Italian audiences (he spoke fluent Italian) explaining how committed the Americans were to winning the war and defeating Germany and the Austro-Hungarian Empire. After the war, he returned to Congress and served there until 1932. Although never a Marine, La Guardia had great respect and affection for the United States Marine Corps.

As the depression deepened, the Hoover administration began to look hard at ways to cut the military. The Marine Corps appeared to many, both in the executive branch and in the Congress, as a place to make some major cuts. Between 1929 and 1933, President Hoover levied upon the Marine Corps a draconian series of manpower cuts that amounted to a reduction of almost 25 percent. This was a disproportionate cut as compared to a 5.6 percent reduction for the Navy; the Army was not cut at all. Just as he was stepping down from power, in December, 1932, Hoover proposed even deeper reductions in Marine Corps manpower. These cuts were to be made in conjunction with planned withdrawals of Marine units from Latin America. If these cuts had been approved, the Marine Corps would have gone from 18,000 to less than 14,000 men. Also, the Marine boot camp at Parris Island was to be closed. In many ways, this was a repeat of 1908, when President Theodore Roosevelt ordered Marines off of all naval ships. Just as in 1908, the Marine Corps launched a vigorous public relations campaign which reminded the nation of past contributions and the value of a separate Marine Corps.

It was at this time that Republican Congressman La Guardia confronted the President from his own party and came to the strong defense of the Marine Corps. Ironically, both La Guardia and

President Hoover had been defeated in the national election of November, 1932, which was a landslide win for Roosevelt and which swept many Republican congressmen out of office. As his last act before he left Congress, La Guardia made a major effort to save the Marine Corps and to reduce these manpower cuts. He elicited the support of other key congressmen such as Carl Vinson and Melvin J. Maas. At an important moment, the House Appropriations Committee voted against the Hoover force reductions and assisted in keeping the Corps at over 15,000 men and, more importantly, in maintaining its institutional integrity. La Guardia, who was such a champion for the poor, the downtrodden and the disadvantaged, was also a champion for important organizations and institutions which were under attack. The United States Marine Corps owes an eternal debt to one of the great figures of the twentieth century, the diminutive former Army officer, Congressman La Guardia.[64]

It was not until later in the 1930s that a fourth remarkable man in the saga of the United States Marine Corps interwar renaissance came to the fore. By no means a military man, Mr. Andrew Jackson Higgins was an inventor and naval architect. Prior to his work with the Marine Corps, Higgins had designed shallow draft boats for use by the fur trappers and oil men who worked in the back bayous of southern Louisiana (in this era of prohibition they were also used widely for rum running).[65] As Marine Corps leaders developed an amphibious warfare doctrine, they realized that there was a need for some highly specialized landing craft to get the Marines safely and efficiently from large ships at sea to the beach. They needed three types of boats: 1. Landing boats that would be used to carry combat troops from ship to shore. 2. Large boats called "lighters" that would carry tanks, trucks and other vehicles to the shore. 3. Amphibians, armed with forward-firing weapons, that would provide supporting fire for the infantrymen, not only as they approached the beach, but also after they came ashore. For the first and second types of boats, the Marines would rely on Higgins. [66]

Higgins worked with the Marines starting in 1934. The early models of the LCVPs (Landing Craft, Vehicle and Personnel) were based on a Higgins design, with flat bottoms and tunnel-shaped sterns. However, these new boats had one fundamental shortcoming. It was difficult for a combat Marine to disembark once these "Higgins boats" had been driven onto the beach. Combat Marines would have to climb over the side and drop down onto the beach. This was not difficult for a young, agile person with no equipment strapped on. However, someone loaded down with a rifle, a heavy load of ammunition, a bayonet, a canteen of water and a full combat pack had a tough time. Carrying gear weighing about eighty pounds, a Marine usually ended up crashing onto his hands and knees, getting himself and his equipment soaking wet and often suffering injury. Clearly, the Marine Corps needed a better way to get the troops off these boats and safely ashore.

In 1939, the Marine Corps again approached Higgins, this time with an idea that might solve the disembarkation problem. Could he design a boat with a hinged ramp in the bow? The idea was not a new one. Ironically, the first nation to fully exploit this idea and use it in combat was Japan. Prior to the Japanese attack on Pearl Harbor, most Americans looked down on Japanese manufacturing skills. The Japanese had a reputation for making cheap, low quality copies of many American commercial products. Yet in the area of amphibious warfare, the Japanese were more advanced than were the Americans. In 1937, the Japanese had used more than 400 "ramp boats" as they successfully attacked the Chinese port city of Tientsin. Marine Corps leaders recognized that they needed an American-made ramp boat; they knew whom to turn to for help—Andrew Higgins.

By 1940, Higgins had succeeded in meeting the design requirements of the Marine Corps. Combat soldiers who stormed the shores of Morocco, Sicily, Anzio, Salerno and Normandy, and combat Marines and soldiers who hit the beaches on the Japanese-held islands throughout the Pacific, benefited greatly from Higgins' design and engineering prowess. The Marine Corps concept for the use of these combat vessels was quite simple. If the Higgins boats did not get hung up on an offshore reef (or get sunk by enemy shells, bombs or mines enroute to the beach), and if the ramp was not dropped too early, swamping the boat, the combat Marines and soldiers had a good chance of reaching the shore, on their feet, dry, in good shape and ready to fight. No longer would they have to climb over the side of an assault boat and jump with full field gear and weapons into the roiling surf.

Andrew Higgins also played a vital role in the design of the lighters that would take vehicles ashore. As the armored tanks got larger and heavier in the late 1930s, the Marines had to design and build larger boats to get these vehicles safely to shore and on to a defended beach. It was Higgins who designed both the boat and the ramp that won the "lighter" competition that was held in May of 1942. The fifty-foot Higgins "lighters" proved to be very seaworthy and soon they were being built by the thousands to support amphibious operations in the Mediterranean, the Pacific and the English channel. These Higgins "lighters" would allow light tanks, half-tracks, trucks, jeeps and other vehicles to drive directly from boat to beach without having their engines flooded out in sea water.[67]

The third type of boat that was essential to Marine Corps operations in the Pacific, the amphibian, was designed by a man with the then famous name of Roebling. The fifth man to make a major contribution to the renaissance of the Marine Corps in the interwar period was, like Higgins, an inventor. Donald Roebling Jr. was the grandson of Colonel Washington Roebling, the man who designed the Brooklyn Bridge. Donald Roebling first used aluminum in order to reduce weight and increase speed at sea and on land, but the final designs were made of steel. Most people called these tracked, amphibious vehicles "alligators".

In February, 1941, a young Marine Captain, Victor Krulak, approached Marine Major General Holland Smith and asked Smith to extend an invitation to the commander of the Atlantic Fleet, Admiral Earnest King, to take his very first ride in an alligator. King, pressed for time, agreed but asked that the ride be a short one. The alligator got stuck on a coral reef, one of the tracks broke, and Admiral King had to jump into four feet of water and wade ignominiously to shore.[68] Despite this inauspicious run for the man who would lead the entire United States Navy in World War II, the alligator had great success in the war. By the end of World War II, 15,654 were built.[69] It was an alligator that took Jimmie Dyess ashore at Roi Namur.

In sum, thanks largely to the efforts of five visionaries, the Marines made enormous strides in the 1920s, 1930s and early 1940s, especially doctrinally and technologically. In fact, the Marine Corps provides a fine historical example of excellent pre-war planning, decision making and strategic action. General Archer Vandergrift, the hero of Guadacanal and Marine Corps Commandant for much of World War II would write in 1948, "Despite its outstanding record as a combat force in the past war, the Marine Corps's far greater contribution to victory was doctrinal; that is, the fact that the basic amphibious doctrine which carried Allied troops over every beachhead of World War II had been largely shaped—often in the face of uninterested or doubting military orthodoxy—by U. S. Marines, and mainly between 1922 and 1935".[70]

With doctrine, tactics and equipment shaping up quite well, what was needed, now that the United States was about to engage in a world-wide war, was tough, realistic training. For the Marines the major focus of attention was on the vast Pacific Ocean and on the Japanese, a potential enemy with an extensive amount of recent combat experience. Japan's wars of territorial expansion had started in 1931 with the capture of Manchuria. From 1937, when the Japanese war against mainland China had commenced, until 1944, when Jimmie Dyess and his fellow Marines engaged them in the Marshall Islands, the Japanese Army had fought the military forces of China, Russia, France, Britain, the Netherlands and America. The Japanese soldier was not only highly disciplined, motivated and battle hardened, but also a ferocious fighter.

The Marines who fought in the early months of World War II were disciplined and well trained, but most lacked combat experience. Consequently losses in combat were high. Compared to the

Marine units who had fought in 1942 and 1943, the 4th Marine Division was indeed fortunate. Unlike the 1st and 2nd Marine Divisions which were thrown into combat early in the war, the 4th Division had ample time to train. When the 4th Marine Division entered combat for the first time on the last day of January, 1944, the United States had been at war for more than two years. Not only was there time for the 4th Marine Division to train, and train well, there also were many combat lessons to draw upon. Both tactics and training were modified and improved as the tough combat experiences of Guadalcanal and Tarawa were examined. But before Dyess had the opportunity to join the 4th Marine Division and to command a combat battalion in that division, he had to face two years that were marked by a series of professional disappointments.

CHAPTER 6:

TWO YEARS
OF FRUSTRATION

The period from the autumn of 1940, when Dyess was called to active duty, to the spring of 1943, when he joined the Fourth Marine Division was marked by numerous professional disappointments for him. First of all, Augusta's 19th Marine Reserve Battalion, which had worked so hard for four years to become combat ready, was broken up and disbanded immediately after it was mobilized in November, 1940. As soon as Augusta's battalion was called to active duty, its officers and enlisted men were sent off in many directions to different active duty units throughout the country. The camaraderie, unit cohesion and mutual respect between and among the Augusta Marines of the 19th Battalion were lost forever.

The policy of the Marine Corps in the autumn of 1940, as the Marine reserve units were being called up for active duty, was very clear and rather harsh. The top leaders in the Marine Corps made a policy decision to disband these Marine Corps reserve units. First, there was a concern that reserve officers might not make good active duty commanders, particularly of those units slated for combat duty. Many of these reserve officers were considered too old or too unfit for the rigors of front-line combat leadership. Also, there was an attitude at Marine Corps Headquarters that there was too much croynism in many of these reserve units and that these units could never be brought up to top combat readiness if they remained intact.[71]

Hence, in November, 1940, newly activated Captain Dyess not only lost the command of Company C of Augusta's 19th Marine Reserve Battalion, but also was placed in a non-combat unit. His first assignment, upon coming on active duty in November, 1940, was at the Marine Barracks at the Norfolk Navy Yard in Virginia where he was given command of a training company. His job was to give basic training to new Marine recruits. Dyess served in this leadership position for five months. Although he would have much preferred an assignment with a combat unit, command of a training company did give him the opportunity to use his leadership skills as he motivated and trained young Marines and sent them off to their combat units. Soon, however, Dyess would face his biggest professional disappointment as a Marine, when, in March, 1941, he received orders for his next assignment.

Instead of moving to a combat infantry unit where he could best use his leadership and marksmanship skills, Dyess was transferred into the barrage balloon specialty. The purpose of barrage balloons was to help defend vital targets such as airfields, command centers and ships (at anchor or in port) from air attacks by the enemy. The barrage balloon concept was quite straightforward. If many large lighter-than-air balloons were suspended by heavy cables above an area which the Marines considered essential, enemy aircraft, as they attempted to make their attacks, would be disrupted. The concept held that enemy aircraft could not accurately drop their bombs or shoot their rockets, machine guns or cannons at targets on the ground without running into the helium-filled balloons or their anchoring cables.

Unfortunately, barrage balloon defense of vital targets, which looked good on paper, was a flawed concept. There was already a considerable amount of evidence amassed by the British during the 1940 Battle of Britain that barrage balloons were not effective in disrupting enemy air attacks. Clever enemy pilots found ways to duck around the balloons and the cables while still attacking ground targets. In fact, the use of these balloons turned out to be counterproductive in that they helped enemy pilots quickly locate and pinpoint vital ground targets, since the balloons were visible to these pilots from many miles away. Nevertheless, the Marines continued to work on a barrage balloon capability until 1943. Dyess would spend two frustrating years, from March, 1941 until February, 1943, first in learning to be a barrage balloon expert and later in training others in this military specialty. He studied hard in the spring of 1941 learning the barrage balloon mission at Quantico, Virginia and at Lakehurst, New Jersey. He had to learn it well because he knew he would soon be teaching large numbers of Marines how to deploy and employ barrage balloon units.

In May, 1941, when his air defense training was complete, Captain Dyess was assigned to permanent duty with the Marine Corps Barrage Balloon School, which had just been established at Parris Island, South Carolina. On arrival at Parris Island, Dyess was assigned as the executive officer; in other words, he became second in command of the school. There was lots of work to do what with getting the equipment shipped in, establishing the various courses of instruction and preparing for the first group of students. By mid-summer of 1941, the classes began flowing through and new operational barrage balloon squadrons were established, trained, equipped and sent off to Panama and the Pacific.

Meanwhile, Germany had invaded the Soviet Union and two of history's greatest tyrants, Adolph Hitler and Joseph Stalin, were locked in massive combat. Many Americans felt that the German attack on Russia in June, 1941, code named Operation Barbarossa, was very good news for the United States. The great hope in America in the summer and fall of 1941 was that Germany and Russia would exhaust each other and that the United States could avoid being sucked into war. The struggle of fascism versus communism was, to many Americans, a case of dog eat dog, and many isolationists argued that America should stand aside while these two evil empires bled themselves to death. In fact, this four-year struggle between Germany and the Soviet Union would cost the lives of more than twenty million soldiers and civilians.[72]

In the meantime, there was ominous news from Asia. In mid-July, 1941, Japan invaded French Indochina with 40,000 troops and quickly conquered the rubber-rich country. President Roosevelt took retaliatory action by freezing all Japanese assets in the United States and cutting off Japan from U. S. produced high octane gasoline. The more the Japanese talked about their need for more land and resources and the more territory they conquered in Asia, the more it appeared to many Americans that war with an aggressive and expansionist Japan was unavoidable.

The late summer of 1941 was a time of great tension in America. The isolationists in America were still very strong politically and they launched a major campaign to discontinue the draft of young Americans into the military. There was also discussion of demobilizing the reserve troops, including Captain Dyess, who had been called up in 1940. August 12, 1941, was a very important date in American history, for on that day, the House of Representatives voted to extend the draft by a single vote (203 to 202). It was also in August that the Atlantic Charter was signed by Churchill and Roosevelt. Many historians now view the Atlantic Charter as the most important political document of the 20th Century. It not only outlined a policy of allied cooperation during wartime but set some specific goals for the cooperation among nations in the postwar world.

Dyess had been on active duty for thirteen months when the attack on Pearl Harbor shocked the world. On Sunday afternoon (Eastern Time) December 7, 1941, Jimmie, Connor and Little Connor, like most Americans, learned over the family radio of the Japanese attack. Little Connor (by 1941, she was no longer called Baby Connor) was six years old at the time. She still remembers sitting by the radio that Sunday afternoon and being shushed by her father and mother (now known as Big Connor) whenever she tried to talk. On that dramatic Sunday, all doubts about America's entering the war were over. Isolationism, which had been such a strong political force in the United States over the past twenty years, completely died that day. In fact, no significant political movement in American history had ever been destroyed so abruptly.

No American who lived through that fateful Sunday will ever forget it. A surge of outrage, patriotism and national unity captured the people of the United States. Even though 2400 Americans had died during the attack on Hawaii, there was one prominent person who was elated when he learned of the attack. Winston Churchill would later write, "To have the United States at our side was to me the greatest joy." As Lord Grey of England had said more than thirty years earlier, the United States was like "... a gigantic boiler. Once the fire is lighted under it there is no limit to the power it can generate."[73] The day after the attack, President Roosevelt made his famous "Date of Infamy" speech. He concluded the speech by saying, "I ask that the Congress declare that since the unprovoked and dastardly attack by Japan on Sunday, December 7,1941, a state of war has existed between the United States and the empire of Japan." Congress took only thirty-three minutes to vote for this declaration of war.[74]

In the next few days, both Germany and Italy declared war on the United States and the die was cast. America, which had tried so hard to avoid war, now would face three enemies. But it would do so with a sense of unity and purpose which was unequaled in American history. If there was ever a time that Americans joined together in a common cause it was the months immediately following the Japanese surprise attack. The world's largest industrial power was joining the fray on the side of the Allies and most of the world breathed a collective sigh of relief. At last, the Americans were involved with rage and sustained determination. The military services would soon be engaged in combat on many fronts. The Marines, more so than the other American military services, could focus its attention on one enemy, the Japanese, and on one area, the Central and Western Pacific.

In the first few months of the war, Japanese airpower, both land-based and carrier-based, seemed extremely formidable. Japan's naval air capability was dramatically demonstrated at Pearl Harbor. This attack was well planned, well executed and extremely accurate. Although it was a strategic disaster since it brought the Americans into the war, the attack produced a brilliant tactical victory. The successful Japanese attack on the air base at Clark Field in the Philippines on December 8th demonstrated another dimension of Japanese combat capability. In this case, they used land-based aircraft stationed on Formosa. For a brief period of time it appeared that the Japanese would present a major naval and airpower threat to the United States. Perhaps Jimmie Dyess and his barrage balloons could, in fact, play a useful role in thwarting Japanese airpower in the upcoming strategic contest in the Pacific.

However, within a few months, most American military leaders realized that neither the carrier-based nor the land-based airpower of Imperial Japan would measure up to the airpower capabilities of the American Navy, Marine Corps and Army Air Corps. Even the fabled German air force, the Luftwaffe, seemed unable to seriously threaten vital American targets on land or sea. After the spring of 1942, American air and naval bases were seldom threatened by enemy air attack either in the Pacific or European theaters. Also, the Americans by the end of 1942 were deploying highly accurate rapid firing antiaircraft guns to defend vital bases overseas. American Marine and Army leaders began questioning, once again, the utility of barrage balloons. Nevertheless, the Marine Corps continued to train officers and enlisted Marines at the Barrage Balloon School and to activate barrage balloon units throughout 1942.

In May 1942, Dyess was promoted to major, but the promotion did not lead to a job change. He stayed on as the executive officer of the Marine Barrage Balloon School. Later that summer, the Marine Corps decided to move the school to the north. It became Dyess's responsibility to pack up and relocate the Barrage Balloon School to New River, North Carolina, get it up and running again and keep the training going. In October, 1942, Major Dyess was moved up from executive officer to officer-in-charge of the school at its new location. He was at last a commander of troops—but still in a training environment and with a military mission which he and his subordinates realized was quickly becoming obsolete.

It was not until November, 1942, two years after he came on active duty, that Dyess learned that a decision had been made at Marine Corps Headquarters to phase out the barrage balloon mission. The school which he had helped to create, taught at, commanded and moved from South Carolina to North Carolina was to be closed. This was the end of an era for the Marines Corps. Never again would they try to defend vital areas using tethered balloons. Shortly thereafter, Dyess learned that he was to be assigned to that part of the Marine Corps that was his real love, the infantry. This was great news; finally he would have the chance to lead Marines with the mission to "close with" and defeat the enemies of the United States. He knew this new assignment was to be the first step toward combat in the Pacific. Many of the staff at the Barrage Balloon School also received assignments to the infantry. Dyess's operations officer, Captain Art Buck, whom Dyess had known since he was a second lieutenant, was also assigned to a combat unit. Like Dyess, Buck was destined to join the 4th Marine Division and fight in the Marshalls.[75]

Major Dyess was assigned to a battalion being formed on the east coast. It was quite an unusual unit for a number of reasons. It was designated a "separate battalion" and was not assigned to a given regiment. In addition to the normal equipment for a Marine infantry battalion, it included some 75 mm light pack howitzers. Also, the battalion had no unit designation. It may have been originally designed as a special unit (perhaps a light raider unit). However, at about the time Dyess joined it, a decision was made that this unit would join a regular infantry regiment, give up its light artillery and deploy en masse to the west coast.[76] Dyess was appointed to the position of battalion executive officer; it appeared that, once again, he was destined to spend another long period as a second-in-command. However, very soon he received wonderful news; he was appointed the acting commander of the battalion. The battalion commander, Major Dolan, had broken his leg. Since Dolan could not go out on maneuvers to provide the personal, hands-on leadership that the battalion needed, Dyess was named the acting commander.

Dyess was anxious to get out into the field and to check out the combat skills of his men. However, there was very little time for infantry combat training for Dyess at New River, for a move was in the offing. This separate battalion, which had been training at New River since the fall of 1942, had received orders to move out. In February, 1943, the officers and enlisted men in the battalion began

96

packing and humming a popular song of that era, "California here I come."

During his first two years on active duty Dyess had moved many times: from Augusta to Norfolk to Quantico to Lakehurst to Parris Island and to New River. Most the these moves were rather simple and straightforward—moving himself and his small family. There was one exception; the move from Parris Island to New River was a major undertaking since he was responsible for transporting the entire Barrage Balloon school and all its personnel and equipment. For the first time, Dyess had gained solid experience in planning movements of large numbers of Marines and their equipment. This first-hand experience would now serve him well. For the trip to California, he was responsible for packing up and moving an entire Marine battalion of eight hundred men.

Although he authorized the few people who owned automobiles to drive them to California, the vast majority of the Marines of his battalion prepared to load up on a railroad train to begin the five-day trip across the country to southern California. One young bachelor officer tried to be a bit manipulative. When he heard of the upcoming train trip, he quickly bought a car in hopes that he could avoid the trip on the crowded train and enjoy a leisurely drive across the country. Dyess would have none of it. He had a finely honed sense of right and wrong and if something smelled a little strange, Dyess was quick to act—firmly but fairly.

Dyess came up with a novel answer to the request he knew he was about to receive. When the officer with the newly purchased car said he had no way to get his car to California, Dyess suggested that he let a fellow officer, who had recently married and did not own a car, drive the car to California. Hence, the married officer was able to accompany his wife as they moved to California. This saved him money and gave him some precious time with his new wife. In addition, all of the men of the battalion learned that their new commander would not allow someone to trifle with the rules which Dyess had established.[77]

Camp Pendleton, just to the north of San Diego, was to be Dyess's home base for almost a year. On arrival in California, he and his battalion joined the 24th Marine Regiment which was to be one of the major combat units of the 4th Marine Division then in the process of forming up. These units were slated for combat duty in the Pacific commencing in early 1944.

The many months of frustration were over for Major Dyess. He was no longer relegated to training people in secondary missions and sending them off to air defense units. At last, he was an integral and important part of the heart and soul of the modern Marine Corps, a combat infantry battalion. Soon after he arrived at Camp Pendleton, Dyess was promoted to lieutenant colonel and, on May 14th, 1944, officially assumed command of the battalion of which he had been the acting commander since March. The separate infantry combat battalion that he had joined at New River now had a name: the 1st Battalion of the 24th Marine Regiment. The men under his command were all full-fledged members of the United States Marine Corps and very proud of it. But, no one was prouder than thirty-four-year-old Lieutenant Colonel Dyess, who had joined the Marine Corps Reserve as a first lieutenant seven years earlier in hopes, one day, of commanding a major operational unit. He now held the leadership position for which he had so long hoped.

When Dyess took command of his battalion, every Marine from private to lieutenant colonel was a volunteer. None were draftees. These men had signed up with their local Marine recruiter to serve with the Marine Corps and with no one else. Although the vast majority of American men who entered the military services in the early years of World War II had been drafted, it was not until the summer of 1943 that the Marine Corps reluctantly started to accept draftees. During the prewar military build-up in 1940 and 1941 and during the early years of World War II, the Marine Corps Commandant had fully supported the Marine Corps tradition of an all volunteer force. Hence, he vigorously opposed the acceptance of draftees within the Corps. He made the strong argument that the Marine Corps was a very special service. Throughout its rich history, the Marine Corps had always been served exclusively by volunteers—patriotic people who were deeply committed to serving their country as Marines.

By 1943 General George C. Marshall, the Chief of Staff of the Army, had become quite concerned that the U. S. Army was receiving too few volunteers and too many draftees. Both the physical and mental qualities of the soldiers in many Army units were seriously deficient. Although he was willing to accept a high percentage of draftees into the Army, Marshall felt that the draftees should be spread among all the military services. Marshall, the most influential military leader in Washington, made a strong case in the Pentagon that the Army should not be the only military service that was forced to accept draftees. Eventually General Marshall won his case and, by late 1943, the Marines started to accept non-volunteers. Even though a few draftees entered the 1st Battalion of the 24th Marines prior to its departure for combat in the Pacific in January, 1944, the vast majority of its enlisted men were volunteers who had joined the Marine Corps prior to the summer of 1943. All of the officers were volunteers.[78]

Who were these men that Dyess would lead into combat and what was their combat training like? It is now time to examine the Marines who joined his battalion at New River, North Carolina or at Camp Pendleton, California.

CHAPTER 7:

THE MARINES OF WORLD WAR II

If there was ever a time in American history when young people made decisions fast, it was in the months immediately following Pearl Harbor. The nation was endangered and many young men, as well as some young women, of all sorts and descriptions understood that it was their time to serve. This was a very special generation of young people. It was a strongly patriotic group, willing to face the hardships of extended military duty to rid the world of the tyrants who had taken control of Germany, Japan and Italy and who were on the march throughout the world. These young American citizens, born during the years immediately following World War I, were the children of the Great Depression. Most had faced hardships as their fathers and mothers had struggled to find enough work and income to keep the family fed, clothed and under one roof. Ever since they were preteenagers, most of these young people had worked after school and on weekends to help cover family expenses.

What inspired these young people to make the decision, soon after Pearl Harbor, to choose the U.S. Marine Corps? There were many reasons. The Marine Corps had a great history and tradition and a strong reputation of public service and discipline. Also, the Marines had been the very first to face the Japanese in close combat. The heroism of the Marines on Wake Island in December, 1941, had inspired many young people to pay a visit to a Marine Corps recruiting station. In addition there were other avenues of inspiration.

In early 1942, there appeared a movie of such extraordinary power that, soon after seeing it, young men flocked by the tens of thousands to Marine recruiters. [79] *The Shores of Tripoli* was a big financial success, but more importantly to the Marine Corps, it quickly became the best military recruiting movie of World War II. This uplifting film starred the darkly handsome, self-assured and athletic John Payne, the voluptuous and vivacious Maureen O'Hara and the ramrod straight Randolph Scott. Payne portrayed the son of a Marine who had served in World War I. He joined the Marines in the fall of 1941 and reported to a Marine sergeant, a battle-hardened veteran of World War I, who was played by Scott. There Payne met and soon fell in love with a Navy nurse, played by the red-headed actress, O'Hara. After going through some very tough training at Camp Pendleton, the young Marine decided that the life of a combat Marine was not for him. He requested and received a cushy job in Washington where he would have a "highball in one hand and an executive secretary in the other." Just before Payne was scheduled to leave for the east coast, he asked O'Hara to marry him and accompany him to Washington. When she realized that he did not have the devotion to duty of the other Marines at Camp Pendleton, she angrily rejected his marriage proposal.

As Payne was about to fly off to Washington with another woman, word reached California of the Japanese attack on Pearl Harbor. As he heard this dramatic news on his car radio, Payne looked through the windshield and saw Randolph Scott and his fellow Marines marching off to war (since Marine Corps units in California did not march off to war on Pearl Harbor day, the Hollywood director was using a considerable amount of poetic license). Payne pulled his car off the road, jumped out and, with the marching troops clustering close around, changed from his civilian clothes into his Marine Corps uniform and dramatically marched to the ship. As he and Scott climbed the gangplank they looked up. High on an upper deck of the ship was O'Hara, in her uniform as a Navy nurse, waiting for the Marines to come on board.

The *Shores of Tripoli* was an immensely popular movie and highlighted the basic patriotism that so motivated young Americans. Many thousands of young men wanted to join such a spirited group, put on their Marine dress blue uniforms and sweep the Maureen O'Haras of America off their feet. There was, of course, a great chasm between expectation and reality. Most of the men of the Fourth Marine Division never owned a dress blue uniform throughout the entire war. Also, there were precious few opportunities to meet, much less sweep off their feet, the gorgeous ladies of their dreams.

The war was well underway when the troops of the Fourth Division began to assemble for their long voyage to that scenic site in southern California known as Camp Pendleton. Dyess was most fortunate since the battalion which he had joined in   early 1943 moved en masse from New River to Pendleton. Unlike Augusta's 19th Battalion, which was broken up in 1940, the First Battalion of the 24th Marine Regiment stayed largely intact from late 1942 until the end of the war. The Marines in the battalion who took the train from New River to Camp Pendleton remember the trip quite well. The battalion boarded railroad cars on the 10th of March, 1943. Although there was a dining car, there were no sleeping facilities whatsoever. It was a long five days as young Marines caught whatever sleep they could on the floor or on the train benches. There were no civilians on board and, most unfortunately, no girls with which to flirt.

As Dyess's battalion moved from the North Carolina to California, they had plenty of time to read newspapers and magazines which were passed from hand to hand on the train. News from the various war fronts was a constant reminder of the stark future that lay ahead. In the South Pacific, Marines were wrapping up the six-month bloody, hand-to-hand battle for the Island of Guadalcanal. To those on that railroad train it seemed clear that the war against the Japanese would be a long and extremely costly one. Hence the training they would soon undertake would have the kind of realism that was unknown in peacetime. Every Marine from the generals to the lowest enlisted ranks knew that the training had to be tough and realistic. Only with superior discipline, great conditioning and fine leadership could the United States Marines prevail against the battle-hardened soldiers of the Japanese Empire.

In 1943 the newspapers were filled with stories from battlefields around the world, and much of the news was bad. The maps showed that the Axis areas of control were very extensive throughout Europe, the Middle East, Asia and the South and Central Pacific. For every Allied victory there were many defeats. The British and Dutch had been badly defeated in Malaya and Singapore and almost all of the Dutch East Indies was, by 1943, under Japanese control.

Although the Allies had eventually defeated General Rommel and his German and Italian troops in North Africa, their casualties were very high. When the Americans entered the war in North Africa in force, the first major engagement was in the mountains of Tunisia. The February, 1943, battle of Kasserine Pass was a shocking defeat for the Americans. The Kasserine debacle highlighted many American deficiencies—in training, doctrine and cooperation among the military services. The Allies regrouped and pushed the Axis forces off the North African territory. Although the Allies won the battle for Sicily in July and August of 1943, many American aircraft had been shot down by friendly fire during the invasion. There were also problems with American military leadership. A number of senior commanders had to be replaced and the U.S. Army's most dynamic leader, Lieutenant General George Patton, was fired for slapping a shell-shocked soldier. Meanwhile, in the summer and fall of 1943, Army Air Corps B-17s and B-24s, unescorted by American fighters on the last portion of their bombing runs over Germany, were being shot down by the scores. When sixty bombers were shot down on a single mission over Schweinfurt in August 1943, six hundred airmen met with death or captivity within less than an hour.

The offensive actions of the Allied armies driving up the Italian boot were slow and painful as the Germans, under the brilliant leadership of General Albrecht Kesselring, used the rough mountains of central Italy to good advantage and stopped the allies for months at Monte Cassino, south of Rome. In the fall of 1943, the invasion of France, which had been discussed publicly ever since the Americans joined the war, was still a long way off. A huge armada of military forces was being assembled in Great Britain. However, the shortage of assault boats to take hundreds of thousands of troops across the English Channel and the fear of another Dunkirk made an invasion of France before the spring of 1944 quite unlikely. Since the Allies had decided that the war against Hitler was of higher priority than the war against Tojo, shortages of supplies and equipment were even more severe for all of the military services fighting (or preparing to fight) in the Pacific .

When on March 15, 1943, the train arrived at its California destination, the weary Marines of Dyess's battalion happily unloaded at the resort area about which they had heard so much. Camp Pendleton would be their home for the next ten months. They moved into tent cities far away from the lovely haciendas of the camp. However, soon afterwards they moved into newly constructed barracks. Their living conditions in the new barracks were much better in sunny California than in the cramped, humid, tin Quonset huts of New River, North Carolina.

This area of Southern California had quite a rich history. On the 13th of June, 1798, a small group of Franciscans established the Mission San Luis Rey de Francis but for most of its history the area was a ranch and farming area. By the 1920s, 25,000 acres were under cultivation and 1500 people were employed growing peas, beans, barley, lettuce, celery and peppers as well as flowers of many types. In addition, 12,000 head of cattle grazed on this huge ranch.

The Second War Powers Act of World War II allowed the federal government to purchase the entire ranch (the price was just over 4 million dollars). The new Marine base was named in honor of Major General Joseph H. Pendleton who had served for 46 years in the Corps. After retirement, he was prominent in civic affairs, serving as mayor and then member of the school board of Coronado. When President Franklin Roosevelt personally dedicated the camp on September 25, 1942, he asked the Marines to preserve, as much as possible, the prewar atmosphere of this lovely ranch.[80]

When the Rancho Santa Margarita y Las Flores was transformed into Camp Pendleton in 1942, the Marine Corps gained one of the largest military camps in the world. With 18 miles of shoreline on the Pacific Ocean and a total of 133,000 acres, Camp Pendleton provided an ideal training area for the Marines who would fight the tough battles in the Pacific. During World War II, the 3rd, 4th and 5th Marine Divisions would accomplish their training here.

These depression-hardened, raw-boned, muscular young men, most of whom were still teenagers, trained and trained and trained at this huge camp. When they sailed off to combat they did so with the expectation that they would fight their way from island to island to island across the Pacific until they finally invaded and captured the Japanese homeland itself. When the men of the 4th Marine Division sailed across the Pacific in January, 1944, they went to war "for the duration." Only when the Japanese were completely defeated could they fathom the possibility of coming home.

CHAPTER 8:

THE 1ST BATTALION, 24TH MARINES

"I won't feed my men this crap, take it back and bring us some good food!" The First Battalion, 24th Marines, had been on a field exercise at Camp Pendleton for several days when, at last, hot food arrived. Lieutenant Colonel Dyess sampled the vittles and found they were not acceptable for human consumption. When nourishing food finally arrived, the hungry men knew that they had a leader who would look after their interests, demand high standards of those who supported them and make good on his promises.

One of the favorite stories of Dyess at Pendleton was when the entire battalion was scheduled to make an arduous 48 hour forced march. When it was time to load up with full combat pack, weapon and ammunition, Dyess noticed that someone had lightened Dyess's pack. He got this fixed in a big hurry with a brief comment, " I wear the same pack as the rest of the troops." About three fourths of the way home, when everyone was at the point of exhaustion, Dyess rose up to his full height and shouted in a loud voice, "When I quit, we all quit." He then went to the front of the battalion and led the march all the way back to camp. The Marines knew he was hurting, for he was limping on the knee he had injured so badly on the football field at Clemson. If the old man could make it, by golly, they could make it too.

In the period from March, 1943, until February, 1944, Dyess would demonstrate on many occasions, both in training and in combat, that the Marine Corps had made an outstanding decision in picking him for this important command. Having held leadership positions in the Boy Scouts and the Sea Scouts, at Richmond Academy, at Clemson, in the Army and Marine Corps Reserves and at the Marine Corps Barrage Balloon School, Dyess had learned a great deal about how to motivate and discipline subordinates. By the time he became a battalion commander, he understood that leadership is, to a very considerable extent, a value that is entrusted to the superior by the subordinate. He fully grasped the relationship between leaders and followers and understood that leadership embodies an emotional, often spiritual, investment by the subordinate in his superior. The mature and wise Lieutenant Colonel Dyess nurtured the relationship of trust and mutual respect between him and his troops, both officer and enlisted.

For the men of the 4th Division, a three-day pass to Los Angeles or San Diego was a rare event. Normally, there was no scheduled transportation to get the young Marines from base to town. Everyone was on his own to get to town and to get back on time. However, the men of the 1st Battalion, Twenty Fourth Marines, were quite fortunate. Lieutenant Colonel Dyess trained his troops with gritty determination but when he granted them a three-day pass, he planned ahead and reserved buses for them. He wanted to

Jimmie and Connor Dyess, 1943. This picture was taken in California when Jimmie was undergoing training at Camp Pendleton. A few months later, Jimmie sailed from San Diego to the Marshall Islands and combat.

be sure that the men could get to town quickly but, more importantly, that they could count on a ride home on Sunday evening. Dyess established a pattern for these Friday through Sunday three-day passes, which occurred about once every six weeks in the summer and fall of 1943.

On the week of the upcoming pass the routine was set. From Monday to Thursday Dyess's battalion trained out in the field, far away from barracks. On Thursday evening, Dyess would lead the entire battalion in a high-speed march with full field equipment. This forced march of about twenty miles lasted straight through the night. By dawn on Friday morning, the battalion was marching into the barracks area at Camp Pendleton. Clean-up of equipment was the next task; this was followed by hot showers for all the troops. Then, bone weary but happy and expectant, the Marines, wearing their fresh uniforms, piled into the waiting buses, eager to check out both the big city and the girls they hoped to find there. In truth, most of the Marines got to see pretty girls but few actually had dates with them. There just were too many young men and too few young women in southern California in those days. Nevertheless there was time for relaxation, a few beers and some time away from camp. Sunday afternoon came quite quickly, but the Marines of the First Battalion knew that the busses would be waiting at the assigned spot to take them back to camp.[81]

In Dyess's battalion of eight hundred Marines there were forty officers, most of whom were young lieutenants. One of these lieutenants had been planning for many months to get married. His future wife lived back East. Since the young officer could not get leave approved to marry in his fiancee's hometown, she planned to take a train to California and come to Camp Pendleton where the wedding would be held. Meanwhile, a Catholic priest, who was attached to the 24th Regiment, helped make arrangements for the event.

The wedding was set for a Saturday and Lieutenant Colonel Dyess decided to make the day very special for the young couple. He arranged a regimental parade and a dinner in honor of the lieutenant and his bride-to-be. He also granted the lieutenant a pass for his honeymoon, giving him the maximum time allowed by wartime regulation—three days. As the wedding day approached, everyone was looking forward to the festivities. But bad news was in the offing. On the Thursday before the scheduled Saturday wedding, an order was received from the Army general who was responsible for defense of the west coast of the United States. This general ordered that all military passes for the upcoming weekend be canceled. He had received an intelligence report that the Japanese were secretly planning some acts of sabotage; therefore he felt it prudent to increase military security and to confine all military forces to their posts and bases. All four of the military services were obliged to comply with this order, with no exceptions whatsoever. Dyess had no choice. It was still permissible to conduct most of planned activities: the parade, dinner and wedding, since all of these were to take place on Camp Pendleton; but Dyess had to cancel the bridegroom's off-base pass for the honeymoon.

Quickly the junior officers of the 1st Battalion devised a plan. After the parade, dinner and wedding, all of the officers (except Dyess) as well as the newly married lieutenant and his bride climbed into a large bus and left Camp Pendleton for a nearby town. The newlyweds checked into a hotel for the night while the other officers bought some soft drinks and beer and waited outside the hotel until early the next morning. When the newly-married lieutenant came out of his hotel, he and his thirty-eight fellow officers climbed back on the bus and were driven back to camp. The scheme worked. If the bride and groom had left the camp by themselves, the young lieutenant might have gotten into a great deal of trouble, even received a court-martial. But the battalion couldn't function if all the officers were thrown into the stockade. The young officers calculated that there was great strength in numbers, and they were right. Lieutenant Colonel Dyess conveniently looked the other way and all turned out well. No one was punished. The lieutenant and his brand new bride had their brief honeymoon and the Marines of the battalion gained still more respect for the silence, wisdom and judgment of their commander.[82]

Although Dyess's battalion was almost up to strength when it arrived at Camp Pendleton, there were a few Marines who joined the battalion in the summer and fall of 1943. In the early fall, a young private by the name of Stephen Hopkins reported in. There was nothing especially noteworthy about this eighteen-year-old Marine except his address. Hopkins's official records indicated that his home of record was Washington, D. C. and that his address was 1600 Pennsylvania Avenue. Captain Irving "Buck" Schechter, Hopkins's company commander, called the young man in and soon learned that his father was Harry Hopkins, President Franklin Roosevelt's closest advisor. By 1943, Harry Hopkins, a classic workaholic, had divorced his wife and had moved permanently into the White House.

Captain Schechter was very blunt in his orientation counseling with young Private Hopkins. Schechter pointed out that with his political connections, Hopkins could probably drop out of the unit at any time. Schechter told Hopkins that he did not want to train a Marine as part of a team and then have him, at the last moment, opt out of going into combat. Schechter told Hopkins that he would rather move him to a support job now rather than later. Hopkins reacted strongly to this suggestion, emphasizing to his new commander that he wanted to serve his nation in combat. He and his older brother, Robert Hopkins, had made a pact. Each would do his best to get into a combat unit and face the enemy. Robert Hopkins had picked the Army; Stephen, the Marines. To his credit, Stephen's outlook represented the views of the vast majority of the Marines at Pendleton. They were apprehensive about combat, but wanted to do their duty—and the duty of Marines, at this moment of American history, was to fight. After listening carefully to what Hopkins had to say, Schechter was convinced of his sincerity and allowed him to stay in his company. He was made a machine gunner in A Company of the First Battalion. As we shall see, the fate of young Stephen Hopkins became inextricably tied to that of his battalion commander.

Lieutenant Colonel Dyess not only had highly motivated enlisted men under his command, he also had many outstanding officers.

He was most fortunate to have an executive officer who had many of his same qualities. Major "Dutch" Schultz was a large man, a college graduate and a fine athlete. In his youth, he had played football for Oregon State. Dyess and Schultz were a real presence on the training field: two strong, strapping athletic men in their early thirties who understood leadership and never asked their men to do anything that they were not willing to do themselves. Both commanded the 1st Battalion, 24th Marines, in combat and both were destined to be killed by enemy fire in 1944: Dyess on Namur and Schultz on Saipan. It is often said that one of the great tragedies of war is that the best and the bravest are the first to fall. This is certainly true of the first two combat commanders of the 1st Battalion, Twenty Fourth Marines.[83]

Dyess's tall stature, his flaming red hair, his self-confidence and his love for the Marine Corps and his men showed through his every activity. His men welcomed having a tough commander, for

Lieutenant Colonel Jimmie Dyess in Marine uniform, 1943. He was commanding the 1st battalion of the 24th Marines at Camp Pendleton.

they knew that they needed to be fully prepared for warfare. If they were to succeed in combat they knew in their hearts there was no one better who could lead them. It was not just Dyess's athletic ability, marksmanship and leadership skills that they respected. They also admired a man with a heart, who loved them and cared for them. They knew that he would stick with them when the going got very tough. They also knew, and this impressed them all, that Dyess would be up front leading by personal example.

It is always helpful for a leader of men in combat to have a deep and abiding self-confidence in himself. Dyess had succeeded often—in saving two lives in heavy seas, in high school and college football, as a fine marksman and as a leader of troops in peacetime. He also had suffered a number of setbacks. Like many great leaders he was not defeated but was strengthened by these reverses. He was the least favored child in the Dyess family. His football career was foreshortened by serious injury. His brief experience as an independent businessman was a failure. The combination of these successes and failures helped make thirty-four-year-old Lieutenant Colonel Dyess a man mature beyond his years.

The summer and fall of 1943 was not just a period for the 24th Marine Regiment to train for combat, but also for the creation and build-up of the newest large combat unit in the Marine Corps, the 4th Marine Division. Whereas Dyess's battalion had 800 men and the 24th Marine Regiment 2,500, the 4th Marine Division had about 17,000. The vast majority of these Marines had had a minimum of six months training in their various combat units before departing for the Central Pacific in January, 1944. The Fourth Marine Division was to fight in four major battles from February, 1944, until May of 1945: Roi Namur, Saipan, Tinian and Iwo Jima. Although the division itself never numbered more than 25,000 at any one time, a total of 81,718 Marines assigned to it saw combat action with the division one or more times. There were 17,722 casualties (killed, wounded or missing in action) in this sixteen-month period, for a casualty rate of 21.6 percent, the highest casualty rate of any Marine division in history. The percentage of the original 17,086 men who left the United States with the Fourth division in January, 1944, and later became casualties was, of course, much higher. In fact, there were some infantry companies which had more than 80 percent of their original members killed or wounded.[84]

As might be expected, the battles conducted by the 4th Marine Division that lasted the longest, Saipan (25 days) and Iwo Jima (26 days), had the highest number of casualties, while Roi Namur (3 days) and Tinian (9 days) had a lower number. With the exception of Iwo Jima, the average casualties per day of combat were about 230. The battle for Iwo Jima was the most deadly, for it cost the division 350 casualties per day. In fact, of all the Marines of the Fourth Marine Division who hit the beaches of Iwo Jima, more than forty percent were killed or wounded in the next 26 days.

Despite these high casualty rates, it is important to reemphasize that the 4th Marine Division was, in the perspective of historical hindsight, quite fortunate. First, it had ample time to train and prepare for combat. Second, it had an opportunity to examine closely the early lessons of the war with Japan and to adjust and improve its tactics, doctrine, ordnance and training accordingly. Third, it was to serve abroad only sixteen months, whereas most of the other Marine divisions would serve overseas twenty-six months or more. Fourth, its zone of combat was exclusively in the Central Pacific. Hence, it did not have to deal with the massive jungles and the oppressive heat that Marines and soldiers faced in other areas in the Pacific. Jungle rot, trench foot and tropical disease were not major problems for the men and the medics of the Fourth Marine Division. Fifth, after each of the combat operations the division took a break. After each battle the division returned to Maui in the Hawaiian Islands for rest, recuperation, resupply and acceptance of replacements as well as individual and unit training. Sixth, during the entire war, the Fourth Marine Division was in actual combat a total of only sixty-three days, a much shorter time than divisions like the First Marine Division, which got bogged down in combat for many months at Guadacanal. Finally, the Fourth Marine

Division was the first Marine division to return to the States and to be deactivated after the war.

Despite all of these advantages, no Marine division participated in more violent action than the Fourth. In its sixty-three days of combat, it saw more close-combat action than any of the other Marine divisions which fought in World War II. Each of its days of combat was a bloody, intense experience. Most days involved round-the-clock fighting. Unlike many units which had the good fortune of attacking beaches that were lightly defended, every beachhead which the 4th Marine Division assaulted was fortified and well defended. Without question, each of the six Marine divisions made a major contribution to the war effort across the vast Pacific. However, the Fourth Marine Division, perhaps more than any division of any nation in the history of armed conflict, proved the viability of amphibious attack against defended beaches.

Although a few of the units of the Fourth Division were activated at New River in North Carolina from the summer of 1942 through the spring of 1943, most were formed in California in 1943. By the time it was formally activated on August 16, 1943, the division included five regiments: the 14th, 20th, 23rd, 24th and 25th Marines. Each of these regiments was commanded by a Marine colonel. In addition to these five regiments, there were two other large units assigned to the Fourth Marine Division: the division special troops and the division service troops, both commanded by a colonel.

In the chain of command immediately above Dyess were his regimental commander, who commanded about 2500 Marines, and his division commander, responsible for the entire 17,000 men of the 4th Marine Division. The regimental commander of the 24th Marines, Colonel Frank Hart, was Dyess's immediate commanding officer. Hart was destined to play an important role in Dyess's life and death. Sixteen years older than Dyess, Colonel Hart had unusually varied experience in both combat operations and international affairs. Hart joined the Army National Guard immediately after graduation from Alabama Polytechnic Institute (now known as Auburn) in 1915. Within a year, he was engaged in combat in America's short war with Mexico. In 1917, he transferred from the Army to the Marine Corps and in the autumn of 1918 was sent to Europe to join a combat unit. Hart arrived in France just two days before the armistice and, hence, did not participate in combat operations in World War I. During the interwar period, he served in Nicaragua where he negotiated the surrender of the bandit general, Cabulla Sequera. Also prior to World War II, Hart served for five years in Haiti.[85]

When the Americans entered World War II, Hart was serving as an American assistant naval attache in London. He participated in one of the great military debacles on World War II, the allied raid against the French port of Dieppe in August 1942. Of the 6100 Canadians, Americans, British and Free French who took part, 4100 were killed, wounded or captured. Having been personally involved in an amphibious operation that was so unsuccessful, Hart had first-hand experience in how not to conduct such landings. This knowledge was useful when it came time for Hart to train and lead the regiment which was destined to face the stiffest opposition on Roi Namur. At a critical moment in combat in the Marshalls, Hart approved Dyess's request to move forward from the beach to the front lines. Hart also was the man who recommended Dyess for the Medal of Honor immediately after the battle for Roi Namur.

Leading the Marines who were tasked to attack and capture Roi Namur was Major General Harry Schmidt, commander of the 4th Marine Division. Schmidt was a large, square-jawed Nebraskan who had been a Marine officer since 1909, the year that Dyess was born. He knew the Pacific region well, having served as a young officer on Guam, in the Philippines and in China.[86] During the training period in 1943 at Camp Pendleton, General Schmidt's primary responsibility was to ensure that all the units of the division would fight as cohesive team. Although much training took place at the company, battalion and regimental level prior to the fall of 1943, beginning in September, 1943, the entire division commenced training together as a coordinated combat unit.

The 132,000 acres of the former Santa Margarita Ranch provided excellent territory for tough, realistic training. The Camp Pendleton terrain, with its hills, canyons and semi-arid desert, provided the setting for field exercises, marches, maneuvers, amphibious assaults and supporting air strikes and artillery fire. During each major exercise the regiments of the division were reinforced with detachments of engineers, medical personnel, assault signalmen and amphibian tractor units. Periodically, the units of the Fourth Division would board transports in San Diego harbor and make a series of practice landings on Alison beach at Camp Pendleton and on the beaches of San Clemente Island off the coast of Southern California. Fortunately, in the 1940s, there was a great deal of open space in Southern California and the nearby islands. The troops could range far and wide as they hit the beaches and moved onshore to attack and capture positions that simulated Japanese military objectives. Today it is hard to imagine how under populated this region was in 1943 and how much terrain was available for exercises and maneuvers.

Benefiting from this extended period of realistic training, the division was destined to set three significant records on its very first combat operation. It was the first Marine division to go directly into combat from the United States. It was the first American unit to capture Japanese owned territory in the Pacific. Thirdly, it secured its primary objective, the Island of Roi Namur, in a shorter time (less than three days) than any other important operation in the entire Pacific War.

CHAPTER 9:

ON TO THE MARSHALLS

The Marshall Islands have a rich history. Occupied by gentle Polynesian people for many millennia, these islands were sighted by white men for the first time in 1526. A Spanish ship captain, Gracia de Loyassa, was the first European to discover them, followed three years later by his countryman, Alvaro de Saavedra. In 1686, Spanish sailors finally got around to claiming for the Spanish crown the four island groups that were later known as the Marshalls, the Gilberts, the Carolines and the Marianas. These island groups were unnamed and largely ignored until 1788 when two Englishmen, Captains Marshall and Gilbert explored the area. It is not surprising that it took so long for these groups of islands to be given names. All of these islands were so small and had such little economic value that they seemed, to every passing ship's captain, to be of little consequence. Of the 2,000 islands in the Marshalls, none exceed 20 feet in elevation and most are only a few acres in size, too small to support native populations.

Although the British gave English names to these island groups, they did not challenge the original Spanish claim to them. They all remained under nominal Spanish control until Spain sold the Marshalls, the Gilberts and the Marianas (except for Guam) to the Germans in 1899. Germany, which had not become a unified country until the 1860s, began its quest for empire much later than the Spanish, Portuguese, British, French, Belgians and Dutch. By the time Germany began its period of imperial expansion, most of the world was already claimed by other European states. But the Spanish, having recently been defeated in the Spanish American War and having lost their major colonies in the Pacific to the United States, were quite willing to sell these groups of tiny islands to the highest bidder, Germany.

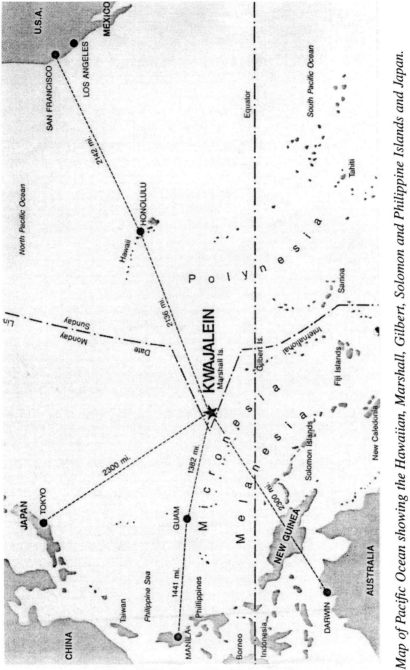

Map of Pacific Ocean showing the Hawaiian, Marshall, Gilbert, Solomon and Philippine Islands and Japan.

Germany wasn't the only nation interested in expanding its influence into the Central Pacific. Japan was even later than Germany in joining the world-wide competition for empire. After its decisive victory in the Russo-Japanese War of 1904-05, opportunistic Japanese military leaders became quite interested in expanding the rather small Japanese empire farther into the central Pacific region. When World War I commenced in 1914, the Japanese, nominal allies of the British, quickly seized the Marshalls. They realized that the Marshalls could serve as a line of departure for attack to the East as well as an outpost line of resistance. By the time American naval planners began to focus their attention on the Marshalls, early in World War II, the Japanese had controlled them for twenty years.

On the 20th of July, 1943, the Joint Chiefs of Staff in Washington directed Admiral Chester W. Nimitz, the Commander in Chief of the Pacific Fleet, to mount an operation in January, 1944, to capture the Marshalls. Planning began immediately in Nimitz's headquarters in Hawaii and by the August 20 a draft plan was ready. By this time Nimitz had a huge force under his command. His three principle subordinate commanders were Admirals Raymond Spruance, Jack Fletcher and William Halsey. Halsey, commander of the South Pacific Fleet, worked extensively with Army General Douglas MacArthur. Fletcher was commander of the North Pacific Fleet while Spruance headed the Central Pacific Fleet and was also the commander of the 5th Fleet. It was Admiral Spruance who would command the joint forces operation against the Marshalls. Each of the military services of the United States would play a significant role in the upcoming campaign.[87]

The campaign for the Marshalls was given the code name "Operation Flintlock." Of all the joint operations that took place against the Japanese in the first twenty-six months of the war, Operation Flintlock would prove to be the most important from both a strategic and an operational perspective. Up until late 1943, the American strategy in the Pacific had been largely defensive— to stop the Japanese from capturing more territory, to keep them out of Australia and New Zealand and to secure the Allied flank in the

119

South Pacific. With the impending amphibious assault on two islands in the Marshalls by the Marine Corps and the United States Army, this strategy was about to make a dramatic change. The new approach was designed to initiate a sustained offensive drive through the Central Pacific in order to secure the bases that would be needed to support a final attack on the Japanese home islands. At last the Navy had the opportunity to implement a strategy that had been under development since 1907. The historical context of the previous forty years helps to explain why Operation Flintlock had such great strategic importance.

The Japanese had initiated war against Russia by a surprise attack on the Russian fleet at Port Arthur on the night of February 8, 1904. The ensuing war is known today as the Russo-Japanese War. In this short war, the Japanese had shown impressive military and naval skill against the world's largest nation. It was a surprise to most observers of the world scene that Japan, a nation mired in feudalism just sixty years earlier, had taken on and defeated so decisively one of the recognized great powers of the world.

Japan, as a result of its victory over Russia, now controlled the Korean peninsula, the Liaotung peninsula of China and the southern half of Sakhalin Island. By 1905 Japan was recognized, for the very first time, as a major military and naval power. Meanwhile, as a result of the Spanish-American War at the turn of the century, America had moved into the Western Pacific and controlled the Philippines and Guam. Thus the two most dynamic powers in the entire Pacific region were flexing their muscles and extending their reach.

The quick and decisive Japanese victory against the Russians caused a panic in America, especially along the West Coast. As early as 1905, it appeared to many, both in the United States and in Japan, that these two countries were moving towards a strategic confrontation which, one day, might lead to war. In addition, a series of events in California in 1906 and 1907 help explain why 1907 was the year that America's War Plan Orange (aimed against Japan) was initiated.

As a direct result of a large immigration of Japanese and Chinese into California in the early years of the 20th Century, a strong anti-oriental movement developed and tried to block further immigration of Asians into America. Labeling Asians as "immoral, intemperate and quarrelsome men bound to labor at a pittance" these racists victimized Orientals by looting and violence in the aftermath of the San Francisco earthquake and fire in April, 1906. Whereas China was considered by most to be a weak power, fear of the Japanese Empire escalated. Anti-Oriental riots in California broke out in the spring of 1907 and a "war scare" hit the headlines. So bad were the relations between Japan and the United States that American war planners seriously began to think of the Japanese as a potential enemy.[88]

Accordingly, the United States Navy, with assistance from the Army, drew up War Plan Orange in 1907. Hence, 1907 is a watershed year in American naval and military history since it marked the time when Japan was officially identified as a future enemy by American naval and military planners. The authors of this war plan made the following geopolitical assumption: in spite of generally friendly relations between the United States and Japan during the fifty years prior to the Russo-Japanese War, a war would someday break out between these two vibrant nations. In developing the war plan, the Americans made a number of specific assumptions about how the Japanese might formulate and carry out its military strategy and how the war might be played out: *1.* The root cause of this presumed war would be Japan's quest for territorial expansion in which she would attempt to dominate the land, people and resources of the Far East. *2.* It would be a war in which neither nation could count on support from allies. *3.* At some point in the future, Japan would fully mobilize for war. *4.* In order to achieve its goal, Japan would find it necessary to remove American power from its southern flank by depriving the United States of its bases in the Philippines and on Guam. *5.* When prepared, she would seize objectives in the Central Pacific but be unwilling or unable to carry the war to the American mainland. *6.* Japan would then settle down into a protracted struggle in the belief that America would eventually grow weary of fighting for such faraway islands. 7. Japan would then sue for peace and, after a period of negotiation, America would concede Japan most of its earlier gains.[89]

War Plan Orange postulated that this Japanese strategy would fail massively. The American planners assumed that the United States would mobilize its considerable industrial resources, counterattack, recover its lost territories and, in the process, completely destroy Japan's military capacity and economic life. War Plan Orange, as originally formulated before World War I, was remarkably accurate in its predictions, not only of what Japan would do, but also of how the United States would respond to the Japanese challenges. War plans are often faulty because they fail to understand the threat, pick an erroneous scenario or fail to accurately predict how their own countrymen will react to the threat and play out the scenario. What is remarkable is that the American war planners had it right in 1907, again in the 1920s and 1930s and, most importantly, in the 1940s.

Admiral Chester Nimitz had first studied War Plan Orange when he was a student at the Naval War College in the early 1920s. There Nimitz, his fellow students and Naval War College faculty members conducted war games to test both the overall strategy and the various campaigns that would be required to defeat Japan. Two of Nimitz's subordinate commanders who would play vital roles in the upcoming campaign for the Marshalls, Admirals Spruance and Kelly Turner, had also studied at the Naval War College during the period between the two world wars. In fact, Spruance and Turner had served on the faculty at Newport together, gaining extensive experience in developing and testing war games relating to a possible military and naval conflict with Japan. Now that war against Japan had become a reality, Nimitz, his staff and his commanders were prepared to use War Plan Orange (somewhat modified in light of the realities of 1943) as the fundamental basis for the advance of the Navy, Marines, Army and Army Air Forces into the Central Pacific.

As the Allies shifted to the offensive, the Marshall Islands presented Admiral Nimitz and his staff with a number of strategic challenges and opportunities. In fact, there was a major controversy concerning the campaign for the Marshalls brewing in Admiral Nimitz's headquarters in Hawaii during the autumn of 1943. The issue was quite straightforward: which islands in the Marshalls should be attacked and which could be bypassed. Admiral Nimitz's three subordinate commanders for Operation Flintlock, Admirals Spruance and Turner and Marine Major General Holland Smith were in agreement with each other. They all felt that the Marshall Islands should be taken in two bites, the first being the attack on and capture of the outer islands of Wotje and Maloelap. Only after these islands were secured by the Allies should follow-on attacks against the central islands of the Marshalls, Kwajalein and Roi Namur, commence. Not satisfied with this step-by-step approach, Nimitz asked his staff to draw up a much bolder strategy. Nimitz wanted to bypass Wotje and Maloelap and go straight for Kwajalein and Roi Namur. Since allied intelligence indicated that the Japanese expected American attacks on Wotje and Maloelap and were busily reinforcing these two outer islands, Nimitz was especially anxious to bypass them and avoid the loss of many American lives.

Nimitz fully understood that the Kwajalein atoll was the pivotal point in the Japanese defensive system for the entire Central Pacific. It was both the command headquarters and the logistical and operational center for the Japanese army and navy. Nimitz felt that through the use of airpower he could prevent the garrisons on the outer Marshalls islands from opposing an American assault on Roi Namur and Kwajalein. By this time, the Allies had gained naval and air superiority in the Central Pacific, and Nimitz was convinced these superiorities could be maintained prior to and during the coming assaults.

The key decision meeting for Operation Flintlock took place in Hawaii on December 14, 1943. Admiral Nimitz, as overall commander, polled his top subordinate commanders. "Raymond," he asked, "what do you think now?" "Outer Islands" Spruance replied. "Kelly?" "Outer Islands," replied Turner. "Holland?" " Outer

Islands," replied Smith. Nimitz continued to query his commanders around the room. Every one of the other commanders urged that the initial assault be made on the outer islands of Wotje and Maloelap. The taciturn Nimitz paused briefly, then said in a firm but soft voice, "Well, gentlemen, our next objective will be Kwajalein." Without asking for any reaction to this bold decision that counteracted the advice of everyone else in the room, Nimitz terminated the meeting and dismissed his commanders.[90]

As the meeting was breaking up, Admirals Spruance and Turner lingered behind to engage Nimitz with additional comments regarding the decision he had just taken. They argued passionately that bypassing the outer islands was both dangerous and reckless. Spruance had been Nimitz's chief of staff prior to assuming his duties as Commander of the Central Pacific Force and 5th Fleet. Nimitz knew him well and had great respect for his judgment. He had an equally high regard for Kelly Turner. But Nimitz was committed to bold action. He listened to their impassioned pleas with great patience. When they had exhausted all of their arguments, Nimitz said calmly, "This is it. If you don't want to do it, the Department will find someone else to do it. Do you want to do it or not?" Kelly turned, smiled, and said, "Sure I want to do it." The dye was cast.[91]

Nimitz's operational strategy for invasion of the Marshalls was thus firmly in place. In the meantime, Japanese overall military strategy at this crucial juncture in World War II had undergone a major change. In September, 1943, the Japanese high command, very concerned by recent Allied victories, had decided to write off the Gilberts, the Marshalls and the Bismarcks and to move the Japanese perimeter of defense farther west. The new Japanese strategy, while sound in its concept, was quite unusual in its execution. Instead of abandoning these threatened and exposed island groups and withdrawing all forces, the Japanese did just the opposite. Reinforcing these islands with ground forces but not with any appreciable addition of air and naval forces, they told their Army commanders to fight to the death to impede the Allied advance.

From a tactical perspective, the Japanese felt that the way to defeat the Americans, as they attacked each defended island, was to engage them on the beaches and prevent them from moving inland. If the Americans should nevertheless establish a lodgment, the Japanese tactic would be to counterattack aggressively in order to destroy the invading force. Japanese commanders, at every location in the Central Pacific, emphasized to their troops that, when the Americans attacked, it would be unpatriotic and an insult to the Emperor for any Japanese soldier to surrender. The highly disciplined Japanese soldiers would follow these draconian orders faithfully.[92]

In retrospect, the Nimitz decision on the 14th of December, 1943 was momentous in several aspects. First, by bypassing the outer islands, Nimitz saved many lives (both Allied and Japanese) which would have been lost if the two heavily defended Japanese islands of Wotje and Maloelap had been attacked and captured. Second, the Japanese garrisons on the outer islands never got a chance to participate in the war. Completely isolated, they practiced survival techniques until the war was over eighteen months later, surrendering peacefully in September, 1945. Third, the less well defended (but strategically more important) islands of Kwajalein and Roi Namur fell quickly with lighter than expected Allied casualties. Fourth, and most important of all, the success of Operation Flintlock convinced Nimitz that he could push across the Central Pacific in rapid order. He gained confidence that he could duplicate his scheme of bypassing heavily defended Japanese islands while capturing strategically important ones.

The beautiful islands of Kwajalein Atoll surround the world's largest landlocked lagoon. The atoll consists of eighty-five islands, extending sixty five miles in length (from north to south) and is eighteen miles across (from east to west). Of these numerous islands two were of major strategic importance; the twin island of Roi Namur and the island of Kwajalein, fifty miles to the south. Both of these islands are quite small—Roi Namur, a mile long and less than a mile wide, Kwajalein, only slightly larger. The atoll lies twenty-four-hundred miles west of Hawaii.

Roi Namur, despite it small size, contained the principal

Japanese military air facility in the Marshalls. The airfield was located on the barren island of Roi while the depots, bunkers, pill boxes, barracks and trenches were largely located on the adjoining island of Namur. A short, man-made, causeway connected the two islands. Admiral Nimitz designated the air base on Roi as the main target of the northern part of a two-pronged amphibious assault scheduled for February 1, 1944. The 4th Marine Division would attack the island of Roi Namur while the U. S. Army's 7th Division would attack the larger island of Kwajalein. The two amphibious landings were scheduled on the same day so that the Japanese on one island would be unable to provide support to the other. This would mark the beginning of what turned out to be a brilliant campaign. It lasted less than a week.

CHAPTER 10:

WAR IN THE PACIFIC

Before examining the specifics of the battle for the Marshalls and the role that Lieutenant Colonel Dyess would play, it is useful to briefly trace the course of the Pacific War from December, 1941 to January, 1944. The island of Roi Namur came into the news on the same day as the Japanese air attack on Pearl Harbor. Five hours after the Japanese bombed Hawaii, the American island of Wake, two thousand miles to the west of Hawaii, was pounded by Japanese bombers. Unlike the carrier-based aircraft that attacked Hawaii, these Japanese bombers were land-based—stationed at Roi Namur. Thirty-six Japanese bombers took off from the Marshalls and flew seven hundred miles to the north to attack the United States Marine garrison on Wake Island. Four days later, a small Japanese invasion force attempted an amphibious attack in an attempt to capture the island. Lacking an aircraft carrier in support, the Japanese assault was repulsed by the Marines. Halleluia! Only four days after the shock of the Pearl Harbor attack, the United States had gained a small victory against the Japanese.[93]

The headlines throughout America on the 12th of December, 1941, all had the same theme: MARINES KEEP WAKE. Journalists compared the defense of Wake by its small American garrison to the defense of the Alamo by Texans in 1836. Millions in America, including Captain Jimmie Dyess at Parris Island, were asking the same question. Could the garrison of Marines, sailors, soldiers and supporting civilian contractors hold out against the Japanese until help arrived? The military complement numbered only three hundred and eighty-eight Marines of the First Defense Battalion. In addition, there were sixty-nine Navy and six Army Air Corps men.

Despite the confusion in Hawaii in the aftermath of the Pearl Harbor attack and the need to protect the Hawaiian Islands from an anticipated Japanese amphibious landing, an American relief force was quickly pulled together and sent west. Under the command of Admiral Fletcher, its mission was simple—save Wake Island. Perhaps this strategically important island in the central Pacific, which had been American owned since 1899, could be held. For the next ten days the determined garrison caught the attention of the world. All over the country, Americans prayed that the relief force would arrive in time and that Wake Island would remain in American hands.

The Japanese resumed air attacks against Wake and by the 22nd of December the last of the twelve Marine Corps fighter planes was destroyed. Even more ominously, on that same day, the garrison on Wake observed a large Japanese invasion force approaching the island. Admiral Fletcher's relief force was still five hundred miles to the east. A few hours later, Admiral Pye, the acting commander-in-chief in the Pacific, received a depressing radio report from the beleaguered garrison on Wake. The Japanese had commenced their assault and had successfully established a beachhead on the island. With a heavy heart, Admiral Pye decided to recall the American relief force; Wake Island and its tiny American garrison were doomed.[94]

Only two weeks after the attack on Pearl Harbor, Americans throughout the country were once again enraged and afraid. The American islands of Guam and Wake had fallen quickly and a massive Japanese invasion of the Philippines had already begun. There was no good news whatsoever. American allies were also receiving bad news. Three days after Pearl Harbor, the British had lost their two most powerful ships in the Pacific, the *Prince of Wales* and the *Repulse*. On Christmas Day, the British Crown Colony of Hong Kong fell to the Japanese. The Allies were in retreat in Europe and Africa and the Japanese military was working its will throughout the Pacific. Christmas, 1941, was a time of great despondency for America. At no time since the embattled days of Valley Forge in the harsh winter of 1777-1778 had the fortunes of America and its embattled warriors seemed so grim.

With the fall of Guam and Wake, the Japanese controlled the major lines of communication throughout the Central Pacific. This meant that the American-owned Philippine Islands could not be reinforced. With a massive force of troops, the Japanese had invaded the island of Luzon in the Philippines on the 22nd of December. Despite a stalwart defense by the garrison of Americans and Filipinos, the final result in the Philippines was never in doubt. On the 6th of May, 1942, the last bastion of American and Filipino resistance, the island of Corregidor, fell to the Japanese. Soon thereafter, news was received in the United States that a tragic march of American and Filipino soldiers had begun (soon labeled graphically but correctly the Battan Death March). Many American and Filipino soldiers were dying of dehydration, deprivation and torture. Absolutely nothing could be done to help them. A massive feeling of fury and frustration once again spread across America. Since the United States was not yet engaged in close combat with the Germans or the Italians, most of the rage in America was concentrated on the Japanese who had attacked Americans directly in Hawaii, Guam, Wake and the Philippines and who were proving so brutal in their treatment of American and Filipino prisoners of war.

Throughout 1942, the Japanese continued their multi-pronged offensive throughout the Pacific and into Southeast Asia. The Solomon Islands, to the north and east of Australia, were captured in January, 1942. The great strategic port of Singapore fell to a major Japanese attacking force on February 15,1942. Indeed, there was nothing but bad news for the Allies in the Pacific until mid-April, 1942. On April 18, to the delight of the Western World, the Americans attacked Tokyo. A small group of sixteen Army Air Force B-25 bombers under the command of Army Lieutenant Colonel "Jimmy" Doolittle, the famous aviation pioneer of the 1920s and 1930s, bombed Japan. Using a daring tactic, Doolittle launched the bombers from the aircraft carrier Hornet in the North Pacific. While the Doolittle raid was of no military significance, it boosted the morale of America and her allies at an especially gloomy time. It also brought war to the Japanese home islands for the very first time. American naval victories at the battles of the Coral Sea and Midway in May and June of 1942 gave America two additional psychological lifts. Even so, most Americans still felt, and rightly so, that the task ahead in the Pacific would be an arduous one that would last for many years.

Whereas the Army Air Corps and the Navy gave America three uplifting moments in 1942, it would be the Marines who would have the primary responsibility of slugging it out across the vast Central Pacific Theater. The years 1942 and 1943 were traumatic for the Marine Corps as they fought two battles of major significance. The battles for Guadalcanal and Tarawa had, in the case of Guadalcanal, been very prolonged, and, in the case of both Guadalcanal and Tarawa, very bloody. Stateside Marines followed these battles and campaigns with keen interest, for they knew that soon they would also be fighting the Japanese and wanted to learn from those battlefield experiences in the Pacific.

For the United States Marine Corps, 1942 was the year of Guadalcanal in the Solomon islands. When the Japanese captured the British-owned Solomons, they threatened both Australia and New Zealand. On the 7th of August, 1942, the Allies commenced a major effort to recapture these strategically important islands. Although the Marines were unopposed as they stormed the beaches of Guadalcanal, this campaign soon became extremely difficult. Two days after the landings, Admiral Fletcher, worried about the Japanese air threat from both carrier- and land-based air forces, withdrew his aircraft carriers. The Marines on shore and those still in their transports off the coast of Guadalcanal were now even more vulnerable to Japanese attack. Although protected by a United States force of battleships, cruisers and destroyers, the unarmed transport ships no longer had the support of carrier aviation.[95]

Two nights after the Americans landed on Guadalcanal, at 1:36 a.m. on August 9, a Japanese battle fleet commenced an attack of devastating proportions against the American fleet. In the next thirty-two minutes, the United States Navy suffered it biggest defeat, in a fair fight, in its long history. This naval battle took place near

Savo Island which was just to the north of Guadalcanal. Four heavy cruisers and one destroyer were sunk and twelve hundred and seventy Americans were killed. While inflicting these losses, the Japanese Navy did not lose a single ship. [96] This defeat made the American lodgment on Guadalcanal even more precarious. Admiral Turner, knowing his transports were now in mortal danger, withdrew them on the afternoon of August 9. The supplies and equipment that the Marines on Guadalcanal had counted on were thus never unloaded. In addition, a reserve regiment of 1400 Marines did not have time to disembark.

Major General Archer Vandergrift, the Marine commander on Guadalcanal, realizing how precarious his position was, moved aggressively to prepare for the Japanese counterattacks which were sure to come. The Marines captured an airfield (quickly named Henderson Field after one of the heroes of the battle of Midway), refurbished it and brought in fighter aircraft. Henderson Field soon became the most important strategic asset on Guadalcanal. With no carrier aviation in the area, the only source of airpower support for the ground troops was this single airfield. The Marines and Army soldiers fought tenaciously and successfully to hold Henderson Field throughout the bloody campaign.

For the next few months, the battle for Guadalcanal was touch and go. The Japanese launched many a number of sustained attacks as well as many Banzai-type assaults. Both sides had great difficulty in resupplying their troops by sea or air. Rations were very short and the Americans often went to sleep hungry in sodden foxholes. The logistical situation for the Japanese was even worse— thousands died of starvation. When the bloody six-month campaign was finally over in February, 1943, and the dead were counted, the Japanese had lost twenty-five thousand troops including nine thousand who had died of starvation or disease. More than fifteen hundred Marines had also perished.[97]

With the victory at Guadalcanal assured, it was time for the Marines to turn their attention to two other sets of strategically important islands, the Gilberts and the Marshalls. These island groups were much closer to the United States than the Solomons and they blocked the westward path of the Allies into the Central Pacific. A strategic decision was made. The Gilberts, to the southeast of the Marshalls, were to be attacked first. Only after the Americans captured the Gilberts would a coordinated Navy, Marine and Army assault on the Marshalls take place.

Tarawa, a strategically important atoll in the Gilbert Islands, proved to be the most significant battle for the United States Marine Corps in 1943. It marked the first time in the war that the Marines had a chance to test their doctrine of amphibious landings against a well-defended beach. Although the Marines captured the atoll in less than a week, two costly mistakes were made: *1.* Americans failed to weaken the Japanese defense sufficiently with a massive, sustained air and naval bombardment. Although many of the big Japanese guns on Tarawa had been knocked out by the short pre-attack bombardment, dug-in Japanese were ready with machine guns and rifles when the Marines launched their assault against the beaches. *2.* The timing of this attack was faulty. It was not high tide when the assault boats approached the island, so many were stopped by an irregular reef some eight hundred yards offshore. Instead of being carried to the beach by landing craft, the Marines were forced to abandon the assault boats and swim (and then wade) in from the reef. They made easy targets as they slowly paddled their way to shore. Many drowned in the attempt and many others were killed or wounded by Japanese gunfire before they could reach the beach and return fire.[98]

The initial Marine beachhead on Tarawa was so precarious that had the Japanese counterattacked the first night they probably would have pushed the invading American force back into the sea. Although American operations were more successful after the first day, the losses were still very high. Whereas fifteen hundred Marines had been killed in the six-month battle for Guadalcanal, over one thousand Marines perished in less than a week at Tarawa. A major difference between the battle for Tarawa and the battle for Guadalcanal, of course, was that the Marines at Tarawa faced heavy opposition as they approached the beach, while those at Guadalcanal landed unopposed.

Although the Marines of the 4th Division at Camp Pendleton did not understand it at the time, they owe a great debt to Admiral Kelly Turner for what he did immediately after the Tarawa battle. It was Turner who undertook a very tough-minded, self-critical analysis of the fight for Tarawa. On November 30, 1943, that analysis was published and flown to Pearl Harbor. It was a remarkable document, for it not only was brutally honest in its analysis of Japanese strengths and American mistakes but it also made some solid recommendations for the upcoming assault on the Marshalls.[99] Turner felt that the key islands in the Marshalls would be reinforced and strengthened by the Japanese in the coming months and that the Americans would face an even more formidable defense than they had faced at Tarawa. He strongly recommended that American forces use more and better air reconnaissance, more submarine scouting, more ships and landing craft. Most importantly, he recommended that at least three times as much bombardment ammunition be used "in order to ensure the troops getting ashore with losses that we can sustain." Admiral Spruance approved all of Turner's recommendations on December 2, 1943, and Admiral Nimitz, in turn, endorsed them all. In order to ensure that these recommendations could be implemented and enough ships, ordnance, aircraft and landing craft would be available, the invasion of the Marshalls was postponed twice: first from January 1 to January 17 and then to January 31.[100]

Another reason for the postponement of the invasion of the Marshalls was a major problem with the field telephones that had been issued to all of the units of the Fourth Division. Most of them did not work. During an investigation to determine what the problem was and how it could be fixed, a major scandal was uncovered. A civilian inspector had been bribed and had agreed to accept the defective radios. To the Marines at Camp Pendleton this scandal was a blessing in disguise. While they waited for their new radios many of them got two weeks of liberty.[101]

By the time the entire complement of forces was pulled together, the Marshall Islands expeditionary forces numbered 297 ships, not counting the fast carrier task groups or the submarines. The troops which would assault the beaches of the Marshalls numbered about 54,000, about twice the number that had attacked the Gilberts.

In addition to more men and much more firepower, the Marshalls campaign would also benefit from a great deal of innovation which took place as a result of the lessons learned from Tarawa. The alligators, which had done so well at Tarawa, were ordered in great quantity. Washington gave very high priority to alligator production and rapid deployment to the Pacific. Two brand new models of alligators were sent to support Operation Flintlock; both were improvements on the models used at Tarawa. The new alligators had better armor to protect the driver and passengers and better fire power to suppress enemy fire coming from the island. The LCIs (Landing Craft Infantry) were also improved. Some of these shallow draft boats were heavily armed and turned into escort craft. On board each of these specially armed boats were five 50 caliber machine guns, two 20 mm and three 40 mm guns. These armed LCIs also had six rocket racks. The crew size of these LCIs was doubled and they no longer carried passengers. They were welcomed by all of the Marines since they provided close-in fire support on the hazardous trip to the beach.

Another innovation that was to have a high payoff in the Marshalls was the arming of fighter planes with air-to-ground rockets. This idea came from Britain's Royal Air Force and was incorporated in the Pacific when it was realized that 50 caliber machine guns on the fighters at Tarawa had been quite ineffective against dug-in Japanese positions. The bullets didn't have the mass to penetrate these positions. The heavy, high velocity rockets would do a much better job. Also, for the first time in American combat history, Navy underwater demolition teams would swim to the island of Roi Namur ahead of the assault landings to check out defenses and blow up underwater barriers to the assault. In the hindsight of more than fifty years, it is remarkable that so much innovation could take place so quickly. Many historians have noted that America won World War II through the use of overwhelming military power. What is often forgotten is that the Americans were extremely creative during the war and were able to cut through bureaucracy in order to get the new military capabilities quickly into the hands of the front-line combat troops.

There was also innovation in training and tactics as a result of the lessons learned from Tarawa.[102] A small island in the Hawaiian group (Kahoolawe) was given to the Navy for use in developing better naval and artillery support. Duplicating what they had found on Tarawa, the Marines built pillboxes, concrete and log bunkers, and other fortifications. Realistic exercises were then held to ensure that the troops would get the most effective fire support possible prior to and during the assault. Rear Admiral James L. Kauffman, Commander of Cruisers and Destroyers for the Pacific Fleet, directed the close fire support for the troops. Particular attention was paid to improving communications between the ships and the troops on the ground who would direct the fire.

In the late fall of 1943, as Dyess read the news reports and after-action reports from Tarawa, he might well have chosen Colonel David Shoup as his role model. Shoup was one of the outstanding Marine leaders at Tarawa, earning the Medal of Honor for his heroism there. Despite sustaining a leg wound that soon became badly infected, Shoup took command of the beachhead on the afternoon of the first day and led the Marines inland on the following day.[103] Jimmie Dyess was to repeat, three months later, the "take charge" leadership approach of Colonel Shoup. There were, however, to be two differences between Shoup's experiences at Tarawa and Dyess's at Roi Namur. Shoup would survive and later become Commandant of the Marine Corps, while Dyess would be killed. Also, on Tarawa the Marine casualties were horrendous. On Roi Namur, the casualties were much lighter.

CHAPTER 11:

THE BATTLE FOR
ROI NAMUR

Packing for the long trip to the Central Pacific was a major undertaking for the men of the 4th Marine Division. These men were headed for long-term combat. Space on board ship was very restricted, so the men had to limit personal items to an absolute minimum. Lieutenant Colonel Dyess made one exception to the tough rules about bringing only essential items. He asked his driver, Willie Turner, to find a large wooden box which was especially sturdy. When Turner brought him such a box, Dyess asked for help in packing it up. To the surprise of Private Turner, the box was to be filled with bottles of whiskey. Dyess never drank alcoholic beverages in the presence of enlisted Marines. Fraternization of officers and enlisted men when alcohol was present was not uncommon in those days, but this was an activity in which Dyess would never participate. Nevertheless, Dyess and Turner carefully packed several cases of liquor into this box. After the job was done, Dyess told Turner, "If anything happens to me, open this box and have a party."[104]

The packing and loading of the ships in San Diego harbor began in December, 1943, but it wasn't until January that the ships carrying the 4th Marine Division sailed for the Central Pacific. The first group of ships to leave San Diego were 15 large LSTs (Landing Ship Tank). These LSTs carried a huge array of trucks, tanks, half-tracks, landing boats and alligators, including the alligator that Dyess would use. The LSTs were accompanied by 7 LCIs, 3 minesweepers and 2 destroyers. This convoy left San Diego on the 5th of January. However, the main complement of ships departed on January 13th. More than one hundred ships sailed that day, including three transport divisions, five fire-support divisions, three escort carriers, nine LCI gunboats and several minesweepers and ocean-going tugs.

These convoys began the long, slow trip from California to the Central Pacific. As they watched the coast disappear over the horizon, the Marines were in the dark as to where they were headed. Operational security was extremely tight. There was much discussion of a campaign that was rumored to be called, "Operation Burlesque and Camouflage." Naturally, there were many rumors concerning the route and final destination of the convoy. One of the favorite rumors was that the division would stop by the Hawaiian Islands to pick up additional supplies and that everyone would get a few days of shore leave. Hopes of rendezvous with lovely Polynesian girls in grass skirts were elevated among the Marines when, on January 21, the convoy pulled into these fabled islands and anchored off the coast of Maui. A few logistical personnel and some supplies were dropped off at Maui so that a permanent training base could be established for the 4th Marine Division. The administrative and training plans were clear: after every battle, the Division would return to the Hawaiian Islands for rest, recuperation, resupply and additional training. Those who were not scheduled to move ashore looked longingly at the beautiful beaches of Maui and waited eagerly for an announcement about liberty. However, the loudspeaker produced only sad news, "There will be no...." Groans and sighs of disappointment could be felt on every ship even before the word "liberty" could be heard. The next day, the convoy was underway for the Marshalls.[105]

By now the routine for the Marines on board ship was well established and carefully followed. Everyone arose at the same time in the morning. Weapons were cleaned each day and there was regular firing of weapons out to sea to make sure that pistols, rifles, carbines and machine guns were in good working order prior to combat. Since there was so little room on deck, physical exercise was done in shifts. Dyess felt very strongly that he must keep his Marines in great physical shape so they would have the extra energy and strength needed to overwhelm the enemy in close combat.

Together with his troops, Lieutenant Colonel Dyess participated in the daily exercises. Most of his men did not realize that this physical training was quite painful for him, since it aggravated the knee that was damaged during his football days at Clemson.

During leisure hours, the men played cards, took naps, stood in long lines for ice cream, wrote letters and held extended bull sessions. The convoy had to travel at the speed of the slowest ship; hence, the embarked Marines would spend more than two weeks in cramped quarters, sleeping in bunks closely stacked, one on top of the other. It was a time of considerable boredom but also a time of great expectation.

Only after the ships left Hawaii were the troops finally informed by their commanders of the destination. Locked safes on each ship were opened, a large panoply of operational plans, photos, maps and models were displayed and serious study of Roi Namur began. Now they knew for sure that they would go directly into combat. Each man was briefed on the details of the operation, where he was *supposed* to land, and what he was expected to do. Since the island was so small, it was easy to memorize the key features, such as the pier, the runway and the major blockhouses and bunkers. Anticipation of the coming trial by fire was palpable. A few of the Marines had previous combat experience in the early battles of World War II and a handful of older Marines had fought in World War I, but the vast majority, including Jimmie Dyess, had no combat experience whatsoever.[106]

The vast armada of ships that approached the Marshalls in late January, 1944, was the largest that had been assembled in the Pacific up to that time. By late 1943, the vast industrial base of the United States was pumping out military equipment at a pace that was totally unprecedented in history. Although the Americans had to supply the British, the Russians, the Free French, the Chinese, the Brazilians and many other allies, they also were able to equip a U. S. military force of more than ten million men who would fight in many theaters. The arsenal of democracy was in full swing and every Marine, sailor and soldier engaged in Operation Flintlock

138

benefited from the quality and the quantity of the military equipment being provided by the hard working and patriotic American workers. America was flexing its individual and collective muscles as no other nation had ever done so massively before.

A major turning point in the war was about to occur and the Marines of Jimmie Dyess's battalion were well trained, well equipped and well led as they prepared to play their part in it. Everyone hoped that the battle of Roi Namur would prove that Americans could overwhelm a heavily defended island quickly with only small number of American casualties.

Command arrangements for Operation Flintlock were clear-cut and well understood. From Nimitz to the front line Marine commanders, it was an impressive group. The commander of the 5th Fleet, Vice Admiral Raymond A. Spruance, was the overall commander. With a nickname of "electric brain", Spruance had a well-deserved reputation of being able to face tough situations with calmness and with a steel-trap, analytical mind, he had distinguished himself as a commander at the two great naval victories of 1942, the battles of the Coral Sea and Midway. Ground operations for the campaign were under the leadership of Major General Holland M. (Howling Mad) Smith. Smith believed strongly that the use of overwhelming force in combination with aggressive, unremitting attack would win battles more quickly and with fewer casualties than any other tactic. He instilled this philosophy into everyone in his command. Smith commanded the Fifth Amphibious Corps which included two major combat units, the U. S. Army's 7th Division and the 4th Marine Division, as well as many supporting units. The Joint Expeditionary Forces were under the operational command of Rear Admiral Richmond Kelly Turner. These forces would conduct simultaneous operations to the north and to the south. The Northern Attack Force, which would assault and capture Roi Namur, was under the tactical command of Rear Admiral Richard L. Conolly.[107]

Crossing the international date line was a big event with traditional ceremonies— a first for almost every Marine. Also, it meant that the islands of the Marshalls would soon appear on the horizon. On the long journey Jimmie Dyess was quite fatalistic. Although he shared his private thoughts with very few, he did tell a couple of people that he thought that he would be killed in combat. He asked his A company commander, Captain Buck Schechter, who had earned a law degree from New York University just prior to the war, to meet with him in private. The two men went to the fantail of the ship. Dyess said to Schechter, "Buck, I know that you're a lawyer. I also know that I'm going to be killed on this operation. I want you to help me make out my will." Schechter replied, "Oh come on Colonel, I'll be glad to help on your will. My fee will be your picking up the check when we have dinner after the war back in the States. You're not going to get killed." Dyess replied, "Thank you, Buck, but I just feel in my bones that I am going to get killed." Dyess signed the will before the ships arrived in the vicinity of the Marshall Islands.[108]

As the ships approached the Marshalls, a trick was played on Dyess. A written order was prepared and given to him that stated that the 1st Battalion of the 24th Marines would not participate in the Roi Namur operation. Instead, the entire battalion would remain offshore until the island was captured. The orders stated that, after the island was secured, Dyess was to bring his battalion on shore to serve as the garrison force while the other battalions were to be shipped to Maui for further training. Dyess was very upset by this turn of events. He let his commanders know, in no uncertain terms, that his battalion had trained hard for combat and should be included in the assault. The order turned out to be a hoax; it was designed to kid Dyess, and it was, of course, successful. After waiting for more than two years, Dyess was anxious to engage the enemy in combat. He was momentarily devastated by the prospect of being held out of the Roi Namur operation.

With the Marine assault of Roi Namur scheduled for the first day of February, it was also important that all the tactical, operational, logistical and ordnance lessons of the bloody battle of Tarawa be applied to the attacks on both Roi Namur and Kwajalein. In addition to the efforts made by the Navy and the Marine Corps to learn and apply the lessons of Tarawa, the Army had also been hard at work. In December, 1943, General George Marshall had made a personal overseas tour to observe military activities firsthand and ascertain how he and other stateside leaders could assist the commanders in the field. He uncovered many problems that demanded his personal attention. Back in the Pentagon on Christmas Eve, he called up some Army ordnance experts from the Aberdeen Proving Ground in Maryland and told them to report to him immediately. After outlining the problems he wanted them to solve, he sent this ordnance team to the Pacific that very night. Even though Christmas was the next day, there was no time to lose with the invasion set for only one month later. Their mission was to make major improvements on the weapons that would soon be used in the battle for the Marshalls.

At a series of meetings in Hawaii, the Army team identified a number of causes of the ordnance problems at Tarawa. Many of the aircraft delivered parachute bombs which had been duds. The team determined that pilots had dropped these bombs at too low an altitude and had not allowed enough time for the time-delay arming mechanism to work. A change in tactics was ordered to ensure that the pilots dropped from a higher altitude so that the bombs would explode normally. Also, 16-inch guns of the Navy's battleships hurled their heavy projectiles at such high velocity that they would often bounce off a target on a small island and explode harmlessly out over the water. This problem was corrected by reducing both the velocity of the shells and the time settings in the time-delay fuse.

The Army experts also found an appalling lack of understanding among all the military services of the proper employment of armament and ammunition. They held training sessions for those who would make the tactical and operational decisions concerning the use of the awesome American firepower. Cooperation between and the among the various military services in January, 1944, was particularly good. No one wanted a duplication of the terrible bloodshed and the unnecessary loss of life which had taken place at Tarawa.[109]

American air attacks against Roi Namur had started in early December, 1943, but it was an air attack on January 29, 1944, just three days before the invasion which was especially noteworthy. The Japanese had eighty-three military aircraft stationed on the airfield on Roi Namur. On that day, every Japanese aircraft was either shot down in air-to-air combat or destroyed on the ground. Only five U. S. Navy aircraft were lost in the process. When the Marines hit the beaches of Roi Namur, they did not have to face one Japanese aircraft sortie. The fact that the Americans didn't just have air superiority, but complete air supremacy, would be an important factor leading to the rapid success in the battle.

For three consecutive nights before the main assault on Roi Namur, the Americans hit the Japanese with lethal fire from an impressive array of naval ships. In addition, the Navy fired star shells throughout each night to track enemy troop movements and to contribute to the fatigue of the Japanese soldiers waiting for the landing which they knew was coming soon. This "softening up" fire helped to insure that the defenders were tired, confused and demoralized. This fire was also responsible for the death and wounding of many Japanese. Again, the lessons of Tarawa were being applied. The Marines did not want to face well-armed and well-rested soldiers when they approached the beaches on D Day.

Although air attacks and naval gunfire support prior to and during the battle were very helpful, Marine artillery support was also important. Since the tiny islands immediately adjacent to Roi Namur were uninhabited, a decision was made to place Marine artillery units on islands with the exotic names of Ennuebing, Mellu, Ennubirr, Ennumennet and Ennugarret. Rather than establish D-Day as the day of the main assault, it was decided that D-Day for the Roi Namur campaign would be the 31st of January, the day before the main attack. Hence, the movement of the Marine artillery men and their guns to these small islands marks the beginning of what was to be a three-day battle for Roi Namur. On January 31, 1944, artillery units were ferried to these five islands. These units, consisting of 75mm and 105mm howitzers from the 14th Marines of the 4th Division, were under the overall command of the 4th Marine Division's assistant commander, Brigadier General James Underhill.[110]

The seizure of these outer islands was the responsibility of two units of the 4th Division: the Scout Company and Regimental Combat Team 25. The honor of being the very first units to land on enemy territory went to Lieutenant Colonel Clarence J. O'Donnell's 1st Battalion of the 25th Marines and to the Scout Company of the division. They went ashore at 0958 on January 31. They chose the seaward side of Ennuebing and Mellu Islands. These islands lay to the southwest of Roi Namur. Unfortunately, these small outer islands were protected by dangerous coral reefs and a number of landing boats hit the reefs and were swamped. Ennuebing was secured within an hour and the larger Mellu by 1209. The artillery came ashore less than an hour after the islands were secured. Dyess's close friend from the Barrage Balloon School, Major Art Buck, was the weapons company commander of the 1st Battalion of the 25th Marines.

The second and third battalions of the 25th Marine Regiment landed on the three islands to the southeast of Roi Namur: Ennubirr, Ennumennet and Ennugarret. All three of these islands were secured by nightfall on the 31st. On Ennubirr, the 2nd battalion of the 25th raised the first American flag in the Marshalls—on a coconut tree. The artillery men had to work all night siting their guns and hauling in ammunition; but, as dawn broke on February 1st, they were ready. Artillery fire on the objective began early on the 1st and continued unabated as the amphibious assault units moved towards Roi Namur in the late morning.

Naval gunfire support was provided by three battleships, the *Tennessee*, the *Maryland* and the *Colorado*, as well as by five cruisers and nineteen destroyers. The naval task force commander played a vital leadership role in supporting the invasion of Roi Namur. The aggressive Rear Admiral Richard L. Conolly, who had done such a fine job of supporting the amphibious landings on Sicily in July, 1943, was a strong believer in close-in naval gunfire. The Marines awaiting the assault on Roi Namur were uplifted when they saw battleships sail to within a mile of the beach to fire their big guns point blank at Japanese positions. Nick-naming the admiral, "Close-in Conolly," the Marines of all ranks admired his boldness and his willingness to run risks to give them the kind of accurate and devastating fire support they wanted. Whereas Tarawa received twenty-four hundred tons of bombs and artillery rounds in the pre-assault bombardment, the smaller island of Roi Namur received six thousand tons. Since the fire was more accurate and there were fewer duds, the comparison between Tarawa and Roi Namur was stark indeed.

One of the important innovations of the Marshalls campaign was the use of Marines in aircraft whose specific role was to direct, control and adjust naval gunfire. One of their primary responsibilities was to cut off this gunfire at just the right moment—when the Marines were a few hundred yards from the beach. This was the first time in the Pacific war that Marine aviators had been used for this purpose. When it became clear that this tactic worked so well, it became standard in future battles in World War II and in every war since.

Phase Two of the operation commenced on the morning of February 1. Two Regimental Combat Teams, the 23rd and the 24th, were responsible for attacking four beaches on Roi Namur simultaneously in order to overwhelm the defenders. The first and second battalions of the 23rd Marines assembled on the left. Their mission was to strike Red 2 and Red 3 beaches on Roi and to secure the airbase.

The second and third battalion of the 24th Marines were on the right. They had a tougher mission and they knew it. Their mission was to hit Green 1 and Green 2 beaches on the much more heavily defended island of Namur and to capture the island. As the men surveyed the islands from off shore, Roi Namur did not appear very impressive to the Marines. In fact, they were little more than sand spits, connected by a man-made causeway. However, as the Marines approached they could see that these seemingly inconsequential islands contained, as they had been briefed, many concrete bunkers and pillboxes and they knew that there were more than 3000 Japanese soldiers dug into well prepared defensive positions on these two interconnected islands. These Marines also had in mind the tales of the agony of Tarawa and the terrible losses suffered just a few months earlier in the water, on the beach and on Tarawa itself.

At 1:30 a.m. on February 1, reveille was sounded for the four battalions which were to lead the assault on Roi Namur. The plan was to reach the beaches early in the morning so that the Marines would have all day to establish a beachhead and to be in a position to repel any counterattacks that the Japanese would launch after dark on the first night. However, this was to be a morning of many delays because of poor radio communications and out-of-gas LVTs. It wasn't until noon that the 23rd Marines hit the beaches of Roi. Three minutes later the 2nd and 3rd battalions of the 24th Marines landed on Namur. Ten minutes before the first landings, an air observer had dropped parachute flares to indicate that the landing craft were within 500 yards of shore. With the exception of the craft in the assault itself, every ship that had been pounding Roi Namur ceased firing.

The approach of Colonel Hart and his 24th Marines to the beach was ragged with many landing craft not yet assembled for a coordinated attack. Admiral Connolly and General Schmidt considered postponing the attack until all the landing craft could be properly lined up but decided to press on. Tarawa was on their minds. A delay in the attack at Tarawa had given the Japanese time to get prepared and had contributed to the high casualty rate. Even though the Marines hit the beaches of Namur in a piecemeal and disorganized fashion, the Japanese did not seem to be able to take full advantage of this weakness. Japanese resistance at the water's edge was ferocious but not well coordinated.

Even though the Japanese defenders had received a heavy pounding from the air and from artillery and naval gunfire, they did their best to repel the invading Marines. They were armed with coastal defense guns, heavy and medium anti-aircraft guns, heavy machine guns and a variety of small arms. The Japanese were firing from a number of reinforced concrete blockhouses, fifty-two pillboxes, numerous anti-tank trenches, thousands of spider holes and many infantry trenches. Barbed wire was deployed tactically to make Marine movement treacherous and painful. Since they had occupied Roi Namur for more than twenty years, the Japanese had had plenty of time to build these heavy fortifications to assist them in repelling invasion.

The most vivid description of the assault on Roi Namur comes from John Chapin who, at the time, was a second lieutenant platoon leader. He has described how he was equipped that day. (Jimmie Dyess's personal equipment that day was about the same as Lieutenant Chapin's).

> *Landings were made with each person loaded with weight. We wore our dungarees, leggings, and boondockers (shoes). Our skivvies (underwear) had been dyed green while we were still in the States. White ones were too good a target. In addition, our packs were loaded with whatever gear we thought we would need, such as extra socks, toilet gear, poncho and our "D" and "K" rations. Extra cigarettes were stuffed in also. Believe it or not, some of us carried books that we were reading. I wore two knives. The K Bar that was issued was tucked into my right legging. The throwing stiletto that I had purchased was on my belt; a leather thong at the bottom of the sheath was tied around my leg so that the knife would not flop around. My bayonet was in its sheath and attached to my pack. On went the loaded pack. Around my waist was the cartridge belt, fully loaded, with ten clips of M1 rifle ammo, each clip holding eight rounds. Over my shoulder were two bandoleers of M1 ammo, holding an additional eighty rounds. Hanging from my pockets were four hand grenades, only requiring a pulled pin to be activated. We donned our helmets with the brown camouflaged covering. Finally we slung our gas masks over our shoulders.*[111]

As the various boats began to form up for the assault there was confusion in many areas. Radio communications was so spotty and uncertain that attack commanders had to race around in their boats giving instructions shouting into handheld megaphones. Once again quoting John Chapin, whose memories remain very vivid.

By now everything was all mixed up, with our assault wave all entangled with the armored tractors around us. I ordered my driver to maneuver around them. Slowly we inched past, as their 37 mm guns and 50 caliber machine guns flamed. The beach lay right before us. However, it was shrouded in such a pall of dust and smoke from our bombardment that we could see very little of it. As a result, we were unable to tell which section we were approaching (after all our hours of careful planning based on hitting the beach at one exact spot). I turned to talk to my platoon sergeant, who was manning the machine gun right beside me. He was slumped over—the whole right side of his head disintegrated into a mass of gore. Up to now, the entire operation had seemed almost like a movie, or like one of the innumerable practice landings we'd made. Now one of my men lay in a welter of blood beside me and the reality of it smashed into my consciousness.[112]

Soon thereafter, Chapin and his men heard a grinding crash to their immediate right. What they saw was a large, 50 foot LVT collide with an alligator right at the water's edge. The LVT then slid upward and rolled on its side. It then hung there on top of the alligator. Immediately thereafter, Chapin's boat ground onto the beach; he and his men raced for the shore. Just as he sprawled onto the sand, his alligator ground its way backwards into the lagoon. Lieutenant Chapin surveyed the situation and realized that his platoon was three hundred yards too far to the right. Only ten feet to his front was a series of trenches that were filled with Japanese soldiers who were firing at his men. Again, Chapin's recollections are vivid and stark.

> *At one point in this swirling maelstrom of action, I was kneeling behind a palm tree stump with my carbine of the deck, a I fished for a fresh clip of bullets in my belt. Something made me look up and there, not ten feet away was a Jap charging me with his bayonet. My hands were empty. I was helpless. The thought that 'this is it' flashed through my brain! Then shots chattered through from all sides of me. My men hit the running Jap in a dozen places. He fell dead three feet from me.*

Small groups of Marines began forming on their own and began to work their way inland. Lieutenant Chapin was not able to keep tight control of his forty-man platoon. Suddenly he dropped to the ground.

> *My first reaction was that someone had hit my right cheek with a baseball bat. With the shock, instinct made me cover my right eye with my hand. Then I realized I'd been hit. Searing in my mind came the question, 'When I take my hand away, will I be able to see?' Slowly I lowered my arm and opened my eye. I could see. Relief flooded through me.... The bullet had gone completely through my helmet just above my right ear, and left a jagged, gapping hole in the steel.*[113]

By the time the Marines hit the beach on Roi Namur, more than half of the 3500 Japanese soldiers on the island were dead. Many others were punchy and weary from days and nights of relentless heavy bombardment. The top Japanese commander on the island, Vice Admiral Yamada, was killed during the intense pre-invasion bombardment and seven other senior Japanese leaders were killed on the day of the landing. The command, control and communications between and among the Japanese defense forces had been disrupted to a much greater extent than during the Tarawa campaign. Although it did not seem so at the time, the Marines of the Fourth Division were in reasonably good tactical shape as they approached the island. They faced an enemy in disarray and they could count on continued fire support from attack aircraft, naval gunfire and four battalions of Marine artillery as they fought their way across the island.

Some of the more lethal pieces of equipment defending the island were the British made heavy guns captured by the Japanese at Singapore in early 1942. After the fall of Singapore, the Japanese made a strategic analysis about how to deploy the heavy weapons they had captured. Since they were chronically short of first-class heavy guns throughout the war, how these guns were to be allocated and deployed was of some importance. They concluded that Roi Namur was more likely to be attacked than Singapore and had shipped the guns more than three thousand miles to the East. The Japanese strategists had figured correctly. The main enemy in the Pacific would be the United States. When the Americans did not sue for peace soon after Pearl Harbor, the top Japanese leaders realized that the Marshalls would be a logical place for the Americans to attack as they fought their way West across the vast Pacific ocean.

The first major obstacle that the Marines faced, on both Roi and Namur, was an anti-tank ditch near the water's edge. This ditch prevented many of the alligators, half tracks and other vehicles from proceeding on shore so the vast majority of the Marines disembarked at the water's edge.[114] The intensity of the gunfire from the Japanese was heaviest on the very far right of the Marine positions on Namur. From that moment to the end of the campaign the next day, the most significant engagements would be in this sector. This is where Frank Pokrop and his patrol would be surrounded, where Dyess would lead his attack the next day and where he would be killed minutes before Roi Namur fell to the Americans.

The delay of the lead battalions had a domino effect on the entire operation and caused a delay for Dyess's battalion as well. The 1st Battalion had to wait until a sufficient number of assault boats could return from the beach, be assembled and loaded with troops and equipment. Originally scheduled to make the landings in the late morning, Dyess's battalion did not head for shore until mid-afternoon.[115]

Major General Harry Schmidt, USMC, commanded the Fourth Marine Division during the training at Camp Pendleton and during the Marshalls campaign in World War II.

Major General Franklin A. Hart, USMC, as a colonel, commanded the 24th Marine Regiment during the training at Camp Pendleton and during the Marshalls campaign during World War II. Hart was Jimmie Dyess's immediate commander.

Dyess's primary responsibility was getting his battalion safely to shore. Even though the regiment's other two battalions had already established a beachhead, Dyess decided to make a preliminary reconnaissance of the route through the reef and to the beach. Before he would lead his 800 troops ashore, he wanted to have an up-to-date understanding of what hazards and opposition they would face on the way to the beach. He directed the crew of his alligator to proceed to the spot where there was a gap in the off-shore reef. Dyess's alligator was accompanied by an armed naval craft that gave him some fire support. Dyess's slow reconnaissance trip to the beach turned out to be very eventful in quite a surprising way.

On Namur, the Japanese had stored large quantities of munitions, including bombs, artillery rounds and torpedo warheads inside a large bunker. The Marines knew that there were munitions stored on Roi Namur, but the intelligence was sketchy as to the location of the storage areas. One of the first Marines to reach the shore threw a satchel charge into a large structure. Unbeknownst to him, this structure was the storage site for a huge supply of ammunition. Instantly, a massive explosion occurred. Large pieces of concrete and other debris flew high into the air and a towering cloud of smoke rose quickly skyward. At that moment, hundreds of Japanese and many Marines were unlucky enough to be so near the exploding bunker that they were killed instantly. As the debris from this huge explosion fell back towards the island, many others, both Japanese and American, were killed or injured. Some of this flying debris landed in the water causing large splashes while the huge mushroom cloud rose high above the island.

To quote from the history of the 4th Marine Division,

> *In addition to the fire of the die-hard defenders, the Marines encountered a staggering misfortune. A large concrete structure they assumed to be a bunker was really a storehouse for heavy munitions, including torpedo warheads. A satchel charge thrown inside caused an explosion of Vesuvian proportions. 'Great God*

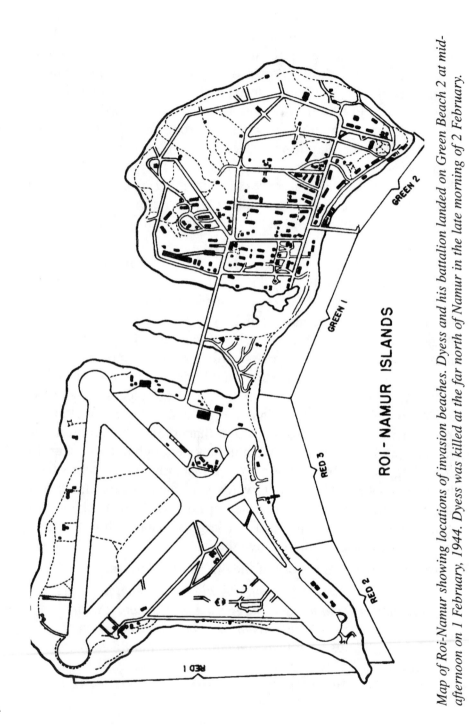

Map of Roi-Namur showing locations of invasion beaches. Dyess and his battalion landed on Green Beach 2 at mid-afternoon on 1 February, 1944. Dyess was killed at the far north of Namur in the late morning of 2 February.

Roi-Namur in 1944. Roi is on the left; Namur is on the right.

Colonel Hart (on the left) briefing key officers on the impending landing on Roi-Namur. Jimmie Dyess is at the far right.

Almighty!' cried an observer in a carrier plane overhead. 'The whole damn island has blown up!' The plane was tossed about a thousand feet farther aloft. As the brown and white mushroom expanded and billowed, according to an officer on one of the offshore destroyers, 'debris and bodies could be seen spinning round like straws in a gale.' The entire island was quickly enveloped, and a Marine approaching shore in a small boat saw 'trees and chunks of concrete flying through the air like match-sticks.' A piece of the concrete killed a Marine in another boat. Within the next half-hour, the arsenal was the source of two more explosions. When it was all over, twenty Marines were dead and 100 were hurt. One man who survived had been blown off the isle and out into the lagoon.[116]

154

Although the explosion grabbed the attention of every Marine and every sailor in his alligator, it did not deter Dyess from continuing his reconnaissance. Shortly after passing through the off-shore reef, his two small boats began to receive sporadic mortar and small arms fire. Dyess realized that some of the Japanese motar men and gunners had recovered from the shock of the explosion and had his two boats bracketed. Acting quickly, he ordered the boats to turn back to sea. They returned to the area where the other boats carrying his battalion were assembling. Shortly thereafter, Dyess led the entire battalion, at four knots, towards Green Beach. Although Dyess had anticipated a difficult journey, good fortune was on his side and on the side of the entire 1st battalion. The seas were rather calm as the assault boats made their way towards the shore; enemy fire from the island was also rather light.

This dramatic munitions bunker explosion took place at 1300 hours on Namur, 1 February, 1944.

An alligator on the beach at Namur, 1 February, 1944. Jimmie Dyess came ashore at Green Beach 2 in an alligator like this one.

On board the alligator with Dyess that afternoon were Private Kenneth W. Jones, his radio operator, and Private Willie Turner, his driver. Both had served directly under Dyess since March, 1943, knew him quite well and were with him much of the time during the battle for Roi Namur. Turner and Jones generously shared with me their memories, which were very vivid. Also on the alligator were some support personnel including a member of the 4th Marine Division band, Private Kenneth L. Schulz. Schulz had fondly remembered Dyess from the Camp Pendleton days since Dyess always complimented the band members each time they played for his battalion. In a November 15, 1989, letter to Jimmie's daughter, Schulz describes what happened:

...as we left the L. S. T. in an Amphtrac and headed for the beach, I was surprised to see Col. Dyess in the same Amphtrac because I didn't expect to see him in the same Amphtrac with bandsmen, corpsmen and other H. & S. personnel. I commented on this to a fellow bandsman.

While we were all scared to death facing our first combat landing, I noted a determined look on your father's face and, if you will, an impression of destiny.

When the Amphtrac hit the beach we all jumped over the side and "hit the deck." After perhaps 20 or 30 seconds, your father raised himself to his knees and yelled, "we can't win the war laying on our bellies." Then in a crouch he darted off the beach towards the heavy action.

I looked around, still on my stomach, at the dead and wounded, both our own and the enemy. A chaplain was administering the last rights to a young marine. The smell of cordite and death was heavy in the air. I could no longer see Col. Dyess and did not see him again, but remember thinking, "that Marine officer has a rendezvous with destiny and knows it.

When Dyess and his first two companies reached Green Beach on Namur, the beachhead was secure and the Marines of the two lead battalions of his regiment were fighting their way across the island. Dyess received orders to send his Able Company to the right to join the Second Battalion and his Baker Company to the left to join the Third Battalion. Both companies were immediately thrown into combat and soon were engaged in heavy fighting. Dyess's third infantry company, Charlie Company, hit the beach at about 1600 hours and within thirty minutes had moved to its right in support of Able Company. The last elements of Dyess's battalion (the Headquarters Company and the Mortar Platoon) reached the beach about 1615. Dyess had accomplished his first major task with considerable success. His battalion had landed, proceeded onshore and incurred only a few casualties.

Once he was sure that his entire battalion was ashore, Dyess sought out and reported to the regimental commander, Colonel Hart, who had established his command post on the beach. The other two battalion commanders (Lieutenant Colonel Francis Brink of the 2nd battalion and Lieutenant Colonel Austin R. Brunelli of the 3rd battalion) had also set up their small command posts on the beach. Although Hart and the three battalion commanders had generally good radio communication with the supporting ships and aircraft and with the artillery units on the adjacent islands, much of the communication with forward units was quite poor. Hence, runners were sent forward in order to maintain contact with the front line company commanders. [117]

Dyess quickly evaluated the situation and determined that there was a need for a senior officer to be with the troops who were actively engaged in close combat with the Japanese. He volunteered to move forward; Colonel Hart quickly agreed. This was an easy decision for Hart, for he had great faith in Dyess's leadership abilities and "Big Red" clearly was anxious to go forward, get close to the action and take charge. From that moment on and until his death the next day, Lieutenant Colonel Dyess was the de facto operational commander of the regiment and its combat battalions. Dyess moved towards the area of heaviest fighting, which was on the extreme right flank. This is where the Second Battalion had met fierce resistance and where Dyess's Able and Charlie Companies were both heavily engaged in combat.

Now it is time to pick up the Frank Pokrop story. When the huge explosion of the munitions bunker occurred (at about 1300), Pokrop was already on shore. The explosion not only caused many casualties but it also caused great confusion on both sides. It was then that Corporal Pokrop organized his patrol and moved forward. In the aftermath of the huge explosion, the Japanese were momentarily confused and demoralized. Many hunkered down by climbing deep into their spider holes. Hence, when Pokrop and his patrol moved forward, they initially encountered little enemy resistance. Without fully realizing it, they had moved through enemy lines and into an area of great danger. A few minutes later, they were spotted by the Japanese. Pokrop and his buddies were far enough behind enemy lines that they began to receive enemy fire from three directions. Very soon all but one of the Marines in Pokrop's patrol were wounded and pinned down by the cross fire of the Japanese.[118]

Dyess, who by that time had moved to the extreme right of the front line of troops, heard the heavy fire. Soon he realized that there were Marines caught beyond enemy lines and that they were under heavy pressure. He also realized that, with darkness setting in, there was not much time left if these Marines were to be rescued. That these Marines were not from his own battalion made no difference to Dyess. Marines were in serious trouble and he knew instinctively that something had to be done, and done quickly, to help them. He organized a small rescue force, which included some infantrymen and a half-track vehicle, and charged forward. Corporal Pokrop and the other Marines in his patrol were in desperate shape. They were pinned down and couldn't move. There were no medics with Pokrop's patrol to tend to the wounded. By using fire and maneuver, Dyess and his rescue party were able to fight through the enemy lines, provide suppressing fire and reach the stranded Marines. Some of his men assisted the wounded Marines back to friendly lines while Dyess and others continued to provide covering fire. There is no question that Dyess saved the lives of these stranded Marines—the Japanese would take no prisoners in the battle for Roi Namur. The rescue was completed just as total darkness engulfed the battered island.[119]

When night set in on the first full day of combat, the Marines were well established on Roi Namur. The Twenty Third Marines, whose mission was to attack and capture the airfield and the island of Roi, had had a rather easy time. Since all the Japanese airplanes had been destroyed by air and artillery attacks and since there were few bunkers and defensive positions on the island of Roi, almost all of the enemy soldiers had fled, prior to the assault, to Namur where there were better defensive positions, bunkers and pillboxes. By nightfall on February 1, all of Roi was in American hands.

The 24th Marines faced much tougher resistance on Namur. In some places, the Japanese defenses were closely coordinated. In others, it was an individual soldier who gave the Marines problems. Late in the afternoon, there was a Japanese soldier who was particularly troublesome to the 1st battalion. Perching on top of a large blockhouse he threw grenades down upon Marine positions. Dyess formulated a plan and sent a patrol into the blockhouse. They worked their way up to the roof to take out the Japanese soldier.

By nightfall on February 1, the Marines of the 4th Division had moved far enough forward that it was clear to most that the battle would last no more than another day or two. Within about eight hours of the first landing, the Marines had secured all of Roi and about half of Namur. As night fell, Dyess moved up and down the line. He made sure that the flanks were protected, that the Marines were well dug in and that fields of fire were established in anticipation of night attacks by the Japanese and, perhaps, a Japanese counterattack at first light the next morning. Dyess established a shift schedule so that each Marine could have the opportunity to grab a couple of hours of sleep that night. Early that evening, the rain began. The Marines got little sleep that night in their soggy fox holes. Throughout the night the Japanese launched small attacks against Marine positions. In addition, there was periodic fire that kept everyone on edge and almost everyone awake.

The second day of the battle, February 2, went well for the Marines. Although Japanese soldiers continued to fight ferociously, most to their death, their situation was increasingly dismal. They were outnumbered, outgunned and were receiving no help from the sea or air. However, they continued to take advantage of their dug-in positions and had good firing positions from the few remaining pillboxes they still controlled. Dyess wanted to finish the battle quickly and secure the island. Also, he realized that the area immediately in front of him was the last bastion of Japanese military strength. Willie Turner, who was with Dyess on both days of the battle, was used as a runner as he took messages to the various company commanders of the three battalions of the regiment. Dyess remained in charge of the front-line infantry battle.

No one seemed to mind that he was playing the role of the regimental commander and not the role of a single battalion commander. Dyess had taken charge and the Marines of the 24th Regiment, who knew him so well, were quite willing to follow his orders. Dyess had a sense of urgency and his fellow Marines were anxious to wrap up the battle so they could take a break, get something to eat and prepare to leave this island of death and destruction.[120]

As the battle continued throughout the morning, Dyess was up front pointing the way toward enemy firing positions as he led seven light tanks up Narcissus Road. The tanks were supported by two of his own infantry companies, Able and Charlie. In addition, he sent three tanks and two half-tracks to the right of the main attack. These elements were proceeding up the beach line while engaging pillboxes and Japanese soldiers. Dyess was a virtual dynamo of energy, encouragement and direction. He was leading men, most of whom were still teenagers, who were experiencing their first days of combat. After two nights with little or no sleep, they were weary and scared. Dyess was not only giving directions and support, he was also firing at Japanese positions. As Dyess moved up and down the line, a number of Marines yelled at him to stay low and to keep his head down. He ignored their pleas. He wanted to direct the fire of his fellow Marines and in order to do so he exposed himself to Japanese rifle and machine gun fire. On that fateful morning, Willie Turner remembered Dyess saying, "Let's go Willie; let's get the chestnuts out of the fire."[121]

At about 1045 on D + 2 (February 2nd), Dyess rose up once again to observe the enemy's firing positions and to direct fire against them. His attention was directed toward the last of the Japanese pillboxes that was still occupied and still sending out deadly fire against the Marines. Within seconds of the time he raised up, Dyess was hit in the head by a Japanese bullet, probably from a machine gun that was firing from the pillbox to his immediate front. Killed instantly, he fell backwards. Moving quickly,

Willie Turner, Bob Fleischauer, and two others grabbed a stretcher and gently placed him on it. Using this stretcher, they lifted Dyess, and, picking their way through the debris on the battlefield, carried him back the half mile distance to the beach.[122]

Word spread quickly among the troops that "Big Red" was dead. The man who had so wished to lead Marines in combat had been cut down less than twenty-four hours after landing on Green Beach. Ironically, only a few minutes after Dyess was killed, the pillbox ceased firing and the battle for Namur was essentially over. By 1300 hours the last of the Japanese positions had been overrun. General Schmidt declared Roi Namur secure at 1418 hours, February 2. During the remainder of the afternoon the only lethal dangers facing the Marines were a few isolated Japanese snipers.

From the very moment of victory, many of the Marines realized that the campaign was a huge success. In less than three days, this strategically important island had fallen. The Fourth Marine Division had lost 313 Marines and corpsmen killed. Another 502 had been wounded. Japanese losses were much higher, some 3472 killed and 264 captured.[123] Journalists and historians would mark this battle as a tactical and strategic success for the Americans. Soon the battle would be forgotten as the world's attention shifted to other areas and other campaigns. Nevertheless, family members of the killed would mark this as a day of great tragedy. Their loved one had been sent into battle and less than two days later, he was dead. For them, February, 1944, would always be remembered not as a moment of great triumph but a time of enduring sadness and loss.

Capturing Kwajalein Atoll required more than just overrunning Roi Namur. There was another objective to be taken. Fifty miles to the south, the Army's Seventh Infantry Division was fighting its way across the largest island in the atoll, Kwajalein. Fortunately, the Army had also learned the lessons of Tarawa and had enjoyed massive and coordinated support from attacking aircraft and from Naval gunfire. Like the Marines of Roi Namur, the Army had also placed artillery on an adjacent island in order to provide constant and responsive support to the infantry troops attacking the island. It took the 7th Division four days to capture Kwajalein.

Nimitz's great gamble had paid off. Each military service had performed well and the coordination among the many and diverse units had been better than in any previous American campaign in the war. The military establishment of the United States, which in 1939 had been so small and so poorly trained and equipped, had evolved in less than five years into a remarkable fighting machine. Americans and their numerous allies in Britain, who were busy preparing for the largest amphibious landing in history, were able to gain confidence in the efficacy of amphibious operations against a heavily defended beach. Since the invasion of Normandy was still four months away, the leaders and planners for Operation Overlord would have time to study the many lessons from this successful campaign in the Marshalls.

Walter Lippmann, one of the most respected journalists of the period, caught the significance of the Marshalls victory in his commentary in the *New York Herald Tribune* three weeks after Operation Flintlock. "In the Marshalls and at Truk the Navy has done more than to win a good victory over the enemy. It was won a resounding victory in the hearts and minds of our people over the anxiety and the doubt which have, since the close of the other war, divided and confused us." If I would critique Mr. Lippmann from the wisdom of today, I would have only changed one thing. Clearly, the Marines and the Army should also have received Lippmann's praise.

At the end of the battle for Roi Namur, the 4th Marine Division spent a few days cleaning up the battlefield. The cleanup operation was very unpleasant for all the Marines. They buried dead comrades as well as thousands of Japanese corpses. Many of the Japanese had been killed by the pre-invasion bombardment and had been dead for several days when the clean-up began. Their bloated and partially decomposed bodies made the burial duty extraordinarily onerous. Hence, all of the Marines were elated when they were told that it was now time to board ship and set sail for the

Hawaiian Islands. Most of the Marines redeployed to Maui for further training in preparation for the next battle. However, Major Art Buck was still on Roi Namur on Lincoln's birthday. He remembered that exactly a year earlier, Dyess and Buck had been together at New River and Dyess had suggested that they both think of each other on Lincoln's birthday in 1944. Buck recalled that conversation and spent part of that day remembering Dyess and how much he had helped him a year earlier as Buck thought through a tough decision about whether to accept a regular commission in the Marine Corps.[124]

After three months on Maui, the 4th Division would sail west again, on May 29 1944, to the next major target in the war in the Central Pacific, Saipan. In the meantime, on Maui there were many things for the Marines to do: cleaning and refurbishing of equipment, processing in replacement Marines, as well as individual and unit training. However, there was also some leisure time. Willie Turner went to see the battalion commander who had replaced Dyess, Lieutenant Colonel Schultz. Having been the executive officer of the First Battalion at Pendleton and on Roi Namur, Schultz knew Turner very well. Turner told him of the box of whiskey and of the request by Lieutenant Colonel Dyess that the enlisted men throw a party and enjoy the liquor. Schultz's reply was harsh. He said that enlisted men are not supposed to have any liquor. Later Schultz changed his mind and told Turner to go ahead but to have the party far away from camp and out of sight. Hence, Turner and his fellow Marines had quite a party and toasted the leadership and courage of Big Red many times that evening. Three months later, at the battle for Saipan, Lieutenant Colonel Schultz, battalion commander of the 1st Battalion of the 24th Marines, was, like his immediate predecessor, killed leading his troops in combat.[125]

Meanwhile at Admiral Nimitz's headquarters, there was great attention on the next island to be captured by the Fourth Marine Division, Saipan. Nimitz was also looking carefully at the best way to quickly capture Tinian, the third island which the Fourth Marine Division would assault. Nimitz was aware that a new military aircraft was becoming operational which could play an important role in the defeat of Japan. War Plan Orange had assumed that bases very close to Japan would have to be captured before a sustained air campaign could be launched. However, a new long-range bomber of the Army Air Corps, the B-29, had been developed early in the war and was now ready for use in the Pacific. If Tinian, a small island in the central Marianas, might quickly be captured, it could be turned into a base for long-range-strategic bombers. Although it was a long distance from the home islands of Japan, Tinian was close enough to serve as a strike base for the B-29s, whose range capabilities greatly exceeded those of any other bomber in the world.

It was to be the 4th Marine Division which would, in nine days in late July, 1944, capture what soon became the most important single island in the Pacific. From Tinian a massive bombing campaign would commence in the fall of 1944. It was also from Tinian that the atomic bombs would be carried to Hiroshima and Nagasaki. When well conceived and well-executed strategy is married to major technological innovation, the result in wartime can be decisive. Nimitz had found the keys to the Japanese locks. He turned the first key at Operation Flintlock.

All the accomplishments in the Marshalls and beyond were possible because a bold commander, Admiral Chester Nimitz, thought and planned strategically and was willing to overrule the collective judgment of his operational commanders. Nimitz's gamble in the Marshalls had a high potential payoff which was fully realized. Although given very little attention by most historians, Operation Flintlock was one of the rare cases in the history of warfare where a campaign went better than expected, both tactically and strategically. Although Admiral Nimitz demonstrated great leadership on many occasions during his distinguished forty-seven-year naval career, the Flintlock decision ranks just behind Midway as his boldest and best. It fully validated War Plan Orange and it encouraged Nimitz to be bold again and again.

By the time Operation Flintlock was completed, the Marine Corps had grown to a size unprecedented in its long history. In early 1944, the Corps numbered 390,000 men and women and included five divisions and four air wings. Before the war ended in September, 1945, a sixth division would be formed. During the entire course of the war 669,000 men and women served as United States Marines. This was ten times the size of the Marine Corps in World War I and one hundred times its size in the Spanish American War. In fact, this figure exceeded the total of all the Marines who had served from 1775 to 1941.

By V-J Day, 98% of the officers and 89% of the enlisted force had served overseas. This compares with 73% for all of the military services combined. Never again would the Marine Corps be so large or so experienced in combat. The successes were many but the costs were high. With less than 5% of the American armed forces, the Marines suffered nearly 10% of all American battle casualties. In the three years and eight months that the war lasted for the Americans, the Marines suffered 67,207 wounded and 19,733 dead.[126]

Of the more than eighty thousand Marines who served with the 4th Marine Division during its sixteen months in the combat theater, only twelve earned Medals of Honor. They were Dyess, First Lieutenant John V. Power (Roi Namur), Private First Class Richard B. Anderson (Roi Namur), Private Richard K. Sorenson (Roi Namur), Gunnery Sergeant Robert H. McCard (Saipan), Private Joseph W. Ozbourn (Tinian), Captain Joseph J. McCarthy (Iwo Jima), Colonel Justice M. Chambers (Iwo Jima), Sergeant Darrell S. Cole (Iwo Jima), Sergeant Ross F. Gray (Iwo Jima), Private First Class Douglas T. Jacobson (Iwo Jima) and Pharmacist's Mate First Class Francis Pierce, Jr. (Iwo Jima) . Although a Navy man, Pierce was assigned to the Fourth Marine Division. Having also earned the Navy Cross and the Silver Star, Pierce was one of the very few individuals in American history to have earned all three of America's highest military awards for heroism. Of these twelve recipients of the Medal of Honor, six died in the actions for which they are cited. The 49th Annual Reunion Publication (September, 1996), entitled "Valor" is dedicated to these twelve men. In this beautiful magazine, there is a page outlining the significance of this medal to the men of the 4th Marine Division. I quote this page in its entirety.

The Medal of Honor

The Medal of Honor, the Nation's highest award for military valor, is given only to those who have acted with supreme courage, with total disregard for their own safety in the face of the most hazardous conditions. It is an award that only a comparative handful of men in the world are entitled to wear. It is bestowed by Act of Congress and reflects the nation's gratitude to those who, in moments of uncommon risk, offered everything they had in her defense, including life itself. The medal itself is but a humble token, a gesture of recognition for sacrifices which cannot be repaid in worldly goods.

Of the twelve men who were awarded the Medal of Honor for "conspicuous gallantry" while serving with the Fourth Marine Division, seven did not live to have the honor bestowed on them personally. Six of these men died in the actions for which they are cited. To them, "above and beyond the call of duty" were not mere words but a challenge which involved their skill, determination, and self-sacrifice in the face of almost certain death. Their reward was the knowledge that they were acting in the tradition of the highest ideals of the Naval Service and of the Nation it represents.

Those who live to wear the Medal of Honor do so proudly and yet with the spirit of humility befitting true heroes. They share the highest glory of which it is a symbol, yet hold it in solemn trust for comrades less fortunate. Whether they live or whether they died, our Nation is richer for their actions.

Although the 4th Marine Division was in the combat theater for only sixteen months, it was awarded two Presidential Unit Citations and a Navy Unit Commendation. It was a sad day for many Marines when the Division was deactivated on the 28th of November, 1945. However, in February, 1966, it was reactivated as the lead division of the Marine Corps Reserve. Major units of the division served with distinction during the Persian Gulf War of 1991. Today, the 4th Marine Division has its headquarters in New Orleans and has units stationed all over the United States. The vast majority of Marines assigned to this division are reservists, but like Jimmie Dyess from 1936 to 1940, they stand ready to serve on active duty when their nation calls. Dyess's regiment, The 24th Marines, is stationed at various locations throughout the Central United States. The headquarters building of the 24th Marines is located outside of Kansas City and is named Dyess Hall in honor of Lieutenant Colonel Dyess.

CHAPTER 12:

THE AFTERMATH

The death of Jimmie Dyess hit Augusta, Clemson College and the Marine Corps bases at New River, Parris Island and Camp Pendleton like a series of huge gut-wrenching explosions. The devastating news came to Augusta first by telephone. This telephonic notification was followed by a telegram and two letters to his widow, all from the Commandant of the Marine Corps, Lieutenant General Archer A. Vandergrift. Vandergrift, who had himself earned the Medal of Honor for heroism while commanding the 1st Marine Division at Guadalcanal, personally signed both letters of condolence.

In his hometown of Augusta, where Dyess was so well known, respected and loved, the news of his death spread like wildfire. Many newspaper articles were written about Dyess, both in the Augusta newspapers and in Marine Corps base newspapers such as "The Buck" at Parris Island. All of the articles pointed out his heroism in combat as he led his men on the assault on the last Japanese position on Roi Namur. Curiously, none of these articles covered the fact that he had previously earned the Carnegie Medal. The articles all had a number of factual mistakes but they caught the essence of his leadership and heroism in combat.

Friends and family reached out to Big Connor and Little Connor and to Jimmie's mother and his two sisters. Connor Cleckley Dyess was now a widow at age thirty two. The only child of Jimmie and Connor, "Little Connor", had lost, at the age of eight, a father whom she had waived goodbye to only a month earlier in California. Sallie Weatherly Dyess, who lost her first son in 1919 and her husband in 1941, now had lost her second son. Louise Dyess and Sarah Ewing had lost their second brother.

Dr. Hervey Cleckley, Connor's older brother, was a tower of strength and support to Big Connor and Little Connor. Big Connor and Hervey had always had a close and loving relationship. The depth, breadth and warmth of their relationship was very helpful at this time of great grief. Dr. Cleckley was forty years old when Jimmie was killed but he was already well known in both Augusta and in his medical specialty, psychiatry. After returning from his studies at Oxford, Hervey had completed both medical school and a psychiatric residency at the Medical College of Georgia in Augusta. By the late 1930s, his psychiatric practice was thriving. His book, *The Mask of Sanity,* published in 1941, had become the definitive study of the psychopathic personality and was being widely used in medical schools throughout the country. Hervey fully understood the personal anguish that the family was going through and gave his personal and professional help when it was so badly needed.

Hervey helped Connor find solace in the A. E. Housman poem, *To an Athlete Dying Young.* In this poem, Housman outlines a paradox: the early death of a young athlete can be a matter for celebration rather than for sorrow. Dyess had led a life of accomplishment, then died in the full flower of his capabilities, doing what he did best: helping others, saving lives and defending freedom. Cleckley fully understood Housman's phrase, "smart lad", for the hero of this poem about a very successful athlete who died in the prime of his life before he would watch others break his records.

However, there is a profound irony here. If Dyess had lived through that battle, he probably would have won the Medal of Honor for saving the lives of the wounded Marines behind enemy lines and for his aggressive front-line leadership throughout the battle. If he had survived the next three battles which were to follow Roi Namur, Dyess could have enjoyed the fruits of his unique accomplishment of having earned the nation's two highest awards for heroism. But it was not to be. With his complete disregard for danger and his commitment never to ask a Marine to do something he would not do himself, Dyess would probably have been killed before the war was out, if not at Roi Namur, then at Saipan, or Tinian or Iwo Jima.

To return to the Housman poem, we see by the beginning of the second stanza that the young athlete is dead. Once again he is held high by the townspeople, just as he had been when he won the great race. "Smart Lad" is he to have died in his prime when his records were fresh and his youth in its full flower.

The time you won your town the race
We chaired you through the market-place
Man and boy stood cheering by,
And home we brought you shoulder-high

Today, the road all runners come,
Shoulder-high we bring you home,
And set you at your threshold down,
Townsman of a stiller town.

Smart lad to slip betimes away
From fields where glory does not stay,
And early though the laurel grows
It withers quicker than the rose.

Eyes the shady night has shut
Cannot see the record cut,
And silence sounds no worse than cheers
After earth has stopped the ears:

Now you will swell the rout
Of lads that wore their honors out,
Runners whom renown outran
And the name died before the man.

So set, before its echoes fade,
The fleet foot on the sill of shade,
And hold to the low lintel up
The still-defended challenge-cup.

And round that early-laurel head
Will flock to gaze the strengths dead,
And find unwithered on its curls
The Garland briefer than a girl's

Yes, the athlete has won the most important race, the race to death. Dyess found death early. But in death he found great glory. The laurel of fame fades even more quickly than the rose of beauty, yet Dyess died when both were in full bloom. For that there was some solace for his family and friends.

The Marine Corps and the Navy moved with considerable speed to honor Dyess in the months following his death. It was clear that General Vandergrift, who understood so well the agonies of combat, realized almost immediately after Dyess was killed that his performance in combat had been quite remarkable. This realization was highlighted in his letter of 15 March, 1944:

> *My dear Mrs. Dyess*
>
> *I have just received a dispatch from the Commander in Chief, Pacific Ocean Area, informing me that the air field at Roi, Namur, Kwajalein Atoll, Marshall Islands, has been named in honor of your husband, the late Lieutenant Colonel Aquilla J. Dyess, U. S. Marine Corps Reserve, in recognition of his conspicuous bravery in personally leading the assault to capture the final enemy stronghold on that Island.*
>
> *It is my fervent hope that this commemoration of your husband's heroism will in some measure comfort you in your sorrow.*
>
> *With renewed assurances of sympathy, I am*
>
> > *Sincerely yours,*
>
> > *A. A. Vandergrift*
> > *Lieutenant General, U. S. M. C.*
> > *Commandant of the Marine Corps*

The Navy was also quick to recognize the extraordinary heroism of Dyess. On April 26, 1944, Admiral Nimitz held a special ceremony to recognize a few heroes of the Pacific War. He made a special point to highlight the heroism of a Marine Corps private and a lieutenant colonel. The lieutenant colonel was Dyess. On July 18,

*Connor Dyess and "Little Connor" Dyess at Orange, Texas, for
the launching of the USS Dyess (DD 880), January 26, 1945.*

an official announcement was made that Lieutenant Colonel A. J.
Dyess had earned the Medal of Honor on Roi Namur. During
World War II, the Marine Corps was especially careful to ensure
that the Medal of Honor was given to only the most deserving of its
many heroes. Although the war in the Pacific had been going on
for more than two and a half years and the Marine Corps had been
heavily engaged ever since December, 1941, Dyess was only the
seventeenth Marine in the war to have earned America's highest

173

Launching of the USS Dyess, (DD 880), January 26, 1945

Picture and portrait of "Little Connor" Dyess, age 9, 1945.

award. His widow chose not to go to Washington to have the medal presented by President Roosevelt. Instead, the award was presented to her in Augusta by a dear friend of the family, Marine Lieutenant Colonel Weedon Barr, who had been the commander of the 19th Battalion in Augusta from 1936 to 1940.[127]

The publicity concerning the awarding of the Medal of Honor highlighted the citation, but did not give the full background of Dyess's heroism. For instance, no mention was made of his taking charge of the entire regiment on the afternoon of February 1. Also, there is no mention in the citation of his risking his life to fight his way through enemy lines to save Frank Pokrop and the other wounded Marines late that same day. It would be forty-four years later before the full story of his heroism in combat was understood by the family and most of his friends.

CHAPTER 13:

THE MEDAL OF HONOR IN PERSPECTIVE

In the more than two hundred and twenty years that the United States of America has existed as an independent nation, over five hundred million people have been American citizens. During our long history more than thirty million American men and women have served on active duty in the military. And yet, fewer than thirty-five hundred individuals have earned the Medal of Honor. The winners comprise such a small number that the vast majority of Americans have never known, met or even seen a recipient. In fact, within the United States military itself, it is very rare to see a Medal of Honor recipient and even rarer to get to know one. To understand the kinds of people who are awarded the Medal of Honor it may be helpful to examine a few other recipients of this award.

Although I spent fifty-one years in close association with the military (seventeen years as a dependent son of an Army officer, four years as a cadet at the United States Military Academy at West Point and thirty years on active duty as an officer and combat pilot in the United States Air Force), I have known only two Medal of Honor winners. Both Vice Admiral James Stockdale of the United States Navy and Colonel Jack Jacobs of the United States Army earned the Medal of Honor during the Vietnam War. However, they earned their award under very different circumstances: Stockdale as a prisoner of war for eight years in North Vietnam and Jacobs in a one-day combat action during the infamous Tet Offensive of 1968. Both stories are well worth examining.

Despite being severely tortured on many occasions, Jim Stockdale provided enlightened leadership to his fellow prisoners of war during many years of deprivation and near starvation. It is an extraordinary story of persistent courage and heroic leadership.

He provided encouragement, support and leadership to hundreds of fellow prisoners even though he was unable to speak to them. His many years in solitary confinement, systematic deprivation and torture did not stop him from communicating and providing leadership, using the "tap code", to his fellow POWs.

Because Admiral Stockdale is a best selling author and was a candidate for Vice President of the United States in 1992, his military record and his heroism during the Vietnam War is well known to many. However, for those who may not be familiar with Stockdale's agonizing but uplifting experiences, I recommend two of his books: *A Vietnam Experience* and the best selling book that he wrote with his wife, Sybil, *In Love and War*.

Unlike Stockdale's, the Jack Jacobs' Medal of Honor story is not well known. He earned America's highest award in 1968 as a twenty-three-year-old infantry first lieutenant. Many years later, Jack Jacobs worked as a faculty member at the National War College in Washington, D. C. As Commandant of the college in the mid-1980s, I taught an elective course on senior level leadership. In my class I had students from the National War College, the Industrial College of the Armed Forces as well as a few international students from the National Defense University. On a number of occasions, I asked Jacobs to help me teach one session of that course—a two hour segment on heroic leadership. Each time I asked, he politely declined. Finally, he told me why. It was very difficult emotionally for him to recall his experiences where so many people died in his presence. Hence, I quit pressing him to join my seminar and he never taught in my course.

Shortly before my retirement from the military in the summer of 1986, I invited Jack over to my quarters at Fort McNair. I told him of my idea of one day writing a book on a Medal of Honor recipient whom I had never known. I explained to Jack that I needed his help in understanding what motivates a person to take the kinds of actions that earn him the Medal of Honor. In reply, he asked me a question. Would I would be willing to listen to him for at least three hours so he could fully relate his experiences on March 9,

1968? I readily agreed. Consequently, I had the distinct privilege of hearing Jack Jacobs tell me his story of profound heroism in combat. I took the opportunity to ask him many specific questions about his actions and his motivations. Let me relate briefly his story and the answers that he gave to my probing questions.

In 1968, Jack was serving his first combat tour in South Vietnam as an infantry first lieutenant in the United States Army. He was an assistant military advisor to a South Vietnamese Army battalion when the Tet Offensive commenced. The Viet Cong, as well as some troops from the North Vietnamese Army, initiated a major, coordinated campaign against the South Vietnamese military and its allies. The offensive raged on for many weeks throughout all of South Vietnam; it was late in this campaign when Jack faced his biggest challenge in combat. As Jack's battalion was working its way across an open field, it was ambushed by a larger enemy unit. The ambush began with coordinated mortar, machine gun and rifle fire. Within a few minutes, many of Jack's fellow soldiers, both South Vietnamese and American, were wounded or killed.

Jacobs, himself, was badly injured by shrapnel from a mortar round. He had two superficial wounds on his face that caused some bleeding. However, he also sustained a serious head injury. Metal shrapnel had cut off a major part of his scalp. He was bleeding profusely. Nearby, lay another American advisor who was in very bad shape. This noncommissioned officer had been hit in the abdomen by three bullets. The man who too heavy for Jacobs to pick up and carry so Jack grabbed both of his wrists and slowly and painfully dragged him off the battlefield. Jacobs pulled him to a spot which was out of danger from direct-fire enemy weapons and where a medical corpsman was available to give the NCO medical assistance. Realizing that there were others on the battlefield who were wounded and in grave danger, Jack went back to try to assist them.

At this point, I interrupted Jack's rendition of his experiences that day. When I asked him why he didn't remain in safety so he could receive care for his wounds, particularly for the severe wound to his head, his answer was simple. Someone had to assist his wounded buddies. Since no one else seemed to be helping out in those early moments of the battle, he dropped off the NCO, grabbed his rifle again and headed back to try to save another buddy.

This led to a pattern of activity that continued for many hours. In the next five hours, Jack Jacobs made twenty-five trips to the battlefield and one by one dragged wounded soldiers, both American and South Vietnamese, to safety. The battlefield was still active, so at times he had to fight his way back to find the next wounded allied soldier. Jack didn't realize how severe his wounds were, was largely operating on adrenaline and stopped only after his battalion commander finally ordered him to lie down and receive care. His battalion commander was very blunt. He told Jack that he would die if he didn't receive medical care immediately.

Considering the severity of his wounds, Jack probably earned the Medal of Honor on the fifth or six trip back to the battlefield. The fact that he made twenty-five trips is truly remarkable (fourteen of the soldiers whom he pulled to the aid station survived). The more I probed Jack on his motivations, the more I realized that they were very simple and straightforward. Jack realized that his buddies desperately needed help. Somebody had to do something so Jack saved one man and the next and the next. He had no plan; he just did what he did without thinking about it much. In Jack's mind it was a "no-brainer" that didn't require a strategic plan or a cosmic insight. He was fighting for his friends and that day they really needed his help. Jimmie Dyess would have understood.

There was one additional aspect of the story that bears telling. As Jack went back and forth from the battlefield to the aid station, he began to realize that the enemy soldiers were moving onto the battlefield, killing the wounded soldiers and stealing equipment from them. This fact added to his urgency to move as fast as he could and to save as many of his fellow soldiers as quickly as possible. Jack was very angry. Adrenaline, time urgency and anger combined to turn Lieutenant Jacobs into a heroic dervish.

When I told Jack that the Medal of Honor citation for Lieutenant Colonel Dyess highlighted actions that were noteworthy but not extraordinarily heroic, Jack suggested that there may well be more to the story of Dyess's heroism than is indicated on the citation. He suggested that in the write-up, which recommended the Medal of Honor to the Marine Corps, there may have been some specific actions that helped justify the award but were not included in the citation. I have not been able to find this write-up so I cannot verify Jack's thesis. However, the Frank Pokrop letter and the specifics which I received from Willie Turner, Bob Fleischauer and others seem to substantiate Jack's hypothesis that key elements of Jimmie Dyess's heroism were not included in the Medal of Honor citation.[128]

The Medal of Honor. Of the more than 80,000 personnel who served in the combat theater with the 4th Marine Division during World War II, twelve earned the Medal of Honor. Eleven were Marines and one was a Navy corpsman.

There is one other Medal of Honor experience that should be related in part. In Somalia in October, 1993, two American soldiers earned the Medal of Honor. Both were killed in their attempt to save the life of another American soldier who was surrounded by a large hostile force of heavily armed Somali irregular soldiers. One of the soldiers who earned the Medal of Honor that day was Master Sergeant Gary Gordon of the United States Army. After her husband was killed, Carmen Gordon, Master Sergeant Gordon's young widow, wrote a letter to her two small children which so exquisitely captures the philosophy of many heroes including Jimmie Dyess, Jack Jacobs, Gary Gordon and Jim Stockdale that it is well worth quoting.

My dearest Ian and Brittany,

I hope that in the final moments of your father's life, his last thoughts were not of us. As he lay dying, I wanted him to think only of the mission to which he pledged himself. As you grow older, if I can show you the love and responsibility he felt for his family, you will understand my feelings. I did not want him to think of me, or of you, because I did not want his heart to break.

Children were meant to have someone responsible for them. No father ever took that more seriously than your dad. Responsibility was a natural part of him, an easy path to follow. Each day after work his truck pulled into our driveway. I watched the two of you run to him, feet pounding across the painted boards of our porch, yelling, "Daddy!" Every day, I saw his face when he saw you. You were the center of his life.

Ian, when you turned 1 year old, your father was beside himself with excitement, baking you a cake in the shape of a train. On your last birthday, Brittany, he sent you a handmade birthday card from Somalia. But your father had two families. One was us, and the other was his comrades. He was true to both.

He loved his job. Quiet and serious adventure filled some part of him I could never fully know. After his death, one of his comrades told me that on a foreign mission, your dad led his men across a snow-covered ridge that began to collapse. Racing across a yawning crevasse to safety, he grinned wildly and yelled, "Wasn't that great?"

You will hear many times about how your father died. You will read what the president of the United States said when he awarded the Medal of Honor: "Gary Gordon ... died in the most courageous and selfless way any human being can act." But you may still ask why. You may ask how he could have been devoted to two families so equally, dying for one but leaving the other.

For your father, there were no hard choices in life. Once he committed to something, the way was clear. He chose to be a husband and father, and never wavered in those roles. He chose the military, and "I shall not fail those with whom I serve" became his simple religion. When his other family needed him, he did not hesitate, as he would not have hesitated for us. It may not have been the best thing for us, but it was the right thing for your dad.

There are times now when that image of him coming home comes back to me. I see him scoop you up, Ian, and see you, Brittany, bury your head in his chest. I dread the day when you stop talking and asking about him, when he seems so long ago. So now I must take responsibility for keeping his life entwined with yours. It is a responsibility I never wanted.

But I know what your father would say. "Nothing you can do about it, Carmen. Just keep going." Those times when the crying came, as I stood at the kitchen counter, were never long enough. You came in the front door, Brittany, saying, "Mommy, you sad? You miss Daddy?" You reminded me I had to keep going.

The ceremonies honoring your dad were hard. When they put his photo in the Hall of Heroes at the Pentagon, I thought, can this be all that is left, a picture? Then General Sullivan read from the letter General Sherman wrote to General Grant after the Civil War, words so tender that we all broke down. "Throughout the war, you were always in my mind. I always knew if I were in trouble and you were still alive you would come to my assistance."

One night before either of you were born, your dad and I had a funny little talk about dying. I teased that I would not know where to bury him. Very quietly, he said, "Up home. In my uniform." Your dad never liked to wear a uniform. And "up home," Maine, was so far away from us.

Only after he was laid to rest in a tiny flag-filled graveyard in Lincoln, Maine, did I understand. His parents, burying their only son, could come tomorrow and the day after that. You and I would not have to pass his grave on the way to the grocery store, to Little League games, to ballet recitals. Our lives would go on. And to the men he loved and died for, the uniform was a silent salute, a final repeat of his vows. Once again, he had taken care of all of us.

On a spring afternoon, a soldier from your dad's unit brought me the things from his military locker. At the bottom of a cardboard box, beneath his boots, I found a letter. Written on a small, ruled tablet, it was his voice, quiet but confident in the words he wanted us to have if something should happen to him. I'll save it for you, but so much of him is already inside you both. Let it grow with you. Choose your own responsibilities in life but always, always follow your heart. Your dad will be watching over you, just as he always did.[129]

CHAPTER 14:

ANATOMY OF COURAGE

Two of the most overused and misused words in the English language are courage and heroism. Sports commentators often praise the "courage" of Jack Nicklaus as he goes for the green on his second shot at the famous 15th hole at the Augusta National. There are lakes in front of and behind the green, the wind is in his face and the distance is 240 yards. The announcers are working hard to emphasize the drama and the tension of the upcoming shot. Since Nicklaus is not risking his life, is in no real danger and is not assisting anyone in dire need, where, one must ask, is the courage. Although I am a great admirer of Jack Nicklaus, who is a fine athlete and a man of considerable dignity, I think the "heroic" golf shot or the "courageous" effort of a professional golfer is a terrible misuse of two of the most sublime and uplifting terms in the English language.

The definitions of heroism and courage found in dictionaries are somewhat helpful. A hero (any person admired for courage, nobility, bravery or exploits especially in war, someone with godlike strength); courage (the attitude of facing or dealing with anything recognized as dangerous, or painful, instead of withdrawing from it; the quality of being fearless or brave; valor; constant readiness to deal with things fearlessly by reasons of a stouthearted temperament or a resolute spirit). Yet to fully understand the activities of Jimmie Dyess and others who have earned the Medal of Honor or the Carnegie Medal we must go far beyond what can be found in dictionaries.

The most important task is not how to define such terms as heroism or courage or bravery or valor or fearlessness. The underlying issue relates to motivation in the time of great danger. What, in fact, motivates a person to act courageously? Even more importantly, what motivates someone to be courageous on more than one occasion. Scholars for thousands of years have probed these questions. First, it was philosophers, historians and theologians. In more recent years, it has been psychiatrists, psychologists and sociologists.

There are many students of human motivation who argue that since every individual is motivated by self-interest, true altruism and empathy do not exist. These scholars feel that even when people act in what appears to be a very caring and altruistic way, their true motivation is fundamentally selfish. They are looking for rewards, for praise or for increased self-esteem. The writings of two major philosophers and political theorists come to mind. The 16th Century Italian, Niccoli Machiavelli, and the 17th Century Englishman, Thomas Hobbes, have both taken this point of view. A second group of scholars, who are somewhat less skeptical about human motivation, feel that most heroism is driven by a quick, unthinking response. In their view, heroism is not motivated by altruism, but simply by an admirable, but largely uncontrolled, human reaction to a crisis situation.

This second group has a point well worth serious consideration. Clearly, some heroic activity is not a result of a thoughtful and carefully reasoned decision, but is a quick response along the lines of, "I didn't think at all; I just pushed the child away from the oncoming train." The heroism of these quick reacting individuals should be recognized, acknowledged and praised even though it may not be motivated by altruism. This type of reactive heroism does not, however, explain the activities of someone who undertakes separate and distinct heroic activity over the distance of time and place. For instance, it does not explain the admirable actions of many Europeans in the late 1930s and early 1940s who, at great personal risk, helped Jewish people hide out from the German Gestapo and the SS.

Over a period of years these caring individuals, most of whom were Christians, took many risks to assist endangered Jews. Some of these Jews who received assistance from others had been long-term friends; however, many were total strangers to the people who risked so much to assist them. Acts of sustained heroism saved the lives of many Jews during the Holocaust. Skeptics might argue that once these Christians made the initial decision to help, all the subsequent acts, no matter how heroic, were simply a continuation of the initial decision which, at the time, might not have been so risky. In other words, inertia and not multiple heroic acts may provide the best explanation of what happened. Yet, somehow, there must be something to the idea that, on occasion, certain people act in truly unselfish and altruistic ways towards others. Even more powerfully, it is clear that some act altruistically at great risk to their health and to their lives and do so on more than one occasion.

If there are truly unselfish, heroic people, what are their characteristics? Where do they find the motivation to take these actions? Is it possible to educate and motivate others so that they would also be willing to be similarly heroic when the occasion came? Since so much research has been accomplished on the Holocaust, this period provide a laboratory for us to examine, understand and explain altruistic, heroic activity. Let's start with someone with whom many people are familiar: a German named Oscar Schindler. The powerful book, *Schindler's List,* by Thomas Keneally and the stark, Academy Award winning movie, *Schindler's List,* highlighted an individual in Nazi occupied Poland, who was very manipulative, ambitious and self-centered. Schindler initially hired talented and hard working Jews for his factories in order to make money and to live a lavish lifestyle. However, this German entrepreneur, slowly and incrementally came to the point in his life when he began to take risks to save the lives of the large number of Jews who worked for him. A major turning point took place the day that he observed a small Jewish girl in a red coat. She was observing at close hand the murder of many Jews on the street very near where she was standing. To his great horror Schindler finally came to the realization of the profound evil of a regime which would not even attempt to shield a three-year-old child from these horrible acts of random murder. In the struggle between good and evil within Schindler, good at last won out. Schindler will be remembered for many generations into the future, not for his many selfish acts but for his acts of selflessness.[130]

Although the Schindler personality is a fascinating one, full of conflicting motivations and irony, it is not one to be pursued in depth, since altruism was not one of the initial motivations of this flawed man. However, there were many others in Europe in the late 1930s and early 1940s who more clearly demonstrate empathic altruism. Samuel and Pearl Oliner in their enlightening book, *The Altruistic Personality: Rescuers of Jews in Nazi Europe*, highlight some of the characteristics of these courageous people. After extensive interviews with 406 rescuers of Jews, the Oliners found that many reported a religious upbringing. They emphasized that religious education and training, which emphasized the common humanity of all, was often important as they made a decision to assist others. Many of these rescuers pointed out how important values, which had been emphasized by their father and/or mother when they were growing up, were in helping them make the decision to assist others.

The people whom the Oliners defined as altruistic rescuers for the purpose of their study had to have the following characteristics: First, the rescuers received no remuneration of any kind, either before, during or after they helped the Jews. Second, they risked their own lives to help. Third, they were motivated by purely humanitarian considerations.[131] Although altruism seemed to be the driving force for many of the rescuers, some rescuers stated that, "It was very satisfying to us." This seems to indicate that they may have been driven as much by ego and self-satisfaction as by unselfish altruism. Yet the fact that these rescuers risked their lives, time and time again, seems to indicate that altruism was probably a major factor behind their sustained commitment to help.

Jimmie Dyess would have been very comfortable with many of the quotes from the Europeans who risked so much to save people in great need, "When you see a need, you have to help." "If you save somebody's life, that's your duty." "I did it out of a feeling of compassion for those who were weaker and who needed help." "I learned to live honestly, to study well in school, to respect others, and to have compassion and generosity toward those who were less well treated by life."

The Oliners also interviewed a large number of non-rescuers—people who might have helped but chose not to do so. These researchers uncovered a very powerful insight from those who chose not to help. It is hard for many people to acknowledge altruism since it requires them to acknowledge that there are people who may be more admirable than they are themselves. For many, it seems to be easier to look down on the evil than to look up to the good. In any case, trying to sort out the complex set of motivations that causes individuals to establish a pattern of courage in their lives is a fascinating and uplifting exercise.

In some ways, courage in combat is easier to understand than courage in peacetime. People who are preparing for combat expect that they will face great personal risks. Most also understand that they may well need to support buddies who are in grave danger. Cohesion is essential if a military unit is going to be successful on the battlefield. Unit cohesion can only be maintained, once the shooting starts, by people willing to risk their lives to support and assist others. The training of military people who are headed for combat emphasizes leadership and followership at every level, the willingness to accept and carry out orders and the expectation of danger. Courage in combat is altruistic in the sense of having great concern for your fellow combatant but it is not altruistic in another sense. In warfare, it is considered legitimate to kill or wound an enemy combatant in order to serve a higher calling. The World War II example is especially illustrative. In the case of the Japanese military, which had engaged in a series of brutalities which were well known, it was easy to justify American participation in the war in the Pacific and the need to destroy the imperialistic and militaristic proclivities of the Japanese government.

There has been a great deal of research on combat heroism, much of it focused on World War I. Lord Moran's classic study, *The Anatomy of Courage*, was based on his extensive diaries as a British medical officer who spent more than two years on the Western Front in France with the First Battalion of the Royal Fusiliers. Lord Moran makes the point that, while it is not true that all men in combat are courageous, it is true that men of courage are essential to unit success on the battlefield. To quote Moran, " A few men had the stuff of leadership in them, they were like rafts to which all of the rest of humanity cling for support and hope."

This single sentence from Moran's book simply, but eloquently, describes Jimmie Dyess in peace and war. In the huge waves off the coast of South Carolina, Dyess was, in fact, a raft for two exhausted and desperate women. He was again a raft to the men of the 24th Regiment, especially to Corporal Frank Pokrop and his wounded buddies caught behind enemy lines. Dyess was more than just courageous, he combined persistent courage with leadership. It is this combination of characteristics that made him such an uncommon man. If Dyess is to serve as a role model for young people, the mutually supporting qualities of leadership and courage should be studied and emphasized.

In the case of Jimmie Dyess, examples of heroism seem to point more to altruism and less to ego. For instance, after he saved the two women in the storm, he gave full credit to the young woman, Barbara Muller, who first dove into the surf to save another. Yet, the Carnegie Hero Fund Commission would not have awarded Dyess the Carnegie Medal if he had not acted selflessly and heroically. Also, he never talked about earning the Carnegie Medal, even to his closest friends. If ego were a factor in his decision to attempt the rescue, it would seem that he would, at least on occasion, have mentioned the fact that as a young man he had done something quite remarkable—that is, saving, at the same time, the lives of two women. A close examination of the those who have earned the Medal of Honor and the Carnegie Medal highlights many examples of altruism at work. In any case, the heroic acts of Jimmie Dyess in peace and war validate the concept that some heroism is based on empathetic altruism.

In addition to the altruistic personality in certain individuals, it may be possible to identify collective or community altruism. Perhaps the best example in the 20th Century was the action of the Danish people as they resisted German efforts to send Danish Jews to concentration camps and the gas ovens. In 1943, when the Germans were about to begin the roundup, the Danish people helped the Jews escape to Sweden. In addition, the Danes protected the Jewish property that was left behind and after the war, the Danish Jews were able to return and reclaim their abandoned homes and businesses. No other country that fell under German occupation in World War II had such a superb record of individual and collective altruism.

Much of the motivation of American Marines (and other military personnel) during World War II was based on fundamentally altruistic motivations. Perhaps at no other time in American history did this nation operate at such a high level of national altruism. The heroism of many men during World War II in the Pacific, from America, China, Britain, Australia, New Zealand and many other nations, had a major positive payoff. In the wisdom of more than fifty years of hindsight, it is clear that liberal democracy now flourishes in Japan as a direct result of the total defeat of the Japanese Empire in combat and the careful insertion and nurturing of democratic institutions in Japan in the years immediately after World War II. The same can be said of Germany and Italy, two countries who had little experience with liberal democracy prior to World War II.

There are those who would argue that the Second World War II, like all wars, accomplished nothing of any long term value. [132] I strongly disagree with this point of view. The world today has a higher percentage of people living in working democracies than at any time in history. Japan, Germany and Italy, the three major fascist powers of World War II, are now all democratic states. They have operated as robust democracies for more than two generations. These great nations join the United States, Great Britain, France, Canada, Australia and many other states in providing democratic role models for other nations to emulate. Hence, it is no exaggeration to state that the heroism of the Marines of the 4th Division and the millions of others who fought for the Allies in World War II probably accomplished more results of lasting value than any group of combatants in world history.

The veterans of World War II and the families who supported them during those desperate years of the early 1940s deserve the respect and appreciation of billions of people who have benefited, directly or indirectly, from their sacrifices. I would like to expand the famous quote from Winston Churchill when he praised the pilots of the Royal Air Force immediately after the Battle of Britain in 1940. Churchill said in the House of Commons, "Never in the field of human conflict was so much owed by so many to so few."[133] If Churchill were alive today, I am sure he would forgive me for saying about the Marines, sailors, soldiers and airmen of the grand alliance, "Never in human history have so many people owed so much to a single group of people—those who fought in World War II to destroy fascism and to expand democracy."

CHAPTER 15:

COMPARING THE TWO AWARDS FOR HEROISM

The Medal of Honor is the highest military award for bravery that can be given to any individual in the United States of America. Conceived in the early 1860s and first presented in 1863, the medal has a colorful and inspiring history.

As a general rule, the Medal of Honor may be awarded for a deed of personal bravery or self-sacrifice above and beyond the call of duty only while the person is a member of the Armed Forces of the United States in action against an enemy of the United States. However, on rare occasions it is awarded while engaged in military operations involving conflict with an opposing foreign force in which the United States is not a belligerent party. The Medals of Honor which were awarded to two Army soldiers who fought and died in Somalia in 1993 are examples of this second category.

There are many misconceptions about the Medal of Honor. For instance, it is often incorrectly called the Congressional Medal of Honor. Its official title is "Medal of Honor." Since it is presented by a high government official "in the name of the Congress of the United States," it is often mislabeled the Congressional Medal of Honor.[134] However, it must be acknowledged that the term "Congressional Medal of Honor" may serve a useful purpose. In recent years many corporations, institutions and clubs pass out a "medal of honor" to people who have served a long period of time with dedication or who accomplished a particularly noteworthy act. Hence, the term Congressional Medal of Honor is one useful way to highlight the *real* Medal of Honor and to differentiate it from other medals of honor.

Another common misconception about the Medal of Honor is that it has always been awarded for "conspicuous gallantry and intrepidity at the risk of life above and beyond the call of duty." These criteria were not established until 1918. Prior to that time, it was easier to earn the Medal of Honor and it did not have the extraordinary distinction which it has today. Of the slightly more than 3400 Medals of Honor awarded since 1863, more than half were awarded during the Civil War. Less than a thousand have been awarded during the period of the more demanding criteria of the last 80 years (including World War I, World War II, Korea, Vietnam and Somalia). Clearly, it has been much more difficult to earn the Medal of Honor since the criteria were changed in 1918. This is a very important point. Today, the Medal of Honor not only stands at the very pinnacle of all military awards for heroism but it is recognized throughout America as the very symbol of heroism above and beyond the call of duty. This was generally not true prior to 1918.[135]

Another misperception is that it is awarded to a military person for bravery above and beyond the call of duty only in combat. Although this is the general rule, there have been Medals of Honor given to a few outstanding pioneers such as Richard Byrd, Charles Lindberg and Billy Mitchell. These men earned their awards for actions totally unrelated to combat. However, it has been more than sixty years since anyone but a legitimate *combat* hero has received the Medal of Honor.

Another misperception is that the Medal of Honor has never been awarded to a woman. Dr. Mary E. Walker's story is quite interesting. She was awarded the Medal of Honor immediately after the Civil War. She had risked her health and her life as a combat nurse in a number of Civil War battles. Also, she was captured and endured many hardships in a prisoner of war camp. In 1917, a Board of Medal Awards, after a careful review of all the more than 2000 Medals of Honor awarded during the Civil War, ruled that 911 of these awards were unwarranted. All of these unwarranted awards, including Dr. Walker's, were revoked. However, in 1977 her award of the Medal of Honor was restored.

Hence, Mary Walker remains the only woman to have earned the Medal of Honor.

In their provisions for judging whether someone is entitled to the Medal of Honor, each of the armed services of the United States has set up regulations which permit no margin of error or doubt. The deed of the person must be proved by incontestable evidence of at least two eyewitnesses. The deed must be so outstanding that it clearly distinguishes gallantry beyond the call of duty from lesser forms of bravery. It must involve the risk of life; and it must be the type of deed which, if the person had not done it, would not subject him or her to any justified criticism.

The Carnegie Medal is not as well known throughout America as is the Medal of Honor, but it stands as the highest award given in this country for heroism by civilians. There is a strong correlation between America's two highest awards for heroism. Fundamentally, there is a strong imperative with both awards to identify and recognize heroism that is extraordinary and much more so than might be expected from any ordinary person. The words "above and beyond the call of duty" ring true for both awards.

However, there are also some differences between the two awards. Canadians, as well as Americans, can earn the Carnegie Medal—this is not true of the Medal of Honor. Although the Medal of Honor predates the Carnegie Medal by more than forty years, there are more than twice as many Carnegie Medal winners as there are Medal of Honor recipients. At first blush, this seems to indicate that it is easier to earn the Carnegie Medal and, hence, that the Carnegie Medal is of lower rank. However, since the Medal of Honor is almost always earned when Americans are engaged in combat, there are many years when no Medal of Honor is earned. For instance, from the end of the Vietnam war in 1975 until the Somali peacekeeping operation in 1993, no act of supreme bravery occurred during these eighteen years that earned someone a Medal of Honor. Between 1975 and 1993, Americans were engaged in combat in Lebanon, Grenada, Panama, Iraq, Kuwait and Saudi

Arabia. Many Marines, soldiers, naval personnel and airmen acted heroically; yet no act of valor was of such significance that a Medal of Honor was earned. By comparison, in this same eighteen-year period, there were approximately 1500 Carnegie Medals awarded. Individuals ran into burning buildings to save someone, grabbed people who were about to be run over by oncoming trains or dove into frigid waters to save drowning people. Many of these heroes died in their attempts to save others. All acted at great risk to their lives and all attempted to save strangers.

Also, there are many similarities in the personalities and the motivations of those who earned either award. When individuals who have earned either the Medal of Honor or the Carnegie Medal are interviewed after their acts of great courage, their remarks are often quite similar, "Someone had to do something," "She was in great danger, I had to help," "I could not let him die." Hence, whenever I think about the Carnegie Medal and the Medal of Honor, I find the similarities outweigh the differences. This nation is served well by these two awards and the stringent criteria which has made them so special. The military services and the Carnegie Hero Fund commissioners are to be congratulated for ensuring that these awards remain held to such a high standard and that those few who earn them fully deserve to be so honored.

CHAPTER 16:

EVENTS SALUTING THE HEROISM OF DYESS

In the more than half a century since he was killed, Jimmie Dyess has been honored a number of times.

1. A few days after the battle, the airfield on the Island of Roi Namur was named in his honor. Today, Dyess Field is a busy airfield indeed, for Roi Namur is the site of a major U. S. space tracking facility. About three hundred men and women (military, federal civil servants and civilian contractors) work on Roi Namur. Some live on the island but many others fly in and out daily from where they live with their families: Kwajalein Island, fifty miles to the south.

2. In the fall of 1944, the Dyess family learned that a ship would be named in his honor. On January 23, 1945, at Orange, Texas, the destroyer, DD 880, The USS Dyess, was launched. Connor Dyess and her nine-year-old daughter were both in attendance for the ceremony.

3. On May 12, 1945, the first commander of the USS Dyess sent a hand-written letter to Connor Dyess inviting her to attend the commissioning ceremony, "tentatively scheduled" for May 18. He warned her the date may... "vary a few days due to the huge amount of work remaining to be accomplished." In fact, the commissioning took place on May 21, 1945. In this letter, he wrote, "It is our sole aim to make the name of U. S. S. Dyess synonymous with the achievements of the late Col. Dyess."

4. On July 4, 1953, Commander John E. Dacey, commanding officer, USS Dyess, hosted a ceremony on board ship in Savannah, Georgia. A memorial plaque, donated by Jimmie's mother, was presented to the ship by his daughter, Miss Connor Cleckley Dyess. She was seventeen at the time. On a number of subsequent occasions, the crew of the USS Dyess held anniversaries and other celebrations. Each time the commander and the crew invited members of the Dyess family to attend and were, without exception, marvelous hosts.

5. On May 16, 1975, the thirtieth anniversary of the commissioning of the USS Dyess was celebrated at the Brooklyn Naval Yard. The commanding officer, Commander Ben D. Katz, invited the entire Dyess family and many came (his daughter, grandson, granddaughter, sister and a number of nephews and nieces). At the time, the USS Dyess was "home ported" in Brooklyn. She was assigned the duty of training members of the Naval Reserve in both weekend exercises and on two-week cruises.

6. In October, 1977, the Augusta chapter of The Military Order of the Purple Heart changed its name to the A. James Dyess chapter in honor of Augusta's greatest hero. This chapter remains active in support of many community activities and maintains the Dyess name today.

7. In the late 1970s, the Dyess family donated some of the land of the family-owned corporation, the Augusta Lumber Company, to the city of Augusta so that a public park could be built. The Augusta Lumber Company had fallen on hard economic times in the 1950s and 1960s and had gone out of business. The buildings had been razed and the property was no longer being used. Dyess Park is located in a part of the city where there are few other recreational facilities. It serves the recreational needs of many Augustans. The City of Augusta does an excellent job of maintaining the park. The swimming pool, ball fields and other recreational facilities are popular places for nearby residents.

8. On May 30, 1981, the mayor of the City of Augusta, Mr. Lewis Newman, issued a proclamation designating this day as " Jimmy Dyess Day". This proclamation asked all citizens of the city to join in honoring "this outstanding Augustan". The proclamation highlighted his " heroism in combat in the Marshall Islands, giving his life in the defense of this country and in protecting the men serving under him." It also "wishes to honor him and the patriotism and values he stood for."

9. On the 20th of October, 1986, the Roi-Namur battlefield was dedicated officially as a National Historic Landmark. Lieutenant General D'Wayne Gray, the commanding general for all the Marines in the Pacific area at the time, paid tribute to the gallant efforts of the Marines who captured the former Japanese outpost. The honor of unveiling the bronze plaque presented by the Department of Interior and the National Park Service was given to Dyess's daughter, Connor Dyess Smith. It was her first visit to the site of her father's death.

10. In June, 1989, at the annual convention of the 4th Marine Division Association was created. Thanks to the suggestion of Harold Quinn and the strong support of Ray Appling and a number of other Georgians who had served in the 4th Marine Division during World War II, this chapter was named the A. James Dyess Chapter in honor of Jimmie Dyess.

11. In the summer of 1990, the then Commandant of the Marine Corps, General Al Gray, officially designated the headquarters building of the 24th Marine Regiment in Kansas City in honor of Colonel Dyess. This is a fitting tribute, since Dyess served in the 24th Marines from the spring of 1943 until he was killed in February, 1944.

12. On September 17, 1990, at Battery Plaza in Augusta, a ceremony was held (and a monument unveiled) to honor the 19th Battalion of the Marine Corps Reserves on the occasion of the 50th anniversary of its call to active duty prior to World War II. It was at this spot that the Marines boarded a train and headed off to their active duty assignments in 1940. The mayor of the City of Augusta in 1990, Mr. Charles Devanney, praised the Marines from Augusta for their commitment to public service and for their heroism in combat. Many who had served in the 19th Battalion from 1936 to 1940 were in attendance as were members of their families. The plaque on one side of the monument honors all the men of the 19th Battalion. The plaque on the other side honors Lieutenant Colonel Dyess.

13. On the 11th of March, 1994, a major ceremony was held at Riverwalk on the Augusta bank of the Savannah River. A Heroes'

Overlook had been established just opposite Augusta's downtown Radisson Hotel. Every person in the Central Savannah River Area who has earned either the Medal of Honor or America's second highest award for military heroism, the Distinguished Service Cross or the Navy Cross, is honored by a plaque with the award citation. Dyess is uniquely honored, since both his Medal of Honor citation and the citation for his Carnegie Medal are displayed.

14. In August, 1994, the Board of Transportation of the State of Georgia made a decision to name a parkway in honor of Dyess. From 1995 through 1998 a new four-lane extension of Bel Air Road was constructed. The Jimmie Dyess Parkway is 3.1 miles long and connects Gate One of the large army post, Fort Gordon, with Interstate Highway I-20. It is an important limited-access artery in the rapidly growing area where Richmond County and Columbia County meet. It is quite appropriate that a road which serves the most important military installation in the region, Fort Gordon, home of the United States Army Signal Corps, has been named for a military hero from Augusta.

15. On the 13th of December, 1994, a moving dedication ceremony for the Jimmie Dyess Parkway was held alongside Gordon Highway near the front gate of Fort Gordon. It was a raw, cold day, yet more than two hundred people attended the forty-minute ceremony. In attendance were many members of Jimmie Dyess's family including his widow, his daughter, his sister and his granddaughter as well as nephews, nieces, grandnieces and grandnephews. There were a number of Augusta contemporaries of Dyess in attendance including Russell Blanchard, a friend since the Boy Scout days of the early 1920s, and Dudley Bowen, a friend since the Richmond Academy days of the mid 1920s. Also many colleagues of Dyess from the Marine Corps were in attendance, including Bert Gary and Frank Pokrop. During the ceremony, a number of short speeches were made. Former United States Congressman Doug Bernard emphasized the important role that Dyess had played as an exemplary model for young people like himself who had grown up in Augusta in the 1930s and 1940s. Jimmie Lester, representing the Board of Transportation, pointed out how pleased Georgians and Augustans were that this new park way would be dedicated for a true hero of Augusta.

Frank Pokrop flew from his home in Milwaukee to tell the story of how Dyess had rescued him and saved his life in combat. The active duty Marine Corps was represented by Major General David Richwine. Richwine emphasized how pleased the Marine Corps was that Dyess was being honored and saluted Lieutenant Colonel Dyess for his heroism and leadership during the desperate days of World War II. Richwine also saluted all the men and women of the armed services, past and present, for their commitment to public service and willingness to risk their lives for the defense of freedom. It was most appropriate that the band of the Academy of Richmond County played for the ceremony, since Dyess was one of the distinguished graduates of that historic institution. The A. James Dyess Chapter of the 4th Marine Division was well represented at the ceremony, as was the Dyess Chapter of the Military Order of the Purple Heart.

16. In April, 1995, a ceremony was held at Jimmie's high school, the Academy of Richmond County. Thanks to the generosity of the Georgia Power Company, a tree of historic importance was planted in honor of Jimmie Dyess. This tree, a Monticello Silver Maple, was a seedling from a silver maple that was planted by President Thomas Jefferson at his home near Charlottesville, Virginia. Andrew Von Plinsky of Georgia Power was responsible for taking this initiative.

17. On the morning of October 25, 1996, a building in Kansas City was dedicated in Dyess's honor. This building serves as the headquarters building for the 24th Marines. Present at the ceremony were many officials from the Marine Corps, including the commander of the 24th Marines, Colonel Cliff Myer, the commander of all Marine Corps Reserve Forces, Major General Thomas Wilkerson and the Assistant Commandant of the Marine Corps, General Richard I. Neal. Four generations of the Dyess family attended this moving ceremony: His widow, Mrs. C. G. Goodrich, Connor Dyess Smith, Serena Connor Verfurth and Dyess McCoy Verfurth. Dyess McCoy Verfurth is Jimmie Dyess's great-granddaughter. She was born on October 17, 1995, and is named after her great grandfather. The week before the ceremony in Kansas City she had celebrated her first birthday.

18. On October 30, 1998, two ceremonies were held in Augusta. The Jimmie Dyess Parkway was officially opened and the Navy/Marine Corps Reserve Center was named in honor of Dyess. It was a time of great celebration for the family and friends Jimmie Dyess.

In future years there will be more opportunities to highlight the remarkable achievements of Jimmie Dyess and to present him to young people as a role model for their future. The life of Jimmie Dyess is one to be celebrated. In an age of general skepticism and of cynicism about the state of the human condition, there is a strong tendency to question the character and motivations of men and women who serve in leadership positions. Yet high on the hill stands Lieutenant Colonel Dyess for all to see. He lived by the simple belief that service to your fellow man and to your nation is such a powerful obligation that it is both fundamental and unconditional.

May we all bask in his reflected glory.

May we marvel at his accomplishments.

May he encourage the young to look to him for inspiration.

Roi Namur battlefield landmark, 1985.

Connor Dyess Smith making remarks at the ceremony dedicating the battlefield of Roi Namur as a National Historic Landmark. 1986.

Frank Pokrop, whose life Dyess saved, at Dyess Field, Roi Namur. In February, 1985, Pokrop visited Iwo Jima on the 40th anniversary of that epic battle. On the way home, he visited the other battlefields of the 4th Division: Tinian, Saipan and Roi Namur.

Roi Namur is an important facility for NASA and for the US military in tracking space vehicles.

Connor Dyess Smith at the dedication ceremony for the Jimmie Dyess Parkway, December 13, 1994. The Dyess Parkway opened in 1998 and provides direct access from the main gate of Fort Gordon to I-20. Fort Gordon is a large military installation and the home of the US Army Signal Corps.

Dyess Parkway sign. This sign appears on the south side of interstate highway I-20, just west of Augusta. It is the first sign of a major highway in the Augusta area. I-20 is the major highway that runs from West Texas through Dallas, Shreveport, Jackson, Birmingham, Atlanta, Augusta and Columbia. The Dyess Parkway opened in 1998. It serves Richmond and Columbia Counties and Fort Gordon.

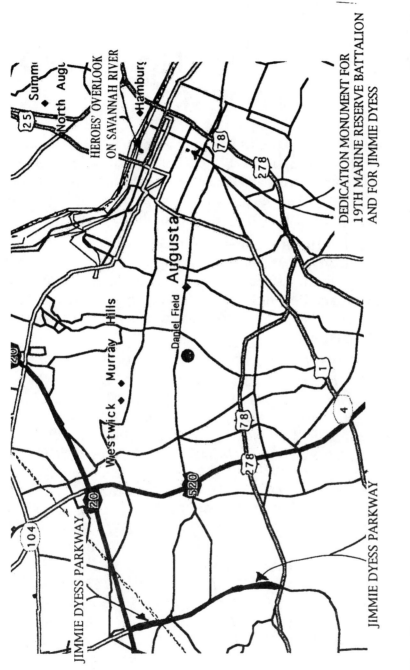

Map of August showing locations of the Jimmie Dyess Parkway, Heroes' Overlook and the dedication monument for both Augusta's 19th Marine Reserve Battalion (1936-1940) and Jimmie Dyess.

205

APPENDIX 1:

NOTABLE CITATIONS AND POEMS

The recognition of Dyess's towering accomplishments continue to grow. The following is a list of citations that highlight both the heroism of Jimmie Dyess and the honors that he has received since his death in 1944. These citations are replicated so that they duplicate, as closely as possible, the lettering of the originals.

1. The Medal of Honor Citation. This citation can be found in two public places. It is permanently displayed at Hero's Overlook along Riverwalk Augusta, on the river side of the Radisson Hotel at 10th Street and Reynolds. It is also displayed in Kansas City, just inside the entrance to Dyess Hall, which is the headquarters for the 24th Marines.

> *FOR CONSPICUOUS GALLANTRY AND INTREPIDITY AT THE RISK OF HIS LIFE ABOVE AND BEYOND THE CALL OF DUTY AS COMMANDING OFFICER OF THE FIRST BATTALION, TWENTY-FOURTH MARINES, REINFORCED, FOURTH MARINE DIVISION, IN ACTION AGAINST ENEMY JAPANESE WEAPONS, LIEUTENANT COLONEL DYESS LAUNCHED A POWERFUL FINAL ATTACK ON THE SECOND DAY OF THE ASSAULT, UNHESITATINGLY POSTING HIMSELF BETWEEN THE OPPOSING LINES TO POINT OUT OBJECTIVES AND AVENUES OF APPROACH AND PERSONALLY LEADING THE ADVANCING TROOPS. ALERT, AND DETERMINED TO QUICKEN THE PACE OF THE OFFENSIVE AGAINST INCREASED ENEMY FIRE, HE WAS CONSTANTLY AT THE HEAD OF ADVANCE UNITS, INSPIRING HIS MEN TO PUSH FORWARD UNTIL*

THE JAPANESE HAD BEEN DRIVEN BACK TO A SMALL CENTER OF RESISTANCE AND VICTORY ASSURED. WHILE STANDING ON THE PARAPET OF AN ANTI-TANK TRENCH DIRECTING A GROUP OF INFANTRY IN A FLANKING ATTACK AGAINST THE LAST ENEMY POSITION, LIEUTENANT COLONEL DYESS WAS KILLED BY A BURST OF ENEMY MACHINE-GUN FIRE. HIS DARING AND FORCEFUL LEADERSHIP AND HIS VALIANT FIGHTING SPIRIT IN THE FACE OF TERRIFIC OPPOSITION WERE IN KEEPING WITH THE HIGHEST TRADITIONS OF THE UNITED STATES NAVAL SERVICE. HE GALLANTLY GAVE HIS LIFE FOR HIS COUNTRY.

2. The resolution that establishes the Jimmie Dyess Parkway which connects the main gate of Fort Gordon with the I-20 Highway to the west of the City of Augusta. It can be found in Perry and Connor Smith's home at 3007 Cedar Hill Lane in Augusta, Ga.

A RESOLUTION
BY THE
STATE TRANSPORTATION BOARD

Whereas, the life and death of Lt. Col. A. James Dyess is an inspiration to all Americans who aspire to patriotism and greatness and

Whereas, Jimmie Dyess, a native Augustan, reflected great credit upon this city and this region by winning the Carnegie Medal for heroism at age 19 by risking his life to save a drowning woman from the Atlantic Ocean; and

Whereas, he brought further distinction on himself and his region by earning the Congressional Medal of Honor for bravery under fire while leading his men in a successful charge against a Japanese stronghold on a Pacific Island during World War II; and

Whereas, comrades in arms gave him their highest accolade by calling him a "true Marine"; and

Whereas, he is the only person in history to win both the Carnegie Medal and the Congressional Medal of Honor by showing his willingness to lay down his life for another both in war and in peace.

Now, therefore, be it resolved that the new extension of Belair Road from I-20 to Gordon Highway in Augusta be designated the "Jimmie Dyess Parkway" in recognition of his many accomplishments, and the Commissioner of Transportation be instructed to install appropriate signs along the roadway.

Be it further resolved that a copy of this resolution be spread upon the minutes of the meeting, and an appropriate copy be presented to the Dyess family.

Unanimously adopted this 20th day of October, 1994.

                                        Approved
                                        Max Goldin, Chairman
                                        State Transportation Board

Attest: Approved
Therol Brown, Secretary   Wayne Shackelford, Commissioner
State Transportation Board   Department of Transportation

3. The plaques that commemorate both the service of Augusta's 19th Marine Battalion and the heroism of Jimmie Dyess are permanently displayed on a monument at the small park in downtown Augusta between Telfair and Walker streets. This was the spot from which the 19th Battalion departed Augusta by train when it was mobilized for active duty in November, 1940.

19TH BATTALION
FLEET MARINE CORPS RESERVE

WE HONOR HERE THE MEN OF THE 19TH BATTALION
MARINE CORPS RESERVE, ORGANIZED DECEMBER
1936. THEY WERE CALLED TO ACTIVE MILITARY
DUTY 7 NOVEMBER 1940 TO MEET THE PREVAILING
THREAT OF WORLD WAR II.

WITH COURAGE AND DISTINCTION THE MEN TOOK
PART IN EVERY BATTLE OF THAT CONFLICT
INVOLVING MARINES.

IN HONOR OF THESE MEN OF THE 19TH
BATTALION, FOR THEIR SERVICE AND DEVOTION,
AND TO THOSE OF THEIR NUMBER WHO MADE THE
ULTIMATE SACRIFICE TO PRESERVE FREEDOM FOR
ALL GENERATIONS, THIS MONUMENT IS DEDICATED
ON BEHALF OF A GRATEFUL COMMUNITY.

NO STONE, NO WORDS CAN REFLECT THE
SACRIFICE AND LOVE OF COUNTRY DISPLAYED BY
THESE MEN. NOR CAN IT VOICE OUR GRATEFUL
PRAYER THAT GOD SHALL BLESS EACH OF THEM.

On the opposite side of this monument is found the following
citation.

A. JAMES DYESS

IN SPECIAL RECOGNITION OF
LIEUTENANT COLONEL A. JAMES DYESS
A MEMBER OF THE 19TH BATTALION, FMCR.

AS A YOUNG MAN, COLONEL DYESS WON
THE CARNEGIE MEDAL FOR
HEROISM BY SAVING THE LIVES OF
TWO DROWNING WOMEN. IN 1944,

AS A BATTALION COMMANDER WITH
THE 4TH MARINE DIVISION,
HE WENT BEHIND ENEMY LINES
TO SAVE THE LIVES OF FOUR WOUNDED MARINES.
THE NEXT DAY, WHILE LEADING HIS MEN
ON THE FINAL ASSAULT
IN THE BATTLE FOR ROI-NAMUR
IN THE MARSHALL ISLANDS, HE WAS KILLED.
HIS VALOR AND COURAGE WERE RECORDED
BY HISTORY AND RECOGNIZED BY
A GRATEFUL COUNTRY.
COLONEL DYESS RECEIVED
THE CONGRESSIONAL MEDAL OF HONOR
POSTHUMOUSLY.
HE IS THE ONLY PERSON IN HISTORY
TO HAVE BEEN AWARDED BOTH
THE CARNEGIE MEDAL AND
THE CONGRESSIONAL MEDAL OF HONOR.
MAY HIS LIFE OF SERVICE AND SELF-SACRIFICE
BE AN INSPIRATION TO ALL
WHO VIEW THIS MONUMENT.

4. The Academy of Richmond County has established two awards as part of the Junior Reserve Officer Training Program at Dyess's high school alma mater. These citations can be found at The Academy of Richmond County.

THE A. JAMES DYESS SABRE

Awarded to the Incoming Battalion Commander in honor of A. James Dyess, a 1927 graduate of the Academy of Richmond County. A past cadet officer and a World War II Medal of Honor Winner. This sabre will be passed to each incoming Cadet Battalion Commander.

APPENDIX 2:

THE USS DYESS:
SERVICE IN WAR, PEACE AND INTERNATIONAL CRISES, 1945 TO 1981.

The story of the USS Dyess is well worth telling. It is a part of the legacy of Lieutenant Colonel Dyess and hence should be included if this biography is to be complete. Those who served on the Dyess knew that their ship was named after someone who had earned the Medal of Honor—it made duty on the Dyess very special indeed.

The USS Dyess (DD 880), was launched in Orange, Texas on the 26th of January, 1945, less than a year after Dyess was killed. Many of the family members were present including Jimmie's older sister, Louise, as well as his wife and daughter, who was nine at the time. Connor Dyess broke the champagne bottle and the ship slid dramatically sideways into the water. The USS Dyess was commissioned on May 21, 1945, with Commander Raymond L. Fulton in command. Over the course of the next 36 years, the USS Dyess was destined to be directly involved in many international crisis as well as the Vietnam War. More than 3000 dedicated sailors served on the Dyess during this long period of public service to her nation and to the defense of freedom throughout the world.

After a short fitting-out period following her commissioning, the Dyess departed Orange for Guantanamo Bay, Cuba, for an extensive shakedown period. In July she sailed for Norfolk and was outfitted with special radar equipment and additional anti-aircraft armament. Following this modification, she was redesignated DDR 880, becoming a radar picket ship. By the time she was ready for combat, World War II had ended. The Dyess would not engage

USS Dyess (DD 880) in 1975 as it sails under the Verrazano Narrows Bridge which connects Staten Island and Brooklyn. The USS Dyess served this nation for 36 years from 1945 until 1981. More than 3000 personel served on the Dyess during those years.

in combat until she had been in the fleet for 21 years. Although she missed combat action in World War II and Korea, the Dyess would have a distinguished record in war, peace and international crises for more than thirty-five years.

In the autumn of 1945, the sparkling new USS Dyess had a short tour of duty as part of the Atlantic fleet. She was stationed at Casco Bay, Maine, and participated in the grand centennial celebration of the US Naval Academy at Annapolis in October. The USS Dyess sailed from Norfolk on the 7th of November, 1945, to join the 5th Fleet at Tokyo Bay. Enroute, she made her first passage through the Panama Canal and stopped at San Diego and Pearl Harbor on her long voyage to Japan. She served for a year as part of the American force that was responsible for the occupation of Japan and the defense of United States' interests in the Pacific in the aftermath of World War II.

But the Dyess was destined to spend the vast majority of the cold war years as a combatant ship of the Atlantic Fleet. On December 16, 1946, she arrived at San Diego from Japanese waters and on January, 1947, sailed for the east coast via the Panama Canal arriving at her new home port of Newport, Rhode Island, by the end of the month. One of her most memorable duties during her first year in the Atlantic was to be part of an escort party for the President of the United States, Harry Truman. As one might expect, Truman loved to sail on the historic battleship the USS Missouri, but as Truman looked out to sea in August, 1947, he would have seen the Dyess proudly sailing in support.

During the next three years Dyess made a number of deployments to the Mediterranean, first in support of unilateral American interests and later as part of the new alliance, NATO. It was in October, 1947, when Dyess made her first cruise across the Atlantic and into the Mediterranean Sea. This was before the implementation of the Marshall Plan and the formulation of NATO. Communist parties in Italy and France were very large and well disciplined and the Greek Civil War was raging. The vast majority of American ground forces, who had fought so magnificently to defeat German and Italian fascism, had been discharged and returned home. Hence, it was the task of American naval power (including the USS Dyess) to play an especially important role in backing up American diplomacy during this delicate period in American-European relations.

Dyess's second cruise to the Mediterranean took place from January to July, 1949. By this time, the Marshall Plan was being implemented and the North Atlantic treaty had been agreed. From this point forward, whenever Dyess entered the Mediterranean, as she did more than ten times, she did so in direct support of NATO. In the autumn of 1949, the Dyess headed north and entered the Arctic circle for the very first time—the exact date was November 12, 1949. The ship and crew became Members of the Royal Order of the Blue Nose upon entering the "Northern Domain of the Polar Bear."

In January, 1950, she entered the Portsmouth Naval Yard for overhaul and when she left the yard, she proceeded to Norfolk, which was to be her new home port. In May, she was off again to the Mediterranean, returning to the United States in October, 1950. By this time the Korean War had broken out and Americans were, once again, engaged in mortal combat. However, the USS Dyess would not see combat in that war. For the next few years, she would serve many long tours in the Mediterranean but would return to Norfolk for refitting, overhauls and additional training exercises. On July 4, 1953, Dyess visited Savannah for the specific purpose of receiving a bronze plaque from the Dyess family in honor of Lieutenant Colonel Dyess. Dyess's daughter, Connor, a teenager at the time, made the presentation.

The next major event in the history of the USS Dyess took place in the fall of 1956 during the Suez crisis. Dyess was on her 7th Mediterranean cruise when serious diplomatic and military crises broke out simultaneously in Egypt and in Hungary. America chose not to get involved militarily in the Hungarian crisis, but since so many American lives were in danger in the Middle East, President Eisenhower felt military action there was necessary. The issue of who controlled the Suez Canal led to a brief war with the British, French and Israelis on one side and the Egyptians on the other. Dyess assisted in the evacuation of many Americans who were put in danger as a result of this war.

During the 1950s, Dyess served in many capacities: as a plane guard during the qualifying of pilots in carrier operations, as a combat ship in practice hunter-killer operations against submarines and as an escort ship in amphibious and large fleet exercises. She not only spent many tours in the Mediterranean, but also conducted exercises in northern Europe, in the North Atlantic, in the South Atlantic and around Cuba. In 1959, her home port was changed and in July she sailed from Norfolk to the south.

On July 25, 1959, she arrived at Charleston, South Carolina, her new home port. Another extensive overhaul took place in the fall and winter of 1960-61. She received a long-range air search radar

during this overhaul. In October, 1962, Dyess became engaged
once again in a major international event. The Russians had secretly placed intermediate range ballistic missiles into Cuba. These
missiles, which had nuclear warheads, could reach most of the
strategic targets in the United States. This was a major escalation in
the Cold War and led to a series of military and diplomatic actions
that quickly became known as the Cuban Missile Crisis. President
Kennedy declared a "quarantine" of Cuba and Dyess was part of a
flotilla of ships which were responsible for stopping the movement
of any more military equipment from the Warsaw Pact nations into
Cuba. President Kennedy's firm diplomacy, backed up by strong
military and naval power, worked and the Soviets backed down.
The Soviet missiles were removed from Cuba and by the end of
1962, this crisis ended. Dyess returned to Charleston.

In 1964, the Dyess sailed into the Boston Naval Shipyard for a
major conversion. Her primary role as a radar picket ship was to be
changed. From 1964 until she was sold to the Greek Navy in 1981,
her role became fundamentally an anti-submarine one. At the
Boston Naval Yard, the Dyess was equipped with a high-powered
sonar, the ASROC (antisubmarine rocket) weapons system and new
torpedo tubes. This overhaul (the Fleet Rehabilitation and
Modernization Program—FRAM) caused her designation to
change. The USS Dyess was again DD 880; she was no longer
DDR 880. In her long and distinguished history, this was Dyess's
most significant overhaul and mission change.

Although 1964 was a landmark year for Dyess, it was 1966 that
was to be the most challenging and most demanding year in
Dyess's history. Just as the new year began, the USS Dyess was
called to combat duty in the escalating war in Southeast Asia. She
sailed through the Panama Canal on January 25, rescued two
downed aviators off Hawaii on February 10, and stopped for resupply at Subic Bay, in the Philippine Islands, in early March. On
March 4, she left Subic Bay for Danang and the war zone. She
served in the combat zone off the coast of Vietnam in two separate
roles: In support of carrier operations in the Tonkin Gulf and in

direct gunfire support in both the Danang area and in the III Corps area of South Vietnam.

Without question, the most challenging combat assignment for Dyess was when she sailed to the Mekong delta to support South Vietnamese military units. Using her four 5 inch guns, she provided fire support to troops in contact with the enemy. Her bombardment was coordinated with air strikes from both fighter jets and armed helicopters. In order to accomplish her mission, she had to sail in the shallow waters of the Saigon River. On several occasions she was hastily summoned to lend emergency support to South Vietnamese army troops who were attacking a large Viet Cong base camp twenty miles up the coast from Vung Tao. In one ten day period in late June 1966, she fired 2391 rounds in an around-the-clock operation.

Upon completion of her combat duty, she set sail for the long journey home. She joined with the other ships in her destroyer squadron and sailed from the Philippine Islands to Newport via the straits of Malacca, the Indian Ocean, the Red Sea, the Suez Canal, the Mediterranean Sea and the Atlantic Ocean. When she arrived at Newport on the afternoon on August 17, 1966, she and her sister ships were greeted by four thousand happy family members and friends. In a period of eight months, Dyess had circumnavigated the world, fought in combat off the coast of North and South Vietnam and in the rivers of South Vietnam and returned home safe and sound. During her world cruise, she steamed some 50,000 miles and spent 76% of her time underway. Her guns fired 2787 rounds in combat and her crew conducted 51 major underway replenishments plus many light-line transfers with other destroyers. The ship's complement of 280 men proved fully capable of dealing with the heavy demands of combat and non-combat operations.

In 1967, the Dyess, once again, returned to the Mediterranean. Although no one knew it at the time she left her home port, her mission was to become an especially sensitive one. On May 12 she completed her journey across the Atlantic and arrived at Gibraltar. At the time, it appeared to all of the crew members that this would be another routine cruise with the Sixth Fleet in the Mediterranean. By late May, Dyess was in the Eastern Mediterranean engaging in a number of "Flag Showing" port visits to various European and Middle Eastern nations. On May 30 she rescued a civilian ship that was disabled in heavy seas and towed her to the Greek island of Rhodes. As she entered the Suez Canal on June 3 and headed for Port Said, Egypt, she expected the normal warm welcome that she had received at each of her port visits throughout the Mediterranean.

To the great surprise of members of the crew, crowds of angry Egyptians gathered on the shore and shouted out anti-American slogans. Small boats sailed along side Dyess and again angry shouts could be heard. Thankfully, Dyess completed her voyage through the Suez Canal just in time. Soon after reaching the Red Sea, Dyess received word that Israel had bombed targets along the canal. Only nine hours after departing the southern extremity of the canal, Dyess was cut off from the rest of the Sixth Fleet. Israel and a number of Arab countries engaged in intense combat which was to last less than a week, with the Israelis victorious. During the Six Day War, Israel gained control of Jerusalem and the West Bank of the Jordan River. The USS Dyess was prominently mentioned in the press as the last warship of any nation to transit the Suez Canal before its closure on June 5, 1967. The Egyptians sank ten ships near the southern end of the Canal during the Six Day War. It was not until 1975 that the Suez was reopened.

After duty in the Indian Ocean and the Persian Gulf, Dyess returned home in August, 1967. Since she could not sail through the Suez Canal she accompanied the aircraft carrier, USS Forrestal (CVA-59), as they made their way around the southern tip of Africa via the Cape of Good Hope.

After an extensive overhaul in the Boston Naval Yard in the winter and spring of 1968, Dyess got underway on April 24 for sea trials. On the way back to Boston the next day, Dyess ran aground. She reentered Boston Naval Shipyard that night for dry-docking and repairs. By September, she had passed her various operational readiness inspections and was sailing to the Mediterranean for another five-month deployment. In December, 1968, Dyess was once again in the news. This time, along with USS Turner (DD 834), she made an historic cruise into the Black Sea. This Black Sea cruise was vigorously condemned by the Soviet Union and the two American destroyers were under continuous surveillance by Soviet naval and air units. However, the ships stayed in international waters throughout the voyage and there were no incidents to deal with or to report.

The year 1970 broke a pattern of yearly deployments to the Mediterranean. From May until October, Dyess conducted exercises and port visits in the Eastern Atlantic and visited ports in Spain, France, Germany, England, Portugal, the Netherlands, Scotland and Norway. Most of her exercises were anti-submarine exercises with the ships and submarines of many of the NATO allies.

The Dyess was upgraded many times in order to insure that she could meet the considerable challenge that the huge Soviet submarine fleet posed. However, by the 1970s she had become one of the older destroyers in the Navy and was reassigned to the Brooklyn Naval Yard for duty with the Naval Reserves. Now she would be manned largely by Naval reservists. These reservists loved the Dyess and looked forward to each one of the two-week training cruises in the Atlantic Ocean.

In 1974, a memorable event occurred at sea. In heavy fog and at night, four destroyers were proceeding quite slowly off the Canadian coast near Halifax. The Dyess was the third ship in line. The second ship (the USS Myles—DD 829) began to have engine troubles. As fate would have it, the officer of the deck for the Myles was the engineering officer. He got so involved in giving instructions to the engineering team that he forgot that his primary responsibility was as officer of the deck. The Myles was slowing down and rather than maneuvering the ship to the side, the officer of the deck kept the Myles on a steady course. Slowly the Dyess was overtaking the Myles. A collision resulted and although is was not much more than a brush of one ship with the other and the damage was minor it had to be reported as an official collision at sea.

On February 27, 1981, a decision that the crew of the Dyess had been dreading for many months was made. The USS Dyess, at the grand old age of 36, was to be decommissioned and transferred to the Greek Navy. In her many years of service with the US Navy, the USS Dyess was home to more than three thousand Naval professionals. Close friendships were made and great affection for the ship was established and maintained through the years. Many of the former crew members of the USS Dyess get together every year to renew acquaintances and to exchange sea stories.

An award winning web site has been constructed by a relative of a former crew member on the Dyess, Ernie Pomeroy. The web site is a delight to visit and has lots of wonderful information on locations of former crew members, the history of the ship, upcoming events, etc. It can be found at http://www.extremezone.com/~pomeroy/dyess/

If Jimmie Dyess were alive today, he would have many things to say to the dedicated professionals of the USS Dyess. He would thank them for staying in contact with his family for so many years and for keeping that contact going even after the decommissioning. He would praise them for their perseverance in helping to win the Cold War and for making possible a world where democracy can find roots, grow, blossom and thrive. But most of all, he would salute them for their commitment to the preservation of liberty, for their dedication to their nation and for their love of a grand ship.

APPENDIX 3:

THE MILITARY RECORD OF A. JAMES DYESS

ARMY CAREER HISTORY OF A.J. DYESS

1931

May 31	Accepted Commission as Second Lieutenant, US Army Reserve

1935

July 1-14	Active Duty for Training
Aug. 13-26	Active Duty for Training

1936

July 15-28	Active Duty for Training

MARINE CORPS HISTORY OF A.J. DYESS

1936

Dec. 5	Accepted Appointment as First Lieutenant, USMCR
Dec. 21	Assigned to Headquarters Company, 19th Battalion, as adjutant

1937

June 13-27	Active duty training at Parris Island, South Carolina
Aug. 7-Sept. 12	Active duty training at Parris Island, South Carolina and a shooter with Marine Corps Reserve Rifle and Pistol Team Detachment at Camp Perry, Ohio

1938

June 12-26   Active duty training at Parris Island, South Carolina

July 20-Aug. 12 Active duty as shooter with Marine Corps Reserve Rifle and Pistol Team at Wakefield, Massachusetts

Aug. 13-Sept 12 Active duty as shooter, Marine Corps Reserve Rifle and Pistol Team Detachment at Camp Perry, Ohio

1939

March 6   Appointed Captain, USMCR, with rank from Feb. 20th, 1939

June 11-25   Active duty as company commander for training at Marine Barracks, Parris Island, South Carolina

1940

July 21-Aug. 4   Active duty for training, Marine Barracks, Quantico, Virginia

Nov. 8   Active duty (battalion mobilization). Proceeded with company to Marine Barracks, Norfolk Navy Yard. Performed duty as company commander, 19th Training Company, until March 31, 1941

1941

March 31   Company Commander, 21st Reserve Company, Marine Barracks, Norfolk Navy Yard. Also served as member Post Council, Post Exchange Council and Surveying Officer

April 12   Assigned to Quantico, Virginia, for duty in Barrage Balloon Training School

May 3-17   Duty at Naval Air Station, Lakehurst, New Jersey, to assemble material for barrage balloons

May 23	Assigned to Parris Island, South Carolina, as Executive Officer, Barrage Balloon School

1942

May 16	Appointed Major (temporary rank) in Marine Corps Reserve with date of rank of May 8, 1942
Sept. 30	Transferred with Barrage Balloon School to New River, North Carolina
Oct. 1	Officer in Charge of Barrage Balloon School, New River

1943

March 10	Departed North Carolina for Camp Pendleton, Oceanside, California
March 15	Joined 1st Battalion, 24th Marines as Battalion Executive Officer
April 1	Appointed Lieutenant Colonel with date of rank of Oct. 5, 1942
May 14	Commanding Officer, 1st Battalion, 24th Marines

1944

Jan. 13	Shipped out from San Diego, California, with his battalion for the Central Pacific
Feb. 2	Killed in action while leading his men in the battle for Roi Namur, the Marshall Islands, during Operation Flintlock.

APPENDIX 4:

THOSE WHO ASSISTED ME

Hundreds of individuals helped me pull this extraordinary story together over the period from 1986 to 1998. I will not list them all but I would like to highlight a few who were especially helpful.

1. Frank Pokrop . Frank provided the inspiration for this book when he wrote a long letter to my wife, Connor, in 1988. He had read about the dedication of the Roi Namur battlefield in which Connor had participated and wanted her to be aware of what Jimmie Dyess had done on the first of February to save his life and the lives of four other Marines. Connor and I, for the very first time, now understood that the Medal of Honor citation did not tell the full story of Dyess's heroism in battle. The entire Dyess family will always be in debt to Pokrop for taking the initiative in writing his powerful letter.

2. Willie Turner. Willie was Jimmie Dyess's driver during the months of training at Camp Pendleton. He also served as Dyess's enlisted assistant from the summer of 1943 until Dyess was killed. Of all the enlisted men in the Marine Corps who knew Dyess, Willie knew him the best. Although it was clearly painful for Willie to share his recollections of training at Camp Pendleton, of the trip by ship to the Marshall Islands and of the two days of combat, he gave me dozens of insights into the kind of man Dyess was in train-ing and in combat.

3. Connor Goodrich. Connor Goodrich was married to Jimmie Dyess for nine years and three months (November, 1934-February, 1944). She was thirty-two years old when he died. She shared her memories of him as best she could, even though some of these memories were painful to recall and went back more than fifty-five years.

4. Connor Dyess Smith. During our trip to the Marshall Islands in the fall of 1986, Connor took the time to write down her memories of her father. She has also related to me in recent years many other memories of her family life with her father in Augusta, New River, Parris Island and in Southern California.

5. George and Sarah Ewing. Although her brother was six years older than she, Sarah has many vivid memories which she generously shared with me. George, who died in 1992, was also very helpful, especially when talking about sports.

6. Members of the 4th Marine Division in World War II. Many of these Marines wrote long, detailed letters of their memories of Dyess. Bob Fleischauer, Kenneth Schulz, Pat Renna, Richard Rothwell, Art Buck, Kenneth Jones, Sam Calano, Tom Kerr, Gene Mundy were especially helpful.

7. Augustans: Mary Creson, Bill Weltch, Russell Blanchard, Bill Eve, Claud Caldwell, Mackie Mulherin, Emma Mason, Campbell Vaiden, Sam Fortson, Roy Simkins, Bert Gary, Frank Robinson, Ed Cashin, Fred Harrison and Jack Widener.

8. Clemson University: Pete Naegel.

9. Marine Corps History Office: Ed Simmons and Bob Aquilina.

10. Cherry Point: Rudy T. Schwanda

11. USS Dyess: Former captain of the USS Dyess, Captain Ben Katz, USN (ret.), Dan Davis and Ernie Pomeroy.

12. Jimmie Dyess Chapter of the 4th Marine Division (World War II). This chapter has been very supportive of my research, encouraging me to write the book and to get it published while many of the veterans of the 4th Marine Division during World War II were still alive. I am particularly in debt to Harold Quinn and Earl Guy.

13. Rear Admiral Jim Stark, USN, who told me of the story of the collision of the USS Dyess and the USS Myles.

14. Art Buck who told me stories of the Barrage Balloon School and gave substantive criticism to a draft manuscript.

15. Tom Kerr who shared with me a number of fascinating recollections and who gave me helpful, substantive comments on a draft manuscript.

16. People who helped with the genealogical search of the Dyess family. P. McCoy Smith, Dudley Bowen, Marcie Wilhelmi, Charles R Lee, Sr., Pam Trammell.

17. Marines on active duty. General Chuck Krulak, General Butch Neal, Major General Dave Richwine, Major General Tom Wilkerson and from the 24th Marines in Kansas City, Major Eric Peterson and Colonel Cliff Myer.

18. The staff of the Marine Corps Association Art and Printing Departments. Jon Dodd, Charlotte Jackson, Macrina Singleton, Shannon Gordon, Tina Dodd, Ron Lunn, Greg Turley and Jeff Lee.

APPENDIX 5:

BACKGROUND ON THE CARNEGIE MEDAL

To understand the purpose of the Carnegie Medal, it is very useful to study the words of Mr. Andrew Carnegie himself when he inaugurated the medal in 1904. This inauguration consisted of a deed of trust to the Hero Fund Commission which Carnegie wrote and signed. Please note the wonderfully colorful language of a man who was supremely successful as an entrepreneur, industrialist and businessman and who was so strongly motivated to reach out and help others.

DEED OF TRUST

To the Hero Fund Commission:

GENTLEMEN: We live in an heroic age. Not seldom are we thrilled by deeds of heroism where men or women are injured or lose their lives in attempting to preserve or rescue their fellows; such the heroes of civilization. The heroes of barbarism maimed or killed theirs.

I have long felt that the heroes and those dependent upon them should be freed from pecuniary cares resulting from their heroism, and, as a fund for this purpose, I have transferred to the Commission five million dollars of First Collateral Five Per Cent Bonds of the United States Steel Corporation, the proceeds to be used as follows:

FIRST. To place those following peaceful vocations, who have been injured in heroic effort to save human life, in somewhat better positions pecuniary than before, until again able to work. In case of death, the widow and children, or other dependents, to be provided for until she remarries, and the children until they reach a self-supporting age. For exceptional children exceptional grants may be made for exceptional education. Grants of sums of money may also be made to heroes or heroines as the Commission thinks advisable-each case to be judged on its merits.

SECOND. No grant is to be continued unless it be soberly and properly used, and the recipients remain respectable, well behaved members of the community, but the heroes and heroines are to be given a fair trial, no matter what their antecedents. Heroes deserve pardon and a fresh start.

THIRD. A medal shall be given to the hero, or widow, or next of kin, which shall recite the heroic deed it commemorates, that descendants may know and be proud of their descent. The medal shall be given for the heroic act, even if the doer be uninjured, and also a sum of money, should the Commission deem such gift desirable.

FOURTH. Many cities provide pensions for policemen, firemen, teachers, and others, and some may give rewards for acts of

heroism. All these and other facts the Commission will take into account and act accordingly in making grants. Nothing could be further from my intention than to deaden or interfere with these most creditable provisions, doubly precious as showing public and municipal appreciation of faithful and heroic service. I ask from the Commission most careful guard against this danger. The medal can, of course, be offered in such cases. Whether something more can not judiciously be done, at the request of, or with the approval of, the city authorities, the Commission shall determine. I hope there can be.

FIFTH. The claims upon the Fund for some years can not exhaust it. After years, however, pensioners will become numerous. Should the Commission find, after allowing liberally for this, that a surplus will remain, it has power to make grants in case of accidents (preferably where a hero has appeared) to those injured. The action taken in the recent Harwick Mine accident, where Heroes Taylor and Lyle lost their lives, is an illustration. The community first raised a fund of forty thousand dollars, which was duplicated by me after waiting until the generosity of the community had full scope.

Here again the Commission should be exceedingly careful, as in this case, not to deaden, but to stimulate employers or communities to do their part, for such action benefits givers themselves as well as recipients.

SIXTH. It seems probable that cities and employers on this continent will ultimately be placed under similar conditions to those of Britain, Germany, and other European States, and required to provide against accidents to employees. Therefore, the Commission, by a two-thirds vote, may devote any surplus that accrues beyond providing for heroes and their dependents (which provision must never be abandoned) to such other modes of benefiting those in want, chiefly caused through no fault of their own (such as drunkenness, laziness, crimes, etc.) but through exceptional circumstances, in such manner and to such extent as the Commission thinks advisable and likely to do more good than if such sums were given to those injured by accident, where the latter may be suitably provided for by law, or otherwise.

SEVENTH. The field embraced by the Fund is the United States of America, the Dominion of Canada, the Colony of New Foundland, and the waters thereof. The sea is the scene of many heroic acts. No action more heroic than that of doctors and nurses volunteering their services in the case of epidemics. Railroad employees are remarkable for heroism. All these and similar cases are embraced. Whenever heroism is displayed by man or woman in saving human life, the Fund applies.

EIGHTH. No personal liability will attach to members for any act of the Commission. The Commission has power to fill vacancies.

NINTH. The Commission has full power to sell, invest, or reinvest all funds; to employ all officials, including Secretary, traveling agents to visit and oversee beneficiaries, etc., and to fix their compensation. Members of the Commission shall be reimbursed all expenses incurred, including traveling expenses attending meetings. The President shall be granted such honoraria as the Commission thinks proper and as he can be prevailed upon to accept.

TENTH. An annual report, including a detailed statement of sums and medals granted and the reasons therefor, shall be made each year and published in at least one newspaper in the principal cities of the countries embraced by the Fund. A finely executed roll of the heroes and heroines shall be kept displayed in the office at Pittsburgh.

(Signed) ANDREW CARNEGIE.

WITNESS
LOUISE WHITFIELD CARNEGIE.
New York, March 12th, 1904.

APPENDIX 6:

BIBLIOGRAPHY

Adams, Henry H. *1942: The Year That Doomed the Axis.* New York: David McKay Co., 1967.

America's Medal of Honor Recipients. Golden Valley, Minnesota: Highland Publishers, 1980.

Ballendorf, Dirk A. and Bartlett, Merrill L. *Pete Ellis: An Amphibious Warfare Prophet.* Naval Institute Press, 1996.

Berry, Henry. Semper Fi Mac: *Living Memories of the U.S. Marines in World War II.* New York: Arbor House, 1982.

Bradley, John H. and Jack W. Dice. *The Second World War: Asia and the Pacific.* Wayne, New Jersey: Avery Publishing Group, 1989.

Bryan, Wright. Clemson: *An Informal History of the University, 1889-1979.* Columbia, South Carolina: The R. L. Bryan Company, 1979.

Cashin, Edward J. *The Story of Augusta.* Augusta, Georgia. Richmond County Board of Education, 1980.

Chapin, John C. *The 4th Marine Division in World War II.* Washington: History and Museums Division Headquarters, U. S. Marine Corps, 1945.

Chapin, John C. *Breaking the Outer Ring: Marine Landings in the Marshall Islands (Marines in World War II Commemorative Series).* Washington: Marine Corps Historical Center, 1994.

Coggins, Jack. *The Campaign for Guadalcanal.* Garden City, NY: Doubleday, 1972.

Davis, Burke. *Marine! The Life of Chesty Puller.* Boston: Little, Brown, 1962.

Frank, Benis M. and Henry I. Shaw, Jr. *Victory and Occupation: History of U.S. Marine Corps Operations in World War II, vol. 5.* Washington, D.C.: Government Printing Office, 1968.

Fussell, Paul. *Wartime: Understanding Behavior in the Second World War.* New York: Oxford University Press, 1989.

Garand, George W. and Truman R. Strobridge. *Western Pacific Operations: History of U.S. Marine Corps Operations in World War II, vol. 4.* Washington, D.C.: Government Printing Office, 1971.

Hanrahan, Gene Z., ed. *Assault! True Action Stories of the Island War in the Pacific.* New York: Berkley, 1962.

Hayashi, Saburo, with Alvin D. Coox. *Kogun: The Japanese Army in the Pacific War.* Quantico, Va.: Marine Corps Association, 1959.

Heinl, Robert D. Jr. and John A. Crown. *The Marshalls: Increasing the Tempo.* Washington, D.C.: Government Printing Office, 1954

Holmes, Richard. *Acts of War: The Behavior of Men in Battle.* New York: The Free Press, 1985.

Hough, Frank O., Verle E. Ludwig, and Henry I. Shaw, Jr. USMC Historical Branch. *Pearl Harbor to Guadalcanal: History of U.S. Marine Corps Operations in World War 11, vol. 1.* Washington, D.C.: Government Printing Office, 1958.

Hoyt, Edwin P. *To the Marianas.* New York: Van Nostrand Reinhold, 1980.

Isely, Jeter A. and Philip A. Crowl. *The U.S. Marines and Amphibious War.* Princeton, NJ: Princeton University Press, 1951.

Keegan, John. *The Second World War.* New York: Penguin, 1989.

Keneally, Thomas. *Schindler's List.* New York: Touchstone, 1993

Kent, Graeme. *Guadalcanal: Island Ordeal.* New York: Ballantine Books, 1971.

King, Ernest J. and Walter Muir Whitehill. *Fleet Admiral King: a Naval Record.* New York:W.W. Norton and Company, Inc., 1952.

Leckie, Robert. *Challenge for the Pacific.* Garden City, N.Y: Doubleday, 1965.

— . *Strong Men Armed: The United States Marines Against Japan.* New York: Random House, 1962.

Letcher, John Seymour. *One Marine's Story.* Verona, Va.: McClure Press, 1970.

Manchester, William. *Goodbye Darkness: A Memoir of the Pacific War.* New York: Dell, 1982.

McKale, Donald M., ed. *Tradition: A History of the Presidency of Clemson University.* Macon, Georgia: Mercer University Press, 1988.

Melted, Frank M. *Old Clemson College: It Was a Hell of a Place.* Rose, Georgia: W. H. Wolf Associates, 1981.

Miller, Edward S. *War Plan Orange.* Annapolis, Maryland: Naval Institute Press. 1991

Moran, Lord. *The Anatomy of Courage.* Garden City Park, New York: Avery Publishing Group, 1987.

Morison, Samuel Eliot. *The Rising Sun in the Pacific: History of United States Naval Operations in World War II, vol. 3.* Boston: Little, Brown, 1959.

___ *Aleutians, Gilberts and Marshalls: History of United States Naval Operations in World War II, vol. 7.* Boston: Little, Brown, 1960.
Victory in the Pacific: History of United States Naval Operations in World War II, vol. 14. Boston: Little, Brown, 1960.

Moskin, J. Robert. *The U.S. Marine Corps Story.* New York: McGraw-Hill, 1977.

Overy, Richard. *Why the Allies Won.* New York. Norton, 1996

Potter, E. B. *Nimitz*. Annapolis, Maryland: Naval Institute Press, 1976.

Pratt, Fletcher. *The Marines' War.* New York: Sloane, 1948.

Proehl, Carl W., ed. *The Fourth Marine Division in World War II. Washington, D.C.* Infantry Journal Press, 1946.

Rowland, Arthur Ray, ed. *Reminiscences of Augusta Marines.* Augusta, Georgia: Richmond County Historical Society, 1985.

Russ, Martin. *Line of Departure: Tarawa.* Garden City, N.Y.: Doubleday, 1975.

Schaffer, Alan. *Visions: Clemson's Yesteryears, 1880s-1960s.* Louisville, Kentucky: Harmony House Publishers, 1990.

Schuon, Karl, ed. *The Leathernecks.* New York: Franklin Watts, 1963.

Shaw, Henry I., Jr. *Tarawa: A Legend Is Born.* New York: Ballantine Books, 1969.

Shaw, Henry I., Jr., Bernard C. Nalty, and Edwin T. Turnbladh. *Central Pacific Drive: History of U.S. Marine Corps Operations in World War 11, vol. 3.* Washington, D.C.: Government Printing Office, 1966.

Simmons, Edwin H. *The United States Marines: The First Two Hundred Years, 1775-1975.* New York: Viking, 1976.

Smith, Holland M., and Percy Finch. *Coral and Brass.* New York: Scribners, 1949.

Smith, S. E., ed. *The United States Marine Corps in World War II.* New York: Random House, 1969.

Toland, John. *But Not in Shame: The Six Months After Pearl Harbor.* New York: Random House, 1961.

———. *The Rising Sun: The Decline and Fall of the Japanese Empire, 1933-1945.* New York: Random House, 1970.

Trammell, Pamela, *The Descendants of the Dyess Brothers of Barnwell, South Carolina.* Privately Published, Texarkana, Texas, 1994

Tregaskis, Richard. *Guadalcanal Diary.* New York: Random House, 1943.

Updegraph, Charles L., Jr. *U.S. Marine Corps Special Units of World War II.* Washington, D.C.: Government Printing Office, 1972.

Vader, John. *New Guinea: The Tide Is Stemmed.* New York: Ballantine Books, 1971.

Vandegrift, A. A., and Robert B. Asprey. *Once a Marine.* New York: Ballantine Books, 1966.

Wheeler, Richard A. *Special Valor: The U. S. Marines and the Pacific War.* New York: Harper and Row, 1983.

Witty, Robert M. and Neil Morgan. *Marines of the Margarita: The Story of Camp Pendleton and the Leathernecks who Train on a Famous California Rancho.* (San Diego: Copley Book, 1970)

FOOTNOTES

1. The Medal of Honor citation can be found at Perry and Connor Smith's home in Augusta, Ga. 3007 Cedar Hill Lane, Augusta, Ga. 30909

2. Pamela K. V. Trammell, *The Descendants of the Dyess Brothers of Barnwell, South Carolina.* p. xviii.

3. Ibid. p. xii.

4. Interview with Connor C. Goodrich

5. Edward J. Cashin, *The Story of Augusta*, p. 205

6. Ibid., p.208

7. Ibid., p. 218

8. John W. Kirshon, *Chronicle of America*, p. 598

9. Cashin, p. 221

10. Ibid., p. 221

11. *Chronicle of America*, p. 612

12. Interview with Connor Dyess Smith

13. Cashin, p. 232

14. Ibid., p. 233

15. Ibid., P. 236

16. Interview with Russell Blanchard and Bill Weltch

17. *The Rainbow* (The Yearbook of the Academy of Richmond County, 1927)

18. Ibid.

19. Interviews with Russell Blanchard, Bill Eve, Bill Weltch, Dudley Bowen, Sam Forston.

20. Cashin, p. 237

21. Wright Bryan, *Clemson: An Informal History of the University, 1889-1979* pp. 106-111.

22. Ibid., pp. 112-117

23. Frank Mellette, *Old Clemson College—It Was a Hell of a Place* pp. 183-184.

24. Interview with Campbell Vaiden
25. Augusta Chronicle, July, 1928
26. Interview with Sarah Ewing
27. Joseph Frazier Wall, *Andrew Carnegie,* pp. 33-60
28. Ibid., p. 73
29. Ibid., pp. 74-79
30. Ibid., pp. 87-90
31. Ibid., p. 138
32. Ibid., pp. 808-808
33. Ibid., pp. 788-789
34. Ibid., pp. 828-829
35. Ibid., pp. 894-896
36. Ibid., p. 896
37. Telephonic interview with the executive vice president of the Carnegie Hero's Fund, Mr. Walter F. Rutkowski.
38. *Carnegie Hero Fund Commission: Seventy-five Years, 1904-1979.*
39. Ibid.
40. Cashin, p. 239
41. Interview with Sarah Ewing
42. Interview with Connor Goodrich
43. Interview with Connor Goodrich
44. Interview with Connor Goodrich
45. Interview with Connor Goodrich
46. Pamphlet from Sweet Briar College
47. Interview with Connor Goodrich
48. Interview with Connor Goodrich
49. Interview with Connor Goodrich
50. Interview with Connor Goodrich
51. Interview with Connor Goodrich
52. Interview with Claud Caldwell

53. Kenneth J. Clifford, *Progress and Purpose: A Developmental History of the United States Marine Corps 1900-1970*, p. 3.

54. Clifford, p. 6

55. Allan R. Millett, Semper Fidelis, pp. 322-323

56. Millett, p. 323

57. Russell F. Weigley, *The American Way of War: a History of United States Military Strategy and Policy.* p. 256

58. Weigley, p. 256

59. Weigley, p. 256

60. Weigley, p. 258

61. Clifford, pp. 64-65

62. Dirk Anthony Ballendorf and Merrill Lewis Bartlett, *Pete Ellis: An Amphibious Warfare Prophet, 1880-1923.* p. 141

63. Specter, p. 25

64. *Laguardia.*

65. Specter, p. 25

66. Clifford, p. 48

67. Clifford, p. 54

68 Clifford, p. 56

69. Clifford, pp. 53-57

70. Eric Larrabee, *Commander in Chief*, p. 277

71. Interview with Ed Simmons

72. Doris Kearns Goodwin, *No Ordinary Time*, p. 255

73. Goodwin, p. 255

74. Goodwin, p. 255

75. Interview with Art Buck

76. Interview with Art Buck

77. Interview with Tom Kerr

78. Interview with Ed Simmons

79. Interview with Bob Fleischauer

80. Allan R. Millett, *Semper Fidelis*, p. 348

81. Interview with Willie Turner
82. Interview with Tom Kerr
83. Interview with Willie Turner
84. *The 4th Marine Division in World War II* p. 235
85. Ibid. p 8
86. Ibid. p 2
87. Morison, pp. 83-84
88. Edward S. Miller, *War Plan Orange* p. 21
89. Miller
90. EB Potter, Nimitz, p. 265
91. Ibid., p. 265
92. Morison, p. 232
93. Wheeler, p. 15
94. Ibid. pp. 17-33
95. Ibid. p. 52
96. Ibid. pp. 51-53
97. Ibid. p. 132
98. Ibid. pp. 164-179
99. Morison, pp. 202-203
100. Morison, p. 203
101. Interview with Tom Kerr
102. Morison, pp. 164-167
103. Ibid. pp. 164-167
104. Interview with Willie Turner
105. John C. Chapin, *Breaking the Outer Ring:Marine Landings in the Marshall Islands.* p. 2
106. Ibid. p. 2
107. Ibid. p. 2
108. Henry Berry, *Semper Fi, Mac: Living Memories of the U. S. Marines in World War II,* p. 223
109. "Planning for Kwajalein: Brigadier General George Eddy's Recollections," Army Magazine, June, 1996

110. Chapin, p. 4
111. Chapin, p. 5
112. Chapin, p. 5
113. Chapin, p. 8
114. Morison, p. 247
115. Interview with Willie Turner
116. *The 4th Marine Division in World War II,* p. 29
117. Interview with Willie Turner
118. Interview with Frank Pokrop
119. Interview with Frank Pokrop
120. Interview with Willie Turner
121. Interview with Willie Turner
122. Interview with Bob Fleischauer
123. Chapin, p. 13
124. Interview with Art Buck
125. Interview with Willie Turner
126. Millett, p. 439
127. Interview with Connor Goodrich
128. Interview with Jack Jacobs
129. This letter appeared in Newsweek Magazine
130. Thomas Keneally, *Schindler's List* p. 129
131. Oliner and Oliner, *The Altruistic Personality* p. 2
132. Paul Fussell is probably the best known author in this category.
133. Winston Churchill, *Their Finest Hour* p. 340
134. *America's Medal of Honor Recipients*, p. 11
135. Ibid. p. 11

ABOUT THE AUTHOR

Perry M. Smith is an internationally known speaker, TV and radio commentator, author and president of Visionary Leadership of Augusta, Ga. He conducts seminars on leadership, strategic planning or ethics for corporations, military colleges and non-profit organizations. He also gives keynote speeches at conferences and conventions. He was military analyst at CNN from January 1991 to June 1998. On 14, June 1998, he resigned from CNN on an issue of ethics.

A retired major general, Smith served for 30 years in the U. S. Air Force. During his military career he commanded an F-15 wing in Europe and served as the top Air Force planner and as the Commandant of the National War College. He flew 180 combat missions in 1968-69 over Laos and North Vietnam.

A graduate of the U. S. Military Academy at West Point, he earned his Ph.D. in International Relations from Columbia University. His dissertation (on planning) earned the Helen Dwight Reid award from the American Political Science Association. He has written five books including *Taking Charge* ; *Rules and Tools For Leaders*; *Assignment Pentagon*; and *How CNN Fought the War.*

Smith lives with his wife in Augusta, Ga. Smith's address is PO Box 15666, Augusta Ga. 30919 (telephone: 706 7389133). His e-mail address is genpsmith@aol. com His web page is http://members aol. com/genpsmith His wife, the former Connor Cleckley Dyess and daughter of Jimmie Dyess, is a lyric soprano who has sung for Presidents Ford and Carter and was the featured soloist at Jimmie Doolittle's 90th birthday party. The Smiths have two children, McCoy and Serena, and two granddaughters, Dyess and Porter.